CAREER EXAMINATION SERIES

MW01198807

THIS IS YOUR **PASSBOOK**® FOR ...

ASSOCIATE ACCOUNTANT/ AUDITOR

NATIONAL LEARNING CORPORATION®
passbooks.com

PASSBOOK® SERIES

THE *PASSBOOK® SERIES* has been created to prepare applicants and candidates for the ultimate academic battlefield – the examination room.

At some time in our lives, each and every one of us may be required to take an examination – for validation, matriculation, admission, qualification, registration, certification, or licensure.

Based on the assumption that every applicant or candidate has met the basic formal educational standards, has taken the required number of courses, and read the necessary texts, the *PASSBOOK® SERIES* furnishes the one special preparation which may assure passing with confidence, instead of failing with insecurity. Examination questions – together with answers – are furnished as the basic vehicle for study so that the mysteries of the examination and its compounding difficulties may be eliminated or diminished by a sure method.

This book is meant to help you pass your examination provided that you qualify and are serious in your objective.

The entire field is reviewed through the huge store of content information which is succinctly presented through a provocative and challenging approach – the question-and-answer method.

A climate of success is established by furnishing the correct answers at the end of each test.

You soon learn to recognize types of questions, forms of questions, and patterns of questioning. You may even begin to anticipate expected outcomes.

You perceive that many questions are repeated or adapted so that you can gain acute insights, which may enable you to score many sure points.

You learn how to confront new questions, or types of questions, and to attack them confidently and work out the correct answers.

You note objectives and emphases, and recognize pitfalls and dangers, so that you may make positive educational adjustments.

Moreover, you are kept fully informed in relation to new concepts, methods, practices, and directions in the field.

You discover that you arre actually taking the examination all the time: you are preparing for the examination by "taking" an examination, not by reading extraneous and/or supererogatory textbooks.

In short, this PASSBOOK®, used directedly, should be an important factor in helping you to pass your test.

ASSOCIATE ACCOUNTANT/ASSOCIATE AUDITOR

DUTIES

An Associate Accountant supervises a staff of professional accountants and clerical support personnel in a large accounting or audit operation with the number supervised varying with the nature of program, or independently performs accounting and/or auditing work requiring a high degree of independent judgment and advanced accounting knowledge.

Associate Auditors are working supervisors and perform systematic examinations and appraisals of the accounting and program records and financial affairs of public, for profit, and non-profit organizations and businesses to ensure that accounts are maintained in compliance with governing laws, rules, regulations, and contracts; determine the ability of the organization to conduct its program efficiently and effectively; and evaluate internal controls and practices. These activities require the application of professional accounting and auditing standards and principles.

SUBJECT OF EXAMINATION

The written test is designed to test for knowledge, skills, and/or abilities in such areas as:
1. General accounting;
2. General auditing;
3. Governmental accounting;
4. Preparing reports and official documents;
5. Supervision; and
6. Understanding and interpreting tabular material.

HOW TO TAKE A TEST

I. YOU MUST PASS AN EXAMINATION

A. *WHAT EVERY CANDIDATE SHOULD KNOW*

Examination applicants often ask us for help in preparing for the written test. What can I study in advance? What kinds of questions will be asked? How will the test be given? How will the papers be graded?

As an applicant for a civil service examination, you may be wondering about some of these things. Our purpose here is to suggest effective methods of advance study and to describe civil service examinations.

Your chances for success on this examination can be increased if you know how to prepare. Those "pre-examination jitters" can be reduced if you know what to expect. You can even experience an adventure in good citizenship if you know why civil service exams are given.

B. *WHY ARE CIVIL SERVICE EXAMINATIONS GIVEN?*

Civil service examinations are important to you in two ways. As a citizen, you want public jobs filled by employees who know how to do their work. As a job seeker, you want a fair chance to compete for that job on an equal footing with other candidates. The best-known means of accomplishing this two-fold goal is the competitive examination.

Exams are widely publicized throughout the nation. They may be administered for jobs in federal, state, city, municipal, town or village governments or agencies.

Any citizen may apply, with some limitations, such as the age or residence of applicants. Your experience and education may be reviewed to see whether you meet the requirements for the particular examination. When these requirements exist, they are reasonable and applied consistently to all applicants. Thus, a competitive examination may cause you some uneasiness now, but it is your privilege and safeguard.

C. *HOW ARE CIVIL SERVICE EXAMS DEVELOPED?*

Examinations are carefully written by trained technicians who are specialists in the field known as "psychological measurement," in consultation with recognized authorities in the field of work that the test will cover. These experts recommend the subject matter areas or skills to be tested; only those knowledges or skills important to your success on the job are included. The most reliable books and source materials available are used as references. Together, the experts and technicians judge the difficulty level of the questions.

Test technicians know how to phrase questions so that the problem is clearly stated. Their ethics do not permit "trick" or "catch" questions. Questions may have been tried out on sample groups, or subjected to statistical analysis, to determine their usefulness.

Written tests are often used in combination with performance tests, ratings of training and experience, and oral interviews. All of these measures combine to form the best-known means of finding the right person for the right job.

II. HOW TO PASS THE WRITTEN TEST

A. NATURE OF THE EXAMINATION

To prepare intelligently for civil service examinations, you should know how they differ from school examinations you have taken. In school you were assigned certain definite pages to read or subjects to cover. The examination questions were quite detailed and usually emphasized memory. Civil service exams, on the other hand, try to discover your present ability to perform the duties of a position, plus your potentiality to learn these duties. In other words, a civil service exam attempts to predict how successful you will be. Questions cover such a broad area that they cannot be as minute and detailed as school exam questions.

In the public service similar kinds of work, or positions, are grouped together in one "class." This process is known as *position-classification*. All the positions in a class are paid according to the salary range for that class. One class title covers all of these positions, and they are all tested by the same examination.

B. FOUR BASIC STEPS

1) Study the announcement

How, then, can you know what subjects to study? Our best answer is: "Learn as much as possible about the class of positions for which you've applied." The exam will test the knowledge, skills and abilities needed to do the work.

Your most valuable source of information about the position you want is the official exam announcement. This announcement lists the training and experience qualifications. Check these standards and apply only if you come reasonably close to meeting them.

The brief description of the position in the examination announcement offers some clues to the subjects which will be tested. Think about the job itself. Review the duties in your mind. Can you perform them, or are there some in which you are rusty? Fill in the blank spots in your preparation.

Many jurisdictions preview the written test in the exam announcement by including a section called "Knowledge and Abilities Required," "Scope of the Examination," or some similar heading. Here you will find out specifically what fields will be tested.

2) Review your own background

Once you learn in general what the position is all about, and what you need to know to do the work, ask yourself which subjects you already know fairly well and which need improvement. You may wonder whether to concentrate on improving your strong areas or on building some background in your fields of weakness. When the announcement has specified "some knowledge" or "considerable knowledge," or has used adjectives like "beginning principles of..." or "advanced ... methods," you can get a clue as to the number and difficulty of questions to be asked in any given field. More questions, and hence broader coverage, would be included for those subjects which are more important in the work. Now weigh your strengths and weaknesses against the job requirements and prepare accordingly.

3) Determine the level of the position

Another way to tell how intensively you should prepare is to understand the level of the job for which you are applying. Is it the entering level? In other words, is this the position in which beginners in a field of work are hired? Or is it an intermediate or advanced level? Sometimes this is indicated by such words as "Junior" or "Senior" in the class title. Other jurisdictions use Roman numerals to designate the level – Clerk I, Clerk II, for example. The word "Supervisor" sometimes appears in the title. If the level is not indicated by the title, check the description of duties. Will you be working under very close supervision, or will you have responsibility for independent decisions in this work?

4) Choose appropriate study materials

Now that you know the subjects to be examined and the relative amount of each subject to be covered, you can choose suitable study materials. For beginning level jobs, or even advanced ones, if you have a pronounced weakness in some aspect of your training, read a modern, standard textbook in that field. Be sure it is up to date and has general coverage. Such books are normally available at your library, and the librarian will be glad to help you locate one. For entry-level positions, questions of appropriate difficulty are chosen – neither highly advanced questions, nor those too simple. Such questions require careful thought but not advanced training.

If the position for which you are applying is technical or advanced, you will read more advanced, specialized material. If you are already familiar with the basic principles of your field, elementary textbooks would waste your time. Concentrate on advanced textbooks and technical periodicals. Think through the concepts and review difficult problems in your field.

These are all general sources. You can get more ideas on your own initiative, following these leads. For example, training manuals and publications of the government agency which employs workers in your field can be useful, particularly for technical and professional positions. A letter or visit to the government department involved may result in more specific study suggestions, and certainly will provide you with a more definite idea of the exact nature of the position you are seeking.

III. KINDS OF TESTS

Tests are used for purposes other than measuring knowledge and ability to perform specified duties. For some positions, it is equally important to test ability to make adjustments to new situations or to profit from training. In others, basic mental abilities not dependent on information are essential. Questions which test these things may not appear as pertinent to the duties of the position as those which test for knowledge and information. Yet they are often highly important parts of a fair examination. For very general questions, it is almost impossible to help you direct your study efforts. What we can do is to point out some of the more common of these general abilities needed in public service positions and describe some typical questions.

1) General information

Broad, general information has been found useful for predicting job success in some kinds of work. This is tested in a variety of ways, from vocabulary lists to questions about current events. Basic background in some field of work, such as sociology or economics, may be sampled in a group of questions. Often these are principles which have become familiar to most persons through exposure rather than through formal training. It is difficult to advise you how to study for these questions; being alert to the world around you is our best suggestion.

2) Verbal ability

An example of an ability needed in many positions is verbal or language ability. Verbal ability is, in brief, the ability to use and understand words. Vocabulary and grammar tests are typical measures of this ability. Reading comprehension or paragraph interpretation questions are common in many kinds of civil service tests. You are given a paragraph of written material and asked to find its central meaning.

3) Numerical ability

Number skills can be tested by the familiar arithmetic problem, by checking paired lists of numbers to see which are alike and which are different, or by interpreting charts and graphs. In the latter test, a graph may be printed in the test booklet which you are asked to use as the basis for answering questions.

4) Observation

A popular test for law-enforcement positions is the observation test. A picture is shown to you for several minutes, then taken away. Questions about the picture test your ability to observe both details and larger elements.

5) Following directions

In many positions in the public service, the employee must be able to carry out written instructions dependably and accurately. You may be given a chart with several columns, each column listing a variety of information. The questions require you to carry out directions involving the information given in the chart.

6) Skills and aptitudes

Performance tests effectively measure some manual skills and aptitudes. When the skill is one in which you are trained, such as typing or shorthand, you can practice. These tests are often very much like those given in business school or high school courses. For many of the other skills and aptitudes, however, no short-time preparation can be made. Skills and abilities natural to you or that you have developed throughout your lifetime are being tested.

Many of the general questions just described provide all the data needed to answer the questions and ask you to use your reasoning ability to find the answers. Your best preparation for these tests, as well as for tests of facts and ideas, is to be at your physical and mental best. You, no doubt, have your own methods of getting into an exam-taking mood and keeping "in shape." The next section lists some ideas on this subject.

IV. KINDS OF QUESTIONS

Only rarely is the "essay" question, which you answer in narrative form, used in civil service tests. Civil service tests are usually of the short-answer type. Full instructions for answering these questions will be given to you at the examination. But in case this is your first experience with short-answer questions and separate answer sheets, here is what you need to know:

1) Multiple-choice Questions

Most popular of the short-answer questions is the "multiple choice" or "best answer" question. It can be used, for example, to test for factual knowledge, ability to solve problems or judgment in meeting situations found at work.

A multiple-choice question is normally one of three types—

- It can begin with an incomplete statement followed by several possible endings. You are to find the one ending which *best* completes the statement, although some of the others may not be entirely wrong.
- It can also be a complete statement in the form of a question which is answered by choosing one of the statements listed.
- It can be in the form of a problem – again you select the best answer.

Here is an example of a multiple-choice question with a discussion which should give you some clues as to the method for choosing the right answer:

When an employee has a complaint about his assignment, the action which will *best* help him overcome his difficulty is to
A. discuss his difficulty with his coworkers
B. take the problem to the head of the organization
C. take the problem to the person who gave him the assignment
D. say nothing to anyone about his complaint

In answering this question, you should study each of the choices to find which is best. Consider choice "A" – Certainly an employee may discuss his complaint with fellow employees, but no change or improvement can result, and the complaint remains unresolved. Choice "B" is a poor choice since the head of the organization probably does not know what assignment you have been given, and taking your problem to him is known as "going over the head" of the supervisor. The supervisor, or person who made the assignment, is the person who can clarify it or correct any injustice. Choice "C" is, therefore, correct. To say nothing, as in choice "D," is unwise. Supervisors have and interest in knowing the problems employees are facing, and the employee is seeking a solution to his problem.

2) True/False Questions

The "true/false" or "right/wrong" form of question is sometimes used. Here a complete statement is given. Your job is to decide whether the statement is right or wrong.

SAMPLE: A roaming cell-phone call to a nearby city costs less than a non-roaming call to a distant city.

This statement is wrong, or false, since roaming calls are more expensive.
This is not a complete list of all possible question forms, although most of the others are variations of these common types. You will always get complete directions for

answering questions. Be sure you understand *how* to mark your answers – ask questions until you do.

V. RECORDING YOUR ANSWERS

Computer terminals are used more and more today for many different kinds of exams.

For an examination with very few applicants, you may be told to record your answers in the test booklet itself. Separate answer sheets are much more common. If this separate answer sheet is to be scored by machine – and this is often the case – it is highly important that you mark your answers correctly in order to get credit.

An electronic scoring machine is often used in civil service offices because of the speed with which papers can be scored. Machine-scored answer sheets must be marked with a pencil, which will be given to you. This pencil has a high graphite content which responds to the electronic scoring machine. As a matter of fact, stray dots may register as answers, so do not let your pencil rest on the answer sheet while you are pondering the correct answer. Also, if your pencil lead breaks or is otherwise defective, ask for another.

Since the answer sheet will be dropped in a slot in the scoring machine, be careful not to bend the corners or get the paper crumpled.

The answer sheet normally has five vertical columns of numbers, with 30 numbers to a column. These numbers correspond to the question numbers in your test booklet. After each number, going across the page are four or five pairs of dotted lines. These short dotted lines have small letters or numbers above them. The first two pairs may also have a "T" or "F" above the letters. This indicates that the first two pairs only are to be used if the questions are of the true-false type. If the questions are multiple choice, disregard the "T" and "F" and pay attention only to the small letters or numbers.

Answer your questions in the manner of the sample that follows:

32. The largest city in the United States is
    A. Washington, D.C.
    B. New York City
    C. Chicago
    D. Detroit
    E. San Francisco

1) Choose the answer you think is best. (New York City is the largest, so "B" is correct.)
2) Find the row of dotted lines numbered the same as the question you are answering. (Find row number 32)
3) Find the pair of dotted lines corresponding to the answer. (Find the pair of lines under the mark "B.")
4) Make a solid black mark between the dotted lines.

VI. BEFORE THE TEST

Common sense will help you find procedures to follow to get ready for an examination. Too many of us, however, overlook these sensible measures. Indeed, nervousness and fatigue have been found to be the most serious reasons why applicants fail to do their best on civil service tests. Here is a list of reminders:

- Begin your preparation early – Don't wait until the last minute to go scurrying around for books and materials or to find out what the position is all about.
- Prepare continuously – An hour a night for a week is better than an all-night cram session. This has been definitely established. What is more, a night a week for a month will return better dividends than crowding your study into a shorter period of time.
- Locate the place of the exam – You have been sent a notice telling you when and where to report for the examination. If the location is in a different town or otherwise unfamiliar to you, it would be well to inquire the best route and learn something about the building.
- Relax the night before the test – Allow your mind to rest. Do not study at all that night. Plan some mild recreation or diversion; then go to bed early and get a good night's sleep.
- Get up early enough to make a leisurely trip to the place for the test – This way unforeseen events, traffic snarls, unfamiliar buildings, etc. will not upset you.
- Dress comfortably – A written test is not a fashion show. You will be known by number and not by name, so wear something comfortable.
- Leave excess paraphernalia at home – Shopping bags and odd bundles will get in your way. You need bring only the items mentioned in the official notice you received; usually everything you need is provided. Do not bring reference books to the exam. They will only confuse those last minutes and be taken away from you when in the test room.
- Arrive somewhat ahead of time – If because of transportation schedules you must get there very early, bring a newspaper or magazine to take your mind off yourself while waiting.
- Locate the examination room – When you have found the proper room, you will be directed to the seat or part of the room where you will sit. Sometimes you are given a sheet of instructions to read while you are waiting. Do not fill out any forms until you are told to do so; just read them and be prepared.
- Relax and prepare to listen to the instructions
- If you have any physical problem that may keep you from doing your best, be sure to tell the test administrator. If you are sick or in poor health, you really cannot do your best on the exam. You can come back and take the test some other time.

VII. AT THE TEST

The day of the test is here and you have the test booklet in your hand. The temptation to get going is very strong. Caution! There is more to success than knowing the right answers. You must know how to identify your papers and understand variations in the type of short-answer question used in this particular examination. Follow these suggestions for maximum results from your efforts:

1) Cooperate with the monitor

The test administrator has a duty to create a situation in which you can be as much at ease as possible. He will give instructions, tell you when to begin, check to see that you are marking your answer sheet correctly, and so on. He is not there to guard you, although he will see that your competitors do not take unfair advantage. He wants to help you do your best.

2) Listen to all instructions

Don't jump the gun! Wait until you understand all directions. In most civil service tests you get more time than you need to answer the questions. So don't be in a hurry. Read each word of instructions until you clearly understand the meaning. Study the examples, listen to all announcements and follow directions. Ask questions if you do not understand what to do.

3) Identify your papers

Civil service exams are usually identified by number only. You will be assigned a number; you must not put your name on your test papers. Be sure to copy your number correctly. Since more than one exam may be given, copy your exact examination title.

4) Plan your time

Unless you are told that a test is a "speed" or "rate of work" test, speed itself is usually not important. Time enough to answer all the questions will be provided, but this does not mean that you have all day. An overall time limit has been set. Divide the total time (in minutes) by the number of questions to determine the approximate time you have for each question.

5) Do not linger over difficult questions

If you come across a difficult question, mark it with a paper clip (useful to have along) and come back to it when you have been through the booklet. One caution if you do this – be sure to skip a number on your answer sheet as well. Check often to be sure that you have not lost your place and that you are marking in the row numbered the same as the question you are answering.

6) Read the questions

Be sure you know what the question asks! Many capable people are unsuccessful because they failed to *read* the questions correctly.

7) Answer all questions

Unless you have been instructed that a penalty will be deducted for incorrect answers, it is better to guess than to omit a question.

8) Speed tests

It is often better NOT to guess on speed tests. It has been found that on timed tests people are tempted to spend the last few seconds before time is called in marking answers at random – without even reading them – in the hope of picking up a few extra points. To discourage this practice, the instructions may warn you that your score will be "corrected" for guessing. That is, a penalty will be applied. The incorrect answers will be deducted from the correct ones, or some other penalty formula will be used.

9) Review your answers

If you finish before time is called, go back to the questions you guessed or omitted to give them further thought. Review other answers if you have time.

10) Return your test materials

If you are ready to leave before others have finished or time is called, take ALL your materials to the monitor and leave quietly. Never take any test material with you. The monitor can discover whose papers are not complete, and taking a test booklet may be grounds for disqualification.

VIII. EXAMINATION TECHNIQUES

1) Read the general instructions carefully. These are usually printed on the first page of the exam booklet. As a rule, these instructions refer to the timing of the examination; the fact that you should not start work until the signal and must stop work at a signal, etc. If there are any *special* instructions, such as a choice of questions to be answered, make sure that you note this instruction carefully.

2) When you are ready to start work on the examination, that is as soon as the signal has been given, read the instructions to each question booklet, underline any key words or phrases, such as *least, best, outline, describe* and the like. In this way you will tend to answer as requested rather than discover on reviewing your paper that you *listed without describing*, that you selected the *worst* choice rather than the *best* choice, etc.

3) If the examination is of the objective or multiple-choice type – that is, each question will also give a series of possible answers: A, B, C or D, and you are called upon to select the best answer and write the letter next to that answer on your answer paper – it is advisable to start answering each question in turn. There may be anywhere from 50 to 100 such questions in the three or four hours allotted and you can see how much time would be taken if you read through all the questions before beginning to answer any. Furthermore, if you come across a question or group of questions which you know would be difficult to answer, it would undoubtedly affect your handling of all the other questions.

4) If the examination is of the essay type and contains but a few questions, it is a moot point as to whether you should read all the questions before starting to answer any one. Of course, if you are given a choice – say five out of seven and the like – then it is essential to read all the questions so you can eliminate the two that are most difficult. If, however, you are asked to answer all the questions, there may be danger in trying to answer the easiest one first because you may find that you will spend too much time on it. The best technique is to answer the first question, then proceed to the second, etc.

5) Time your answers. Before the exam begins, write down the time it started, then add the time allowed for the examination and write down the time it must be completed, then divide the time available somewhat as follows:

- If 3-1/2 hours are allowed, that would be 210 minutes. If you have 80 objective-type questions, that would be an average of 2-1/2 minutes per question. Allow yourself no more than 2 minutes per question, or a total of 160 minutes, which will permit about 50 minutes to review.
- If for the time allotment of 210 minutes there are 7 essay questions to answer, that would average about 30 minutes a question. Give yourself only 25 minutes per question so that you have about 35 minutes to review.

6) The most important instruction is to *read each question* and make sure you know what is wanted. The second most important instruction is to *time yourself properly* so that you answer every question. The third most important instruction is to *answer every question.* Guess if you have to but include something for each question. Remember that you will receive no credit for a blank and will probably receive some credit if you write something in answer to an essay question. If you guess a letter – say "B" for a multiple-choice question – you may have guessed right. If you leave a blank as an answer to a multiple-choice question, the examiners may respect your feelings but it will not add a point to your score. Some exams may penalize you for wrong answers, so in such cases *only*, you may not want to guess unless you have some basis for your answer.

7) Suggestions
   a. Objective-type questions
      1. Examine the question booklet for proper sequence of pages and questions
      2. Read all instructions carefully
      3. Skip any question which seems too difficult; return to it after all other questions have been answered
      4. Apportion your time properly; do not spend too much time on any single question or group of questions
      5. Note and underline key words – *all, most, fewest, least, best, worst, same, opposite,* etc.
      6. Pay particular attention to negatives
      7. Note unusual option, e.g., unduly long, short, complex, different or similar in content to the body of the question
      8. Observe the use of "hedging" words – *probably, may, most likely,* etc.
      9. Make sure that your answer is put next to the same number as the question
      10. Do not second-guess unless you have good reason to believe the second answer is definitely more correct
      11. Cross out original answer if you decide another answer is more accurate; do not erase until you are ready to hand your paper in
      12. Answer all questions; guess unless instructed otherwise
      13. Leave time for review

   b. Essay questions
      1. Read each question carefully
      2. Determine exactly what is wanted. Underline key words or phrases.
      3. Decide on outline or paragraph answer

4. Include many different points and elements unless asked to develop any one or two points or elements
5. Show impartiality by giving pros and cons unless directed to select one side only
6. Make and write down any assumptions you find necessary to answer the questions
7. Watch your English, grammar, punctuation and choice of words
8. Time your answers; don't crowd material

8) Answering the essay question

Most essay questions can be answered by framing the specific response around several key words or ideas. Here are a few such key words or ideas:

M's: manpower, materials, methods, money, management
P's: purpose, program, policy, plan, procedure, practice, problems, pitfalls, personnel, public relations
    a. Six basic steps in handling problems:
        1. Preliminary plan and background development
        2. Collect information, data and facts
        3. Analyze and interpret information, data and facts
        4. Analyze and develop solutions as well as make recommendations
        5. Prepare report and sell recommendations
        6. Install recommendations and follow up effectiveness

    b. Pitfalls to avoid
        1. *Taking things for granted* – A statement of the situation does not necessarily imply that each of the elements is necessarily true; for example, a complaint may be invalid and biased so that all that can be taken for granted is that a complaint has been registered
        2. *Considering only one side of a situation* – Wherever possible, indicate several alternatives and then point out the reasons you selected the best one
        3. *Failing to indicate follow up* – Whenever your answer indicates action on your part, make certain that you will take proper follow-up action to see how successful your recommendations, procedures or actions turn out to be
        4. *Taking too long in answering any single question* – Remember to time your answers properly

IX. AFTER THE TEST

Scoring procedures differ in detail among civil service jurisdictions although the general principles are the same. Whether the papers are hand-scored or graded by machine we have described, they are nearly always graded by number. That is, the person who marks the paper knows only the number – never the name – of the applicant. Not until all the papers have been graded will they be matched with names. If other tests, such as training and experience or oral interview ratings have been given, scores will be combined. Different parts of the examination usually have different weights. For example, the written test might count 60 percent of the final grade, and a rating of training and experience 40 percent. In many jurisdictions, veterans will have a certain number of points added to their grades.

After the final grade has been determined, the names are placed in grade order and an eligible list is established. There are various methods for resolving ties between those who get the same final grade – probably the most common is to place first the name of the person whose application was received first. Job offers are made from the eligible list in the order the names appear on it. You will be notified of your grade and your rank as soon as all these computations have been made. This will be done as rapidly as possible.

People who are found to meet the requirements in the announcement are called "eligibles." Their names are put on a list of eligible candidates. An eligible's chances of getting a job depend on how high he stands on this list and how fast agencies are filling jobs from the list.

When a job is to be filled from a list of eligibles, the agency asks for the names of people on the list of eligibles for that job. When the civil service commission receives this request, it sends to the agency the names of the three people highest on this list. Or, if the job to be filled has specialized requirements, the office sends the agency the names of the top three persons who meet these requirements from the general list.

The appointing officer makes a choice from among the three people whose names were sent to him. If the selected person accepts the appointment, the names of the others are put back on the list to be considered for future openings.

That is the rule in hiring from all kinds of eligible lists, whether they are for typist, carpenter, chemist, or something else. For every vacancy, the appointing officer has his choice of any one of the top three eligibles on the list. This explains why the person whose name is on top of the list sometimes does not get an appointment when some of the persons lower on the list do. If the appointing officer chooses the second or third eligible, the No. 1 eligible does not get a job at once, but stays on the list until he is appointed or the list is terminated.

X. HOW TO PASS THE INTERVIEW TEST

The examination for which you applied requires an oral interview test. You have already taken the written test and you are now being called for the interview test – the final part of the formal examination.

You may think that it is not possible to prepare for an interview test and that there are no procedures to follow during an interview. Our purpose is to point out some things you can do in advance that will help you and some good rules to follow and pitfalls to avoid while you are being interviewed.

What is an interview supposed to test?

The written examination is designed to test the technical knowledge and competence of the candidate; the oral is designed to evaluate intangible qualities, not readily measured otherwise, and to establish a list showing the relative fitness of each candidate – as measured against his competitors – for the position sought. Scoring is not on the basis of "right" and "wrong," but on a sliding scale of values ranging from "not passable" to "outstanding." As a matter of fact, it is possible to achieve a relatively low score without a single "incorrect" answer because of evident weakness in the qualities being measured.

Occasionally, an examination may consist entirely of an oral test – either an individual or a group oral. In such cases, information is sought concerning the technical knowledges and abilities of the candidate, since there has been no written examination for this purpose. More commonly, however, an oral test is used to supplement a written examination.

Who conducts interviews?

The composition of oral boards varies among different jurisdictions. In nearly all, a representative of the personnel department serves as chairman. One of the members of the board may be a representative of the department in which the candidate would work. In some cases, "outside experts" are used, and, frequently, a businessman or some other representative of the general public is asked to serve. Labor and management or other special groups may be represented. The aim is to secure the services of experts in the appropriate field.

However the board is composed, it is a good idea (and not at all improper or unethical) to ascertain in advance of the interview who the members are and what groups they represent. When you are introduced to them, you will have some idea of their backgrounds and interests, and at least you will not stutter and stammer over their names.

What should be done before the interview?

While knowledge about the board members is useful and takes some of the surprise element out of the interview, there is other preparation which is more substantive. It *is* possible to prepare for an oral interview – in several ways:

1) Keep a copy of your application and review it carefully before the interview

This may be the only document before the oral board, and the starting point of the interview. Know what education and experience you have listed there, and the sequence and dates of all of it. Sometimes the board will ask you to review the highlights of your experience for them; you should not have to hem and haw doing it.

2) Study the class specification and the examination announcement

Usually, the oral board has one or both of these to guide them. The qualities, characteristics or knowledges required by the position sought are stated in these documents. They offer valuable clues as to the nature of the oral interview. For example, if the job involves supervisory responsibilities, the announcement will usually indicate that knowledge of modern supervisory methods and the qualifications of the candidate as a supervisor will be tested. If so, you can expect such questions, frequently in the form of a hypothetical situation which you are expected to solve. NEVER go into an oral without knowledge of the duties and responsibilities of the job you seek.

3) Think through each qualification required

Try to visualize the kind of questions you would ask if you were a board member. How well could you answer them? Try especially to appraise your own knowledge and background in each area, *measured against the job sought*, and identify any areas in which you are weak. Be critical and realistic – do not flatter yourself.

4) Do some general reading in areas in which you feel you may be weak

For example, if the job involves supervision and your past experience has NOT, some general reading in supervisory methods and practices, particularly in the field of human relations, might be useful. Do NOT study agency procedures or detailed manuals. The oral board will be testing your understanding and capacity, not your memory.

5) Get a good night's sleep and watch your general health and mental attitude

You will want a clear head at the interview. Take care of a cold or any other minor ailment, and of course, no hangovers.

What should be done on the day of the interview?

Now comes the day of the interview itself. Give yourself plenty of time to get there. Plan to arrive somewhat ahead of the scheduled time, particularly if your appointment is in the fore part of the day. If a previous candidate fails to appear, the board might be ready for you a bit early. By early afternoon an oral board is almost invariably behind schedule if there are many candidates, and you may have to wait. Take along a book or magazine to read, or your application to review, but leave any extraneous material in the waiting room when you go in for your interview. In any event, relax and compose yourself.

The matter of dress is important. The board is forming impressions about you – from your experience, your manners, your attitude, and your appearance. Give your personal appearance careful attention. Dress your best, but not your flashiest. Choose conservative, appropriate clothing, and be sure it is immaculate. This is a business interview, and your appearance should indicate that you regard it as such. Besides, being well groomed and properly dressed will help boost your confidence.

Sooner or later, someone will call your name and escort you into the interview room. *This is it.* From here on you are on your own. It is too late for any more preparation. But remember, you asked for this opportunity to prove your fitness, and you are here because your request was granted.

What happens when you go in?

The usual sequence of events will be as follows: The clerk (who is often the board stenographer) will introduce you to the chairman of the oral board, who will introduce you to the other members of the board. Acknowledge the introductions before you sit down. Do not be surprised if you find a microphone facing you or a stenotypist sitting by. Oral interviews are usually recorded in the event of an appeal or other review.

Usually the chairman of the board will open the interview by reviewing the highlights of your education and work experience from your application – primarily for the benefit of the other members of the board, as well as to get the material into the record. Do not interrupt or comment unless there is an error or significant misinterpretation; if that is the case, do not hesitate. But do not quibble about insignificant matters. Also, he will usually ask you some question about your education, experience or your present job – partly to get you to start talking and to establish the interviewing "rapport." He may start the actual questioning, or turn it over to one of the other members. Frequently, each member undertakes the questioning on a particular area, one in which he is perhaps most competent, so you can expect each member to participate in the examination. Because time is limited, you may also expect some rather abrupt switches in the direction the questioning takes, so do not be upset by it. Normally, a board member will not pursue a single line of questioning unless he discovers a particular strength or weakness.

After each member has participated, the chairman will usually ask whether any member has any further questions, then will ask you if you have anything you wish to add. Unless you are expecting this question, it may floor you. Worse, it may start you off on an extended, extemporaneous speech. The board is not usually seeking more information. The question is principally to offer you a last opportunity to present further qualifications or to indicate that you have nothing to add. So, if you feel that a significant qualification or characteristic has been overlooked, it is proper to point it out in a sentence or so. Do not compliment the board on the thoroughness of their examination – they have been sketchy, and you know it. If you wish, merely say, "No thank you, I have nothing further to add." This is a point where you can "talk yourself out" of a good impression or fail to present an important bit of information. Remember, *you close the interview yourself.*

The chairman will then say, "That is all, Mr. _____, thank you." Do not be startled; the interview is over, and quicker than you think. Thank him, gather your belongings and take your leave. Save your sigh of relief for the other side of the door.

How to put your best foot forward

Throughout this entire process, you may feel that the board individually and collectively is trying to pierce your defenses, seek out your hidden weaknesses and embarrass and confuse you. Actually, this is not true. They are obliged to make an appraisal of your qualifications for the job you are seeking, and they want to see you in your best light. Remember, they must interview all candidates and a non-cooperative candidate may become a failure in spite of their best efforts to bring out his qualifications. Here are 15 suggestions that will help you:

1) Be natural – Keep your attitude confident, not cocky

If you are not confident that you can do the job, do not expect the board to be. Do not apologize for your weaknesses, try to bring out your strong points. The board is interested in a positive, not negative, presentation. Cockiness will antagonize any board member and make him wonder if you are covering up a weakness by a false show of strength.

2) Get comfortable, but don't lounge or sprawl

Sit erectly but not stiffly. A careless posture may lead the board to conclude that you are careless in other things, or at least that you are not impressed by the importance of the occasion. Either conclusion is natural, even if incorrect. Do not fuss with your clothing, a pencil or an ashtray. Your hands may occasionally be useful to emphasize a point; do not let them become a point of distraction.

3) Do not wisecrack or make small talk

This is a serious situation, and your attitude should show that you consider it as such. Further, the time of the board is limited – they do not want to waste it, and neither should you.

4) Do not exaggerate your experience or abilities

In the first place, from information in the application or other interviews and sources, the board may know more about you than you think. Secondly, you probably will not get away with it. An experienced board is rather adept at spotting such a situation, so do not take the chance.

5) If you know a board member, do not make a point of it, yet do not hide it

Certainly you are not fooling him, and probably not the other members of the board. Do not try to take advantage of your acquaintanceship – it will probably do you little good.

6) Do not dominate the interview

Let the board do that. They will give you the clues – do not assume that you have to do all the talking. Realize that the board has a number of questions to ask you, and do not try to take up all the interview time by showing off your extensive knowledge of the answer to the first one.

7) Be attentive

You only have 20 minutes or so, and you should keep your attention at its sharpest throughout. When a member is addressing a problem or question to you, give him your undivided attention. Address your reply principally to him, but do not exclude the other board members.

8) Do not interrupt

A board member may be stating a problem for you to analyze. He will ask you a question when the time comes. Let him state the problem, and wait for the question.

9) Make sure you understand the question

Do not try to answer until you are sure what the question is. If it is not clear, restate it in your own words or ask the board member to clarify it for you. However, do not haggle about minor elements.

10) Reply promptly but not hastily

A common entry on oral board rating sheets is "candidate responded readily," or "candidate hesitated in replies." Respond as promptly and quickly as you can, but do not jump to a hasty, ill-considered answer.

11) Do not be peremptory in your answers

A brief answer is proper – but do not fire your answer back. That is a losing game from your point of view. The board member can probably ask questions much faster than you can answer them.

12) Do not try to create the answer you think the board member wants

He is interested in what kind of mind you have and how it works – not in playing games. Furthermore, he can usually spot this practice and will actually grade you down on it.

13) Do not switch sides in your reply merely to agree with a board member

Frequently, a member will take a contrary position merely to draw you out and to see if you are willing and able to defend your point of view. Do not start a debate, yet do not surrender a good position. If a position is worth taking, it is worth defending.

14) Do not be afraid to admit an error in judgment if you are shown to be wrong

The board knows that you are forced to reply without any opportunity for careful consideration. Your answer may be demonstrably wrong. If so, admit it and get on with the interview.

15) Do not dwell at length on your present job

The opening question may relate to your present assignment. Answer the question but do not go into an extended discussion. You are being examined for a *new* job, not your present one. As a matter of fact, try to phrase ALL your answers in terms of the job for which you are being examined.

Basis of Rating

Probably you will forget most of these "do's" and "don'ts" when you walk into the oral interview room. Even remembering them all will not ensure you a passing grade. Perhaps you did not have the qualifications in the first place. But remembering them will help you to put your best foot forward, without treading on the toes of the board members.

Rumor and popular opinion to the contrary notwithstanding, an oral board wants you to make the best appearance possible. They know you are under pressure – but they also want to see how you respond to it as a guide to what your reaction would be under the pressures of the job you seek. They will be influenced by the degree of poise you display, the personal traits you show and the manner in which you respond.

ABOUT THIS BOOK

This book contains tests divided into Examination Sections. Go through each test, answering every question in the margin. At the end of each test look at the answer key and check your answers. On the ones you got wrong, look at the right answer choice and learn. Do not fill in the answers first. Do not memorize the questions and answers, but understand the answer and principles involved. On your test, the questions will likely be different from the samples. Questions are changed and new ones added. If you understand these past questions you should have success with any changes that arise. Tests may consist of several types of questions. We have additional books on each subject should more study be advisable or necessary for you. Finally, the more you study, the better prepared you will be. This book is intended to be the last thing you study before you walk into the examination room. Prior study of relevant texts is also recommended. NLC publishes some of these in our Fundamental Series. Knowledge and good sense are important factors in passing your exam. Good luck also helps. So now study this Passbook, absorb the material contained within and take that knowledge into the examination. Then do your best to pass that exam.

EXAMINATION SECTION

EXAMINATION SECTION
TEST 1

DIRECTIONS: Each question or incomplete statement is followed by several suggested answers or completions. Select the one that BEST answers the question or completes the statement. *PRINT THE LETTER OF THE CORRECT ANSWER IN THE SPACE AT THE RIGHT.*

1. The Donaldson Company's cash balance includes a sum of $1,200,000 appropriated by the Board of Directors for the purchase of new equipment.
On its financial statements, this amount should be included on the

    A. balance sheet as a current asset
    B. balance sheet as a non-current asset, specifically identified
    C. balance sheet as a fixed asset, included as part of plant cost
    D. income statement as a non-operating expense

1.____

2. The trial balance of the Davis Corporation as of June 30, 2016, the end of its fiscal year, included opposite the title *Estimated Federal Income Taxes Accrued* the amount of $35,000, which included the company's estimate of the Federal income tax it would have to pay for its 2016 fiscal year and the amount of an unpaid additional assessment for the 2013 fiscal year.
This amount should appear on the balance sheet as a(n)

    A. general reserve
    B. reduction of current assets
    C. current liability
    D. allocation of retained income

2.____

3. A weekly payroll check was issued to an hourly employee based upon 88 hours of work instead of the normal 38 hours. The time card was somewhat illegible, and the number looked like it could have been 88.
The BEST control procedure to prevent such an error would be

    A. desk checking   B. a hash total
    C. a limit test   D. a code check

3.____

4. In preparing a bank reconciliation, outstanding checks should be

    A. *deducted* from the balance per books
    B. *deducted* from the balance per bank statement
    C. *added* to the balance per books
    D. *added* to the balance per bank statement

4.____

5. Independence is essential and is expected under the generally accepted auditing standards.
The fact and appearance of integrity and objectivity are BEST maintained if

    A. the auditor is unbiased
    B. the auditor is aware of the problem of third party liability
    C. there is no financial relationship between the client and the auditor
    D. all financial relationships between the auditor and the client are reported in footnote form

5.____

6. An audit program is a plan of action and is used to guide the auditor in planning his work.   6.____
Such a program, if standardized, must be modified to

     A. observe limits that management places on the audit
     B. counteract internal control weaknesses
     C. meet the limited training of the auditor
     D. limit interference with work of the firm being audited

7. In auditing the *Owner's Equity* section of any company, the section related to a publicly-   7.____
held corporation which uses a transfer agent and registrar would be more intricate than
the audit of a partnership.
Therefore, the procedure that an auditor should use in this case is to

     A. obtain a listing of the number of shares of securities outstanding
     B. make a count of the number of shareholders
     C. determine that all stock transfers have been properly handled
     D. count the number of shares of stock in the treasury

8. In recent years, it has become increasingly more important to determine the correct   8.____
number of shares outstanding when auditing the owner's equity accounts.
This is TRUE because

     A. there has been more fraud with respect to securities issued
     B. there are increased complexities determining the earnings per share
     C. there are more large corporations
     D. the auditor has to test the amount of invested capital

9. In auditing corporation records, an auditor must refer to some corporate documents that   9.____
are NOT accounting documents. The one of the following to which he is LEAST likely to
refer is

     A. minutes of the board of directors meeting
     B. articles of incorporation of the corporation
     C. correspondence with public relations firms and the shareholders
     D. the by-laws of the corporation

10. A generally accepted auditing procedure which has been required by AICPA require-   10.____
ments is the observation of inventories.
Since it is impossible to observe the entire inventory of a large firm, the auditor may
satisfy this requirement by

     A. establishing the balance by the use of a gross profit percentage method
     B. using sampling procedures to verify the count made by the client
     C. accepting the perpetual inventory records, once he has established that the entries
        are arithmetically accurate
     D. accepting the management statement that the inventory is correct as to quantity
        where observation is difficult

11. Materiality is an important consideration in all aspects of an audit examination. Attention   11.____
must be given to accounts with small and zero balances when examining accounts pay-
able.
This does not conflict with the concept of materiality because

A. the size of a balance is no clue to possible understatement of a liability
B. the balance of the account is not a measure of materiality
C. a sampling technique may suggest examining those accounts under consideration
D. the total of the accounts payable may be a material amount and, therefore, no individual account payable should be eliminated from review

12. In establishing the amount of a liability recorded on the books, which of the following types of evidence should an auditor consider to be the MOST reliable?   12.____

    A. A check issued by the company and bearing the payee's endorsement which is included with the bank statement
    B. Confirmation of an account payable balance mailed by and returned directly to the auditor
    C. A sales invoice issued by the client with a delivery receipt from an outside trucker attached
    D. A working paper prepared by the client's accountant and reviewed by the client's controller

13. Prior period adjustments as defined by APB Opinion #9 issued by the AICPA never flow through the income statement.   13.____
The one of the following which is NOT one of the four criteria established by APB #9 for meeting the qualifications for treatment as a prior period adjustment is that the adjustment item

    A. is not susceptible to reasonable extension prior to the current period
    B. must be determined primarily by someone other than company management
    C. can be specifically identified with and directly related to the business activities of a particular prior period
    D. when placed in the current period would give undesirable results of operations

14. The subject caption which does NOT belong in a report of a financial audit and review of operations of a public agency is   14.____

    A. Audit Program
    B. Description of Agency Organization and Function
    C. Summary Statement of Findings
    D. Details of Findings

15. At the inception of an audit of a public assistance agency, you ascertain that the one-year period of your audit includes 240,000 serially numbered payment vouchers.   15.____
The sample selection which would enable you to render the MOST generally acceptable opinion on the number of ineligible persons receiving public assistance is

    A. the number of vouchers issued in a one-month period
    B. every hundredth voucher
    C. a random statistical selection
    D. an equal size block of vouchers from each month

16. Of the following, the one which BEST describes an internal control system is the   16.____

    A. division of the handling and recording of each transaction into component parts so as to involve at least two persons, with each performing an unduplicated part of each transaction

    B. expansion of the worksheet to include provisions for adjustments to the books of account prior to preparation of the financial statements

    C. recording of transactions affecting negotiable instruments in accordance with the principles of debit and credit, and giving these instruments special treatment if they are interest or non-interest bearing notes

    D. taking of discounts, when properly authorized by the vendor, as an incentive for prompt payment

17. During audits of small businesses, an accountant is less likely to find that these establishments have a system of internal control comparable to larger firms because small businesses GENERALLY   17.____

    A. can absorb the cost of small fraudulent acts which may be perpetrated
    B. benefit more than larger firms by prevention of fraud than by detection of fraud
    C. have limited staff and the costs of maintaining the system are high
    D. use a double entry system which serves as a substitute for internal control

18. In the performance of a financial audit, especially one where there is a need for a thorough knowledge of law, an accountant would BEST be advised to   18.____

    A. rely on the testimony of witnesses, as they may be found during the course of the audit, in preference to the written record

    B. rely on the presumption that the client's actions are illegal when the audit discloses meager facts or evidence

    C. be aware of the specific legal objectives he is attempting to attain by means of his audit

    D. be aware of different conclusions he can reach depending upon what facts are stressed or discounted in his audit

19. There are various types of budgets which are used to measure different government activities.
The type of budget which PARTICULARLY measures input of resource as compared with output of service is the _____ budget.   19.____

    A. capital   B. traditional
    C. performance   D. program

20. Bank balances are usually confirmed through the use of a standard bank confirmation form as authorized by the AICPA and the Bank Administration Institute.
In addition to bank balances, these confirmations ALSO confirm   20.____

    A. the credit rating of the client
    B. details of all deposits during the past month
    C. loans and contingent liabilities outstanding
    D. securities held by the bank as custodian for the client

KEY (CORRECT ANSWERS)

1.	B	11.	A
2.	C	12.	B
3.	C	13.	D
4.	B	14.	A
5.	C	15.	C
6.	B	16.	A
7.	A	17.	C
8.	B	18.	C
9.	C	19.	C
10.	B	20.	C

———

TEST 2

DIRECTIONS: Each question or incomplete statement is followed by several suggested answers or completions. Select the one that BEST answers the question or completes the statement. *PRINT THE LETTER OF THE CORRECT ANSWER IN THE SPACE AT THE RIGHT.*

Questions 1-3.

DIRECTIONS: Questions 1 through 3 are based on the classification of items into the appropriate section of a corporation balance sheet. The list of sections to be used is given below:

Current assets	Investments
Current liabilities	Long-term liabilities
Deferred credits	Paid-in capital
Deferred expenses	Plant assets
Intangible assets	Retained earnings

1. With respect to *Bonds Payable Due* in 2015, the PROPER classification is   1.____

    A. Investments
    C. Retained earnings
    B. Paid-in capital
    D. Long-term liabi

2. With respect to *Premium on Common Stock,* the PROPER classification is   2.____

    A. Intangible assets
    C. Retained earnings
    B. Investments
    D. Paid-in capital

3. With respect to *Organization Costs,* the PROPER classification is   3.____

    A. Intangible assets
    C. Plant assets
    B. Investments
    D. Current liabilities

4. J. Frost operates a small, individually owned repair service and maintains adequate double entry records. A review of his bank accounts and other available financial records yields the following information: 4.____
Deposits made during 2015 per bank statements totalled $360,000. Deposits included a bank loan of $25,000 and an additional investment by Frost of $5,000. Disbursements during 2015 per bank statements totalled $305,000. This amount includes personal withdrawals of $28,500 and repayment of debt of $15,000.
The Net Equity of J. Frost at January 1, 2015 was determined to be $61,000.
Net Equity of J. Frost at December 31, 2015 was determined to be $67,000.
Based upon the *Net Worth* method, Frost's net income for the year ended December 31, 2015 was

    A. $6,000   B. $29,500   C. $41,500   D. $55,000

Questions 5-8.

DIRECTIONS: Questions 5 through 8 are based on the following Balance Sheet, Income Statement, and Notes relating to the books and records of the Hartman Corporation.

BALANCE SHEET (000 omitted)

	September 30, 2015 Debit	Credit	September 30, 2016 Debit	Credit
Cash	$ 18		$ 31	
Accounts receivable	28		26	
Inventory	10		15	
Land	40		81	
Building and equipment (Net)	60		65	
Accounts payable		$ 10		$ 11
Notes payable - short-term		2		2
Bonds payable		50		50
Mortgage payable		20		46
Common stock		50		86
Retained earnings		24		23
	$156	$156	$218	$218

INCOME STATEMENT FOR FISCAL YEAR ENDING SEPTEMBER 30, 2016

Income :
Sales		$85
Cost of sales		40
Gross margin		$45

Expenses :
Depreciation	$ 5	
Loss on sale of fixed assets	2	
Other operating expenses	32	
Total expenses		$39
Net income		$ 6

NOTES:
1. Dividend declared during the year 2016, $7,000.
2. Acquired land; gave $36,000 common stock and cash for the balance.
3. Wrote off $1,000 accounts receivable as uncollectible.
4. Acquired equipment; gave note secured by mortgage of $26,000.
5. Sold equipment; net cost per books, $16,000, sales price $14,000.

5. The amount of funds provided from net income for the year ended September 30, 2016 is   5.____

   A. $6,000   B. $7,000   C. $13,000   D. $14,000

6. Financing and investing activities not affecting working capital are reported under the   6.____
rules of APB #19. Notes 1 through 5 refer to various transactions on the books of the
Hartman Corporation.
Select the answer which refers to the numbers reflecting the concept mentioned here.

A. Notes 1, 3, and 5   B. Notes 2 and 4
C. Notes 2, 4, and 5   D. All five notes

7. Funds applied for the acquisition of the land are   7.____

    A. $5,000   B. $36,000   C. $41,000   D. None

8. The net change in working capital from 2015 to 2016 is   8.____

    A. $6,000   B. $16,000   C. $22,000   D. $35,000

9. Sales during July 2015 for the Magnum Corporation, operating in Los Angeles, were   9.____
$378,000, of which $150,000 were on account. The sales figures given include the total
sales tax charged to retail customers. (Assume a sales tax rate on all sales of 8%.)
The CORRECT sales tax liability for July 2015 should be shown as

    A. $3,024   B. $18,240   C. $28,000   D. $30,240

10. Of the following statement ratios, the one that BEST represents a measure of cost effi-   10.____
ciency is

    A. Acid Test Ratio
    B. Operating Costs to Net Sales Ratio
    C. Cost of Manufacturing to Plant Assets ratio
    D. Earnings Per Share

Questions 11-13.

DIRECTIONS: Answer Questions 11 through 13 on the basis of the following information.

An examination of the books and records of the Kay May Corporation, a machinery
wholesaler, reveals the following facts for the year ended December 31, 2015:

    a. Merchandise was sold and billed F.O.B. shipping point on December 31, 2015 at a
sales price of $7,500. Although the merchandise costing $6,000 was ready for shipment on that date, the trucking company did not call for the merchandise until January
2, 2016. It was not included in the inventory count taken on December 31, 2015.
    b. Merchandise with a sales price of $5,500 was billed and shipped to the customer on
December 31, 2015. The merchandise costing $4,800 was not included in the inven-
tory count taken on that day. Terms of sale were F.O.B. destination.
    c. Merchandise costing $5,000 was recorded as a purchase on December 26, 2015.
The merchandise was not included in the inventory count taken on December 31,
2015 since, upon examination, it was found to be defective and was in the process of
being returned to the vendor.
    d. Merchandise costing $2,500 was received on December 31, 2015. It was included in
the inventory count on that date. Although the invoice was dated January 3, 2016, the
purchase was recorded in the December 2015 Purchases Journal.
    e. Merchandise costing $4,000 was received on January 3, 2016. It was shipped F.O.B.
destination, and the invoice was dated December 30, 2015. The invoice was recorded
in the December 2015 Purchases Journal, and the merchandise was included in the
December 31, 2015 inventory.

11. The net change to correct the inventory value as of December 31, 2015 is: 11.____

    A. *Increase* $800   B. *Increase* $5,800
    C. *Increase* $6,800   D. *Decrease* $12,055

12. The net change to correct the sales figure for the year 2015 is: 12.____

    A. *Increase* $2,000   B. *Decrease* $5,500
    C. *Decrease* $7,500   D. *Decrease* $13,000

13. The net change to correct the purchases figure for the year 2015 is: 13.____

    A. *Decrease* $11,500   B. *Decrease* $4,000
    C. *Decrease* $5,000   D. *Decrease* $9,000

Questions 14-18.

DIRECTIONS: Each of the following Questions 14 through 18 consists of a description of a transaction that indicates a two-fold effect on the Balance Sheet. Each of these transactions may be classified under one of the following categories:

    A. Assets are Understated, Retained Earnings are Understated
    B. Assets are Overstated, Retained Earnings are Overstated
    C. Liabilities are Understated, Retained Earnings are Overstated
    D. Liabilities are Overstated, Retained Earnings are Understated

Examine each question carefully. In the correspondingly numbered space at the right, print the letter preceding the category above which BEST describes the effect of each transaction on the Balance Sheet as of December 31, 2015.

14. A major equipment purchase was made at the beginning of 2015. The equipment had an estimated six-year useful life, and depreciation was overlooked at December 31, 2015.   14.____

15. Unearned Rental Income was properly credited when received early in the year. No year-end adjustment was made to transfer the earned portion to an appropriate account.   15.____

16. Goods on hand at a branch office were excluded from the year-end physical inventory. The purchase of these goods had been properly recorded.   16.____

17. Accrued Interest on Notes Receivable was overlooked as of December 31, 2015.   17.____

18. Accrued Federal Income Taxes for 2015 have never been recorded.   18.____

19. The following are account balances for the dates shown: 19.____

	Dec. 31, 2016	Dec. 31, 2015
Current Assets :		
Cash	$168,000	$ 60,000
Short-term investments	16,000	20,000
Accounts receivable (net)	160,000	100,000
Inventory	60,000	40,000
Prepaid expenses	4,000	0

Current Liabilities:

Accounts payable	110,000	80,000
Dividends payable	30,000	0

Given the above account balances, the CHANGE in working capital is a(n)

A. *increase* of $128,000
B. *decrease* of $128,000
C. *increase* of $188,000
D. *decrease* of $188,000

20. In conducting an audit of plant assets, which of the following accounts MUST be examined in order to ascertain that additions to plant assets have been correctly stated and reflect charges that are properly capitalized?   20.____

A. Accounts receivable
B. Sales income
C. Maintenance and repairs
D. Investments

KEY (CORRECT ANSWERS)

1.	D		11.	A
2.	D		12.	B
3.	A		13.	D
4.	B		14.	B
5.	C		15.	D
6.	B		16.	A
7.	A		17.	A
8.	B		18.	C
9.	C		19.	A
10.	B		20.	C

EXAMINATION SECTION
TEST 1

DIRECTIONS: Each question or incomplete statement is followed by several suggested answers or completions. Select the one that BEST answers the question or completes the Statement. *PRINT THE LETTER OF THE CORRECT ANSWER IN THE SPACE AT THE RIGHT.*

1. Gross income of an individual for Federal income tax purposes does NOT include 1.____

    A. interest credited to a bank savings account
    B. gain from the sale of sewer authority bonds
    C. back pay received as a result of job reinstatement
    D. interest received from State Dormitory Authority bonds

2. A cash-basis, calendar-year taxpayer purchased an annuity policy at a total cost of $20,000. Starting on January 1 of 2015, he began to receive annual payments of $1,500. His life expectancy as of that date was 16 years.
The amount of annuity income to be included in his gross income for the taxable year 2015 is 2.____

    A. none   B. $250   C. $1,250   D. $1,500

3. The transactions related to a municipal police retirement system should be included in a(n) 3.____

    A. intra-governmental service fund
    B. trust fund
    C. general fund
    D. special revenue fund

4. The budget for a given cost during a given period was $100,000. The actual cost for the period was $90,000. Based upon these facts, one should say that the responsible manager has done a better than expected job in controlling the cost if the cost is 4.____

    A. variable and actual production equaled budgeted production
    B. a discretionary fixed cost and actual production equaled budgeted production
    C. variable and actual production was 90% of budgeted production
    D. variable and actual production was 80% of budgeted production

5. In the conduct of an audit, the *most practical* method by which an accountant can satisfy himself as to the physical existence of inventory is to 5.____

    A. be present and observe personally the audited firm's physical inventory being taken
    B. independently verify an adequate proportion of all inventory operations performed by the audited firm
    C. mail confirmation requests to vendors of merchandise sold to the audited firm within the inventory year
    D. review beforehand the adequacy of the audited firm's plan for inventory taking, and during the actual inventory-taking stages, verify that this plan is being followed

Questions 6-7.

DIRECTIONS: The following information applies to Questions 6 and 7.

For the month of March, the ABC Manufacturing Corporation's estimated factory overhead for an expected volume of 15,000 lbs. of a product was as follows:

	Amount	Overhead Rate Per Unit
Fixed Overhead	$3,000	$.20
Variable Overhead	$9,000	$.60

Actual volume was 10,000 lbs. and actual overhead expense was $7,700.

6. The Spending (Budget) Variance was   6._____

   A. $1,300 (Favorable)   B. $6,000 (Favorable)
   C. $7,700 (Favorable)   D. $9,000 (Favorable)

7. The Idle Capacity Variance was   7._____

   A. $300 (Favorable)   B. $1,000 (Unfavorable)
   C. $1,300 (Favorable)   D. $8,000 (Unfavorable)

Questions 8-11.

DIRECTIONS: Answer Questions 8 through 11 on the basis of the information given below.

A bookkeeper, who was not familiar with proper accounting procedures, prepared the following financial report for Largor Corporation as of December 31, 2015. In addition to the errors in presentation, additional data below was not considered in the preparation of the report. Restate this balance sheet in proper form, giving recognition to the additional data, so that you will be able to determine the required information to answer Questions 8 through 11.

LARGOR CORPORATION
December 31, 2015

Current Assets			
Cash		$110,000	
Marketable Securities		53,000	
Accounts Receivable	$261,400		
Accounts Payable	125,000	136,400	
Inventories		274,000	
Prepaid Expenses		24,000	
Treasury Stock		20,000	
Cash Surrender Value of Officers' Life Insuranc Policies		105,000	$722,400
Plant Assets			
Equipment		350,000	
Building	200,000		
Reserve for Plant Expansion	75,000	125,000	
Land		47,500	522,500
TOTAL ASSETS			$1,244,900

Liabilities

Salaries Payable		16,500	
Cash Dividend Payable		50,000	
Stock Dividend Payable		70,000	
Bonds Payable	200,000		
Less Sinking Fund	90,000	110,000	
TOTAL LIABILITIES			$246,500

Stockholders' Equity:

Paid In Capital

Common Stock		350,000	

Retained Earnings and Reserves

Reserve for Income Taxes	90,000		
Reserve for Doubtful Accounts	6,500		
Reserve for Treasury Stock	20,000		
Reserve for Depreciation Equipment	70,000		
Reserve for Depreciation Building	80,000		
Premium on Common stock	15,000		
Retained Earnings	366,900	648,400	998.400

TOTAL LIABILITIES & EQUITY		$1,244,900

Additional Data

A. Bond Payable will mature eight (8) years from Balance Sheet date.

B. The Stock Dividend Payable was declared on December 31, 2015.

C. The Reserve for Income Taxes represents the balance due on the estimated liability for taxes on income for the year ended December 31.

D. Advances from Customers at the Balance Sheet date totaled $13,600. This total is still credited against Accounts Receivable.

E. Prepaid Expenses include Unamortized Mortgage Costs of $15,000.

F. Marketable Securities were recorded at cost. Their market value at December 31, 2015 was $50,800.

8. After restatement of the balance sheet in proper form and giving recognition to the additional data, the Total Current Assets should be   8.____

A. $597,400   B. $702,400   C. $712,300   D. $827,300

9. After restatement of the balance sheet in proper form and giving recognition to the additional data, the Total Current Liabilities should be   9.____

A. $261,500   B. $281,500   C. $295,100   D. . D. $370,100

10. After restatement of the balance sheet in proper form and giving recognition to the additional data, the net book value of plant and equipment should be   10.____

A. $400,000   B. B, $447,500   C. $550,000   D. $597,500

11. After restatement of the balance sheet in proper form and giving recognition to the additional data, the Stockholders Equity should be   11.____

A. $320,000   B. $335,000   C. $764,700   D. $874,700

12. When preparing the financial statement, dividends in arrears on preferred stock should be treated as a   12._____

    A. contingent liability   B. deduction from capital
    C. parenthetical remark   D. valuation reserve

13. The IPC Corporation has an intangible asset which it values at $1,000,000 and has a life expectancy of 60 years. The *appropriate* span of write-off, as determined by good accounting practice, should be _____ years.   13._____

    A. 17   B. 34   C. 40   D. 60

14. The following information was used in costing inventory on October 31:   14._____

October				
1 -	Beginning inventory -	800 units	@	$1.20
4 -	Received	200 units	@	$1.40
16 -	Issued	400 units		
24 -	Received	200 units	@	$1.60
27 -	Issued	500 units		

    Using the LIFO method of inventory evaluation (end-of-month method), the total dollar value of the inventory at October 31 was   14._____

    A. $360   B. $460   C. $600   D. $1,200

15. If a $400,000 par value bond issue paying 8%, with interest dates of June 30 and December 31, is sold in November 1 for par plus accrued interest, the cash proceeds received by the issuer on November 1 should be *approximately*   15._____

    A. $405,000   B. $408,000   C. $411,000   D. $416,000

16. The TOTAL interest cost to the issuer of a bond issue sold for more than its face value is the periodic interest payment   16._____

    A. *plus* the discount amortization
    B. *plus* the premium amortization
    C. *minus* the discount amortization
    D. *minus* the premium amortization

17. If shareholders donate shares of stock back to the company, such stock received by the company is *properly* classified as   17._____

    A. Treasury stock
    B. Unissued stock
    C. Other assets - investment
    D. Current assets - investment

18. Assume the following transactions have occurred: 18._____
    1. 10,000 shares of capital stock of Omer Corp., par value $50, have been sold and issued on initial sale @ $55 per share during the month of June
    2. 2,000 shares of previously issued stock were purchased from shareholders during the month of September @ $58 per share.

    As of September 30, the stockholders' equity section TOTAL should be

    A. $434,000   B. $450,000   C. $480,000   D. $550,000

19. Mr. Diak, a calendar-year taxpayer in the construction business, agrees to construct a building for the Supermat Corporation to cost a total of $500,000 and to require about two years to complete. By December 31, 2015, he has expended $150,000 in costs, and it was determined that the building was 35% completed.
    If Mr. Diak is reporting income under the completed contract method, the amount of gross income he will report for 2015 is

19.____

    A. none   B. $25,000   C. $175,000   D. $350,000

20. When the Board of Directors of a firm uses the present-value technique to aid in deciding whether or not to buy a new plant asset, it needs to have information reflecting

20.____

    A. the cost of the new asset only
    B. the increased production from use of new asset only
    C. an estimated rate of return
    D. the book value of the asset

KEY (CORRECT ANSWERS)

1.	D	11.	D
2.	B	12.	C
3.	B	13.	C
4.	A	14.	A
5.	D	15.	C
6.	A	16.	D
7.	B	17.	A
8.	C	18.	A
9.	C	19.	A
10.	B	20.	C

TEST 2

DIRECTIONS: Each question or incomplete statement is followed by several suggested answers or completions. Select the one that BEST answers the question or completes the statement. *PRINT THE LETTER OF THE CORRECT ANSWER IN THE SPACE AT THE RIGHT.*

Questions 1-3.

DIRECTIONS: The following information applies to Questions 1 through 3.

During your audit of the Avon Company, you find the following errors in the records of the company:

1. Incorrect exclusion from the final inventory of items costing $3,000 for which the purchase was not recorded.
2. Inclusion in the final inventory of goods costing $5,000, although a purchase was not recorded. The goods in question were being held on consignment from Reldrey Company.
3. Incorrect exclusion of $2,000 from the inventory count at the end of the period. The goods were in transit (F.O.B. shipping point); the invoice had been received and the purchase recorded.
4. Inclusion of items on the receiving dock that were being held for return to the vendor because of damage. In counting the goods in the receiving department, these items were incorrectly included. With respect to these goods, a purchase of $4,000 had been recorded.

The records (uncorrected) showed the following amounts:
1. Purchases, $170,000
2. Pretax income, $15,000
3. Accounts payable, $20,000; and
4. Inventory at the end of the period, $40,000.

1. The *corrected* inventory is

   A. $36,000   B. $42,000   C. $43,000   D. $44,000

1.____

2. The *corrected* income for the year is

   A. $12,000   B. $15,000   C. $17,000   D. $18,000

2.____

3. The *correct* accounts payable liabilities are

   A. $16,000   B. $17,000   C. $19,000   D. $23,000

3.____

4. An auditing procedure that is *most likely* to reveal the existence of a contingent liability is

   A. a review of vouchers paid during the month following the year end
   B. confirmation of accounts payable
   C. an inquiry directed to legal counsel
   D. confirmation of mortgage notes

4.____

Questions 5-6.

DIRECTIONS: The following information is to be used in answering Questions 5 and 6.

Mr. Zelev operates a business as a sole proprietor and uses the cash basis for reporting income for income tax purposes. His bank account during 2015 for the business shows receipts totaling $285,000 and cash payments totaling $240,000. Included in the cash payments were payments for three-year business insurance policies whose premiums totaled $1,575. It was determined that the expired premiums for this year were $475. Further examination of the accounts and discussion with Mr. Zelev revealed the fact that included in the receipts were the following items, as well as the proceeds received from customers:

$15,000 which Mr. Zelev took from his savings account and deposited in the business account.

$20,000 which Mr. Zelev received from the bank as a loan which will be repaid next year.

Included in the cash payments were $10,000 which Mr. Zelev took on a weekly basis from the business receipts to use for his personal expenses.

5. The amount of net income to be reported for income tax purposes for calendar year 2006 for Mr. Zelev is   5.____

   A. $21,100   B. $26,100   C. $31,100   D. $46,100

6. Assuming the same facts as those reported above, Mr. Zelev would be required to pay a self-employment tax for 2006 of   6.____

   A. $895.05   B. $1,208.70   C. $1,234.35   D. $1,666.90

7. For the year ended December 31, 2015, you are given the following information relative to the income and expense statements for the Sungam Manufacturers, Inc.:   7.____
   Sales $1,000,000
     Sales Returns 95,000

   Cost of Sales
   Opening Inventories $200,000
   Purchases During the Year   567,000
   Direct Labor Costs   240,000
   Factory Overhead   24,400
   Inventories End of Year   235,000

   On June 15, 2015, a fire destroyed the plant and all of the inventories then on hand. You are given the following information and asked to ascertain the amount of the estimated inventory loss.

   Sales up to June 15 $545,000
   Purchased to June 15   254,500
   Direct Labor   233,000
   Overhead   14,550
   Salvaged Inventory   95,000
   The *estimated* inventory loss is

   A. $95,000   B. $162,450   C. $189,450   D. $257,450

8. Losses and excessive costs with regard to inventory can occur in any one of several operating functions of an organization.
The operating function which bears the GREATEST responsibility for the failure to give proper consideration to transportation costs of material acquisitions is

   A. accounting
   C. receiving
                  B. purchasing
                  D. shipping

8._____

Questions 9-17.

DIRECTIONS: Questions 9 through 17 are to be answered on the basis of the information given below.

You are conducting an audit of the PAP Company, which has a contract to supply the municipal hospitals with specialty refrigerators on a cost-plus basis. The following information is available:

Materials purchased	$1,946,700
Inventories, January 1	
Materials	268,000
Finished Goods (100 units)	43,000
Direct Labor	2,125,800
Factory Overhead (40% variable)	764,000
Marketing Expenses (all fixed)	516,000
Administrative Expenses (all fixed)	461,000
Sales (12,400 units)	6,634,000
Inventories, March 31	
Materials	167,000
Finished Goods (200 units)	(omitted)
No Work In Process	

9. The *net income* for the period is

   A. $755,500
   C. $1,732,500
            B. $1,237,500
            D. $4,980,500

9._____

10. The *number* of units manufactured is

   A. 12,400   B. 12,500   C. 12,600   D. 12,700

10._____

11. The *unit cost* of refrigerators manufactured is *most nearly*

   A. $389.00   B. $395.00   C. $398.00   D. $400.00

11._____

12. The *total* variable costs are

   A. $305,600
   C. $4,479,100
            B. $764,000
            D. $4,937,500

12._____

13. The *total* fixed costs are

   A. $458,400
   C. $1,471,800
            B. $1,435,400
            D. $1,741,000

13._____

While you are conducting your audit, the PAP Company advises you that they have changed their inventory costing from FIFO to LIFO. You are interested in pursuing the matter further because this change will affect the cost of the refrigerators. An examination of material part 2-317 inventory card shows the following activity:

May 2 - Received 100 units @ $5.40 per unit
May 8 - Received 30 units @ $8.00 per unit
May 15 - Issued 50 units
May 22 - Received 120 units @ $9.00 per unit
May 29 - Issued 100 units

14. Using the FIFO method under a perpetual inventory control system, the *total* cost of the units issued in May is   14.____

    A. $690   B. $960   C. $1,590   D. $1,860

15. Using the FIFO method under a perpetual inventory control system, the *value* of the clos-ing inventory is   15.____

    A. $780   B. $900   C. $1,080   D. $1,590

16. Using the LIFO method under a perpetual inventory control system, the *total* cost of the units issued in May is   16.____

    A. $1,248   B. $1,428   C. $1,720   D. $1,860

17. Using the LIFO method under a perpetual inventory control system, the *value* of the clos-ing inventory is   17.____

    A. $612   B. $780   C. $1,512   D. $1,680

Questions 18-20.

DIRECTIONS: For Questions 18 through 20, consider that the EEF Corporation has a fully integrated cost accounting system.

18. Unit cost of manufacturing dresses was $7.00. Spoiled dresses numbered 400 with a sales value of $800. When it is not customary to have a Spoiled Work account, the *most appropriate* account to be credited is   18.____

    A. Work In Process   B. Cost of Sales
    C. Manufacturing Overhead   D. Finished Goods

19. Overtime premium for factory workers (direct labor) totaled $400 for the payroll period. This was due to inadequate plant capacity. The account to be *debited* is   19.____

    A. Work In Process   B. Cost of Sales
    C. Manufacturing Overhead   D. Finished Goods

20. A month-end physical inventory of stores shows a shortage of $175. The account to be *debited* to correct this shortage is   20.____

    A. Stores   B. Work In Process
    C. Cost of Sales   D. Manufacturing Overhead

KEY (CORRECT ANSWERS)

1.	A		11.	B
2.	A		12.	C
3.	C		13.	B
4.	C		14.	B
5.	A		15.	B
6.	D		16.	A
7.	B		17.	A
8.	B		18.	A
9.	A		19.	C
10.	B		20.	C

EXAMINATION SECTION
TEST 1

DIRECTIONS: Each question or incomplete statement is followed by several suggested answers or completions. Select the one that BEST answers the question or completes the statement. *PRINT THE LETTER OF THE CORRECT ANSWER IN THE SPACE AT THE RIGHT.*

1. The independent auditor's PRIMARY objective in reviewing internal control is to provide   1.____
   A. assurance of the client's operational efficiency
   B. a basis for reliance on the system and determination of the scope of the auditing procedures
   C. a basis for suggestions for improving the client's accounting system
   D. evidence of the client's adherence to prescribed managerial policies

2. If there is an increase in work-in-process inventory during a period,   2.____
   A. cost of goods sold will be greater than cost of goods manufactured
   B. cost of goods manufactured will be greater than cost of goods sold
   C. manufacturing costs (production costs) for the period will be greater than cost of goods manufactured
   D. manufacturing costs for the period will be less than cost of goods manufactured

Questions 3-4.

DIRECTIONS: Questions 3 and 4 are to be answered on the basis of the information given below about the Parr Company and the Farr Company.

The Parr Company purchased 800 of the 1,000 outstanding shares of the Farr Company's common stock for $80,000 on January 1, 2018. During 2018, the Farr Company declared dividends of $8,000 and reported earnings for the year of $20,000.

3. Using the equity method, the investment in Farr Company on the Parr Company's books should show a balance, at December 31, 2018, of   3.____
   A. $89,600   B. $86,400   C. $80,000   D. $73,600

4. If, instead of using the equity method, the Parr Company uses the cost method, the balance, at December 31, 2018, in the investment account, should be   4.____
   A. $96,000   B. $86,400   C. $80,000   D. $73,600

Questions 5-6.

DIRECTIONS: Questions 5 and 6 are to be answered on the basis of the information given below about the Fame Corporation.

The Fame Corporation has 50,000 shares of $10 par value common stock authorized, issued and outstanding. The 50,000 shares were issued at $12 per share. The retained earnings of the company are $60,000.

5. Assuming that the Fame Corporation reacquired 1,000 of its common shares at $15 per share and the par value method of accounting for treasury stock was used, the result would be that
   A. stockholders' equity would increase by $15,000
   B. capital in excess of par would decrease by at least $2,000
   C. retained earnings would decrease by $5,000
   D. common stock would decrease by at least $15,000

5.____

6. Assuming that the Fame Corporation reissued 1,000 of its common shares at $11 per share and the cost method of accounting for treasury stock was used, the result would be that
   A. book value per share of common stock would decrease
   B. retained earnings would decrease by $11,000
   C. donated surplus would be credited for $5,500
   D. a gain on reissue of treasury stock account would be charged

6.____

7. On January 31, 2018, when the Montana Corporation's stock was selling at $36 per share, its capital accounts were as follows:
   Capital Stock (par value $20; 100,000 shares issued) $2,000,000
   Premium on Capital Stock   800,000
   Retained earnings   4,550,000
   If the corporation declares a 100% stock dividend and the par value per share remains at $20, the value of the capital stock would
   A. remain the same   B. increase to $5,600,000
   C. increase to $5,000,000   D. decrease

7.____

8. In a conventional form of the statement of sources and application of funds, which one of the following would NOT be included?
   A. Periodic amortization of premium of bonds payable
   B. Machinery, fully depreciated and scrapped
   C. Patents written off
   D. Treasury stock purchased from a stockholder

8.____

Questions 9-11.

DIRECTIONS: Questions 9 through 11 are to be answered on the basis of the balance sheet shown below for the Argo, Baron and Schooster partnership.

Cash	$ 20,000
Other assets	180,000
Total	$200,000
Liabilities	$ 50,000
Argo Capital (40%)	37,000
Baron Capital (40%)	65,000
Schooster Capital (20%)	48,000
Total	$200,000

9. If George is to be admitted as a new 1/6 partner without recording goodwill or bonus, George should contribute cash of   9.____
   A. $40,000   B. $36,000   C. $33,333   D. $30,000

10. Assume that Schooster is paid $51,000 by George for his interest in the partnership.   10.____
    Which of the following choices shows the CORRECT revised capital account for each partner?
    A. Argo, $38,500; Baron, $66,500; George, $51,000
    B. Argo, $38,500; Baron, $66,500; George, $48,000
    C. Argo, $37,000; Baron, $65,000; George, $51,000
    D. Argo, $37,000; Baron, $65,000; George, $48,000

11. Assume that George had not been admitted as a partner but that the partnership was dissolved and liquidated on the basis of the original balance sheet. Non-cash assets with a book value of $90,000 were sold for $50,000 cash. After payment of creditors, all available cash was distributed.   11.____
    Which of the following choices MOST NEARLY shows what each of the partners would receive?
    A. Argo, $0; Baron, $13,333; Schooster, $6,667
    B. Argo, $0; Baron, $3,000; Schooster, $17,000
    C. Argo, $6,667; Baron, $6,667; Schooster, $6,666
    D. Argo, $8,000; Baron, $8,000; Schooster, $4,000

12. Which one of the following should be restricted to ONLY one employee in order to assure proper control of assets?   12.____
    A. Access to safe deposit box
    B. Placing orders and maintaining relationship with a principal vendor
    C. Collection of a particular past due account
    D. Custody of the petty cash fund

23

13. To assure proper internal control, the quantities of materials ordered may be omitted from that copy of the purchase order which is
    A. sent to the accounting department
    B. retained in the purchasing department
    C. sent to the party requisitioning the material
    D. sent to the receiving department

13.____

14. The Amey Corporation has an inventory of raw materials and parts made up of many different items which are of small value individually but of significant total value.
    A BASIC control requirement in such a situation is that
    A. perpetual inventory records should be maintained for all items
    B. physical inventories should be taken on a cyclical basis rather than at year end
    C. storekeeping, production, and inventory record-keeping functions should be separated
    D. requisitions for materials should be approved by a corporate officer

14.____

15. In conducting an audit of plant assets, which of the following accounts MUST be examined in order to ascertain that additions to plant assets have been correctly stated and reflect charges that are properly capitalized?
    A. Accounts Receivable   B. Sales Income
    C. Maintenance and Repairs   D. Investments

15.____

16. Which one of the following is a control procedure that would prevent a vendor's invoice from being paid twice (once upon the original invoice and once upon the monthly statement)?
    A. Attaching the receiving report to the disbursement support papers
    B. Prenumbering of disbursement vouchers
    C. Using a limit or reasonable test
    D. Prenumbering of receiving reports

16.____

17. A "cut-off" bank statement is received for the period December 1 to December 10, 2017. Very few of the checks listed on the November 30, 2017 bank reconciliation cleared during the cut-off period.
    Of the following, the MOST likely reason for this is
    A. kiting
    B. using certified checks rather than ordinary checks
    C. holding the cash disbursement book open after year end
    D. overstating year-end bank balance

17.____

18. "Lapping" is a common type of defalcation.
    Of the audit techniques listed below, the one MOST effective in the detection of "lapping" is
    A. reconciliation of year-end bank statements
    B. review of duplicate deposit slips
    C. securing confirmations from banks
    D. checking footings in cash journals

18.____

19. Of the following, the MOST common argument against the use of the negative   19.____
accounts receivable confirmation is that
    A. cost per response is excessively high
    B. statistical sampling techniques cannot be applied to selection of the
       sample
    C. client's customers may assume that the confirmation is a request for
       payment
    D. lack of response does not necessarily indicate agreement with the
       balance

Questions 20-21.

DIRECTIONS: Questions 20 and 21 are to be answered on the basis of the information in the
Payroll Summary given below. This Payroll Summary represents payroll for a
monthly period for a particular agency.

PAYROLL SUMMARY

| Employee | Total Earnings | Deductions | | | | Net Pay |
		FICA	Withhold. Tax	State Tax	Other	
W	450.00	26.00	67.00	18.00	6.00	333.00
X	235.00	14.00	33.00	8.00	2.00	178.00
Y	341.00	20.00	52.00	14.00	5.00	250.00
Z	275.00	16.00	30.00	6.00	2.40	220.60
Totals	1,301.00	76.00	182.00	46.00	15.40	981.60

20. Based on the data given above, the amount of cash that would have to be   20.____
available to pay the employees on payday is
    A. $1,301.00   B. $981.60   C. $905.60   D. $662.60

21. Based on the data given above, the amount required to be deposited with a   21.____
governmental depository is
    A. $334.00   B. $182.00   C. $158.00   D. $76.00

Questions 22-23.

DIRECTIONS: Questions 22 and 23 are to be answered on the basis of the information given
below concerning an imprest fund.

Assume a $1,020 imprest fund for cash expenditures is maintained in your agency. As an
audit procedure, the fund is counted and the following information results from that count.

Unreimbursed bills properly authorized	$345.00
Check from employee T. Jones	125.00
Check from Supervisor R. Riggles	250.00
I.O.U. signed by employee J. Sloan	100.00
Cash counted – coins and bills	200.00
TOTAL	$1,020.00

6 (#1)

22. A PROPER statement of cash on hand based upon the data shown above should show a balance of
A. $1,020   B. $1,000   C. $545   D. $200

22.____

23. Based upon the data shown above, the account reflects IMPROPER handling of the fund because
A. vouchers are unreimbursed
B. the cash balance is too low
C. employees have used it for loans and check-cashing purposes
D. the unreimbursed bills should not have been authorized

23.____

Questions 24-25.

DIRECTIONS: Questions 24 and 25 are to be answered on the basis of the following information.

The following information was taken from the ledgers of the Past Present Corporation: Common stock had been issued for $6,000,000. This represented 400,000 shares of stock at a stated value of $5 per share. Fifty-thousand shares are in the treasury. These 50,000 shares were acquired for $25 per share. The total undistributed net income since the origin of the corporation was $3,750,000 as of December 31, 2017. Ten-thousand of the treasury stock shares were sold in January 2018 for $30 per share.

24. Based only on the information given above, the TOTAL stockholders' equity that should have been shown on the balance sheet as of December 31, 2017 was
A. $2,000,000   B. $6,000,000   C. $8,500,000 D. $9,750,000

24.____

25. Based only on the information given above, the Retained Earnings as of December 31, 2018 will be
A. $2,000,000   B. $3,750,000   C. $3,800,000 D. $4,050,000

25.____

Questions 26-29.

DIRECTIONS: Questions 26 through 29 are to be answered on the basis of the following information.
A statement of income for the Dartmouth Corporation for the 2018 fiscal year follows:

Sales	$89,000	
Cost of Goods Sold	20,000	
Gross Margin		$34,000
Expenses		20,000
Net Income Before Income Taxes		$14,000
Provision for Income Taxes (50%)		7,000
Net Income		$7,000

The following errors were discovered relating to the 2018 fiscal year:
- Closing inventory was overstated by $2,100
- A $3,000 expenditure was capitalized during fiscal year 2018 that should have been listed under Expenses. This was subject to 10% amortization taken for a full year.
- Sales included $3,500 of deposits received from customers for future orders.
- Accrued salaries of $850 were not included in Cost of Goods Sold.
- Interest receivable of $500 was omitted.

Assume that the books were not closed and that you have prepared a corrected income statement. Answer Questions 26 through 29 on the basis of your corrected income statement.

26. The gross margin after accounting for adjustments SHOULD BE　　　26.____
    A. $37,500　　　B. $35,400　　　C. $31,900　　　D. $27,550

27. The adjusted income before income taxes SHOULD BE　　　27.____
    A. $5,350　　　B. $9,550　　　C. $15,000　　　D. $15,850

28. The adjusted income after provision for a 50% tax rate SHOULD BE　　　28.____
    A. $7,925　　　B. $7,500　　　C. $4,500　　　D. $2,675

29. After making adjustments, sales to be reported for fiscal year 2018 SHOULD BE　　　29.____
    A. unchanged　　　　　　　　　B. increased by $3,500
    C. decreased by $3,500　　　　D. reduced by $2,100

Questions 30-33.

DIRECTIONS:　Questions 30 through 33 are to be answered on the basis of the following budget for the Utility Corporation for 2017:

Sales	$550,000
Cost of Goods Sold	320,000
Selling Expenses	75,000
General Expenses	60,000
Net Income	95,000

30. If sales are actually 12% above the budget, then ACTUAL sales will be　　　30.____
    A. $550,000　　　B. $562,000　　　C. $605,000　　　D. $616,000

31. If actual costs of goods sold exceed the budget by 10%, then the cost of goods sold will be　　　31.____
    A. $294,400　　　B. $320,000　　　C. $345,600　　　D. $352,000

32. If selling expenses exceed the budget by 10%, the INCREASE in the selling expenses will be　　　32.____
    A. $750　　　B. $3,750　　　C. $7,500　　　D. $8,333

33. If general expenses are under budget by 5%, they will amount to   33.____
   A. $3,000   B. $57,000   C. $60,000   D. $63,000

Questions 34-35.

DIRECTIONS: Questions 34 and 35 are to be answered on the basis of the following information.

The Yontiff Company began business on January 2, 2018. During the first month, credit sales totaled $100,000. During February, credit sales totaled $125,000. 70% of credit sales are paid during the month of sale, and the balance is collected during the following month.

34. During the month of January, cash collections on credit sales totaled   34.____
   A. $70,000   B. $95,000   C. $100,000   D. $125,000

35. During the month of February, cash collections on credit sales totaled   35.____
   A. $70,000   B. $87,500   C. $117,505   D. $125,000

Questions 36-38.

DIRECTIONS: Questions 36 through 38 are to be answered on the basis of the following information taken from the balance sheet of the F Corporation.

   Common Stock $200 Par $1,400,000
   Premium on Common Stock   115,000
   Deficit   50,000

36. The number of shares of common stock outstanding is   36.____
   A. 200   B. 700   C. 7,000   D. 14,000

37. The total equity is   37.____
   A. $50,000   B. $115,000   C. $1,400,000   D. $1,465,000

38. The book value per share of stock is MOST NEARLY   38.____
   A. $160   B. $200   C. $209   D. $312

Questions 39-40.

DIRECTIONS: Questions 39 and 40 are to be answered on the basis of the following statement.

You are examining the expense accounts of a contractor and you discover that, although his payroll records show proper deductions from employees, he has never provided for the payroll tax expenses for these employees.

39. As a result of the oversight described in the above statement, the Costs of   39.____
   Construction in Progress as given on the balance sheet will be _____ on the balance sheet.
   A. understated   B. overstated   C. unaffected   D. omitted

40. As a result of the oversight described in the above statement, the balance sheet   40.____
for the firm will reflect an
A. overstatement of liabilities   B. understatement of liabilities
C. overstatement of assets   D. understatement of assets

_____

KEY (CORRECT ANSWERS)

1.	B	11.	D	21.	A	31.	D
2.	C	12.	D	22.	D	32.	C
3.	A	13.	D	23.	C	33.	B
4.	C	14.	C	24.	C	34.	A
5.	B	15.	C	25.	B	35.	C
6.	A	16.	A	26.	D	36.	C
7.	A	17.	C	27.	A	37.	D
8.	B	18.	B	28.	D	38.	C
9.	D	19.	D	29.	C	39.	A
10.	D	20.	B	30.	D	40.	B

_____

TEST 2

DIRECTIONS: Each question or incomplete statement is followed by several suggested answers or completions. Select the one that BEST answers the question or completes the statement. *PRINT THE LETTER OF THE CORRECT ANSWER IN THE SPACE AT THE RIGHT.*

Questions 1-4.

DIRECTIONS: Questions 1 through 4 are to be answered on the basis of the following information.

In the audit of the Audell Co. for the calendar year 2017, the accountant noted the following errors:

- An adjusting entry for $10 for interest accrued on a customer's $4,000, 60-day, 6% note was not recorded at the end of December 2016. In 2017 the total interest received was credited to Interest Income.
- Equipment was leased on December 1, 2016 and rental of $300 was paid in advance for the next three months and charged to Rent Expense.
- On November 1, 2016, space was rented at $75 per month. The tenant paid six months rent in advance which was credited to Rent Income.
- Salary expenses in the amount of $60 were not recorded at the end of 2016.
- Depreciation in the amount of $80 was not recorded at the end of 2016.
- An error of $200 in addition on the year-end 2016 physical inventory sheets was made. The inventory was overstated.

1. The amount of the net adjustment to Net Income for 2016 is   1._____
     A. Credit $430   B. Debit $430   C. Credit $600   D. Credit $560

2. The net change in asset values at December 31, 2016 is   2._____
     A. Credit $70   B. Debit $70   C. Debit $110   D. Credit $60

3. The net change in liabilities at December 31, 2016 is   3._____
     A. Debit $360   B. Credit $430   C. Debit $560   D. Credit $360

4. The net change in Owner's Equity at December 31, 2016 is   4._____
     A. Debit $710   B. Debit $430   C. Credit $320   D. Credit $710

5. As of October 2, 2017, the Mallory Company's books reflect a balance of   5._____
$2,104.75 in its account entitled, Cash in Bank. A comparison of the book entries with the bank statement showed the following:

- A check in the amount of $76.25 outstanding at the end of September 2017 had not been returned.
- One check, which was returned with the October bank statement, in the amount of $247 had been recorded in the October cash book as $274.
- A total of $139 of checks issued in October had not been returned with the October bank statement.
- A deposit of $65 was returned by the bank because of insufficient funds.

- The bank charged a service charge of $3.25 for the month of October which was not reported on the books until November.
- The bank had credited $247 representing a note collected in the amount of $250 which was not picked up on the books until November.
- A deposit of $305.50 was recorded on the books in October but not on the bank statement.

The balance in the bank as shown on the bank statement at October 31, 2017 is

    A. $2,220.25   B. $2,104.75   C. $2,006.25 D. $2,315.25

Questions 6-8.

DIRECTIONS: Questions 6 through 8 are to be answered on the basis of the following information.

    A company purchased three cars at $3,150 each on April 2, 2018. Depreciation is to be computed on a mileage basis. The estimated mileage to be considered is 50,000 miles, with a trade-in value of $650 for each car.
    After having been driven 8,400 miles, car #1 was completely destroyed on November 23, 2017 and not replaced. The insurance company paid $2,500 for the loss.
    As of December 31, 2017, of the two remaining cars, car #2 had been driven 10,300 miles and car #3 was driven 11,500 miles.
    On July 10, 2018, after having been driven a total of 24,600 miles, car #2 was sold for $1,800.
    Car #3, after having been driven a total of 27,800 miles, was traded in on December 28, 2018 for a new car (#4) that had a list price of $3,000. On the purchase of car #4, the dealer allowed a trade-in value of $1,850.

6.   The balance in the Allowance for Depreciation account at December 31, 2017 is   6._____
    A. $1,850   B. $910   C. $1,090   D. $1,110

7.   The depreciation expense for the calendar year 2018 is   7._____
    A. $1,530   B. $2,000   C. $2,500   D. $3,000

8.   The book value of the new car (car #4), using the income tax method, is   8._____
    A. $1,850   B. $3,000   C. $2,500   D. $2,910

Questions 9-10.

DIRECTIONS: Questions 9 and 10 are to be answered on the basis of the following information.

    The Pneumatic Corp. showed the following balance sheets at December 31, 2017 and December 31, 2018:

	12/31/2017	12/31/2018
Cash	$6,700	$9,000
Accounts Receivable	12,000	11,500
Merchandise Inventory	31,500	32,000
Prepaid Expenses	800	1,000
Equipment	21,000	28,000
	$72,000	$81,500
Accumulated Depreciation	$4,000	$5,500
Accounts Payable	17,500	11,500
Common Stock - $5 Per Share	10,000	5,000
Premium on Common Stock	40,000	50,000
Retained Earnings	10,500	13,000
	$72,000	$81,500

Additional Information:
A further examination of the Pneumatic Corp.'s transactions for 2018 showed the following:
- Depreciation on equipment, $2,500
- Fully depreciated equipment that cost $1,000 was scrapped, and cost and related accumulated depreciation eliminated.
- Two thousand shares of common stock were sold at $6 per share.
- A cash dividend of $10,000 was paid.

9. A statement of funds provided and applied for the calendar year 2018 would 9.____
    show that net income provided funds in the amount of
    A. $2,500   B. $9,500   C. $15,000   D. $22,500

10. The funds applied to the acquisition of equipment during the calendar year 10.____
    2018 amounts to
    A. $21,000   B. $28,000   C. $1,000   D. $8,000

11. A company's Wage Expense account had a $19,100 debit balance before 11.____
    any adjustment at the end of its December 31, 2017 fiscal year. The company
    employs five individuals who earn $15 per day and were paid on Friday for the
    five days ending on Friday, December 26, 2017. All employees worked during
    the week ending January 2, 2018.
    The adjusted balance in the Wage Expense account at December 31, 2017 is
    A. $22,300   B. $19,100   C. $19,250   D. $19,325

Questions 12-13.

DIRECTIONS: Questions 12 and 13 are to be answered on the basis of the following
                        information.

        The Peach Corp.'s books reflect an account entitled "Allowance for Bad Debts" showing a
credit balance of $1,510 as of January 1, 2017.
        During 2017, it wrote off $735 of bad debts and increased the allowance for bad debts by
an amount equal to ¼ of 1% of sales of $408,000.
        During 2018, it wrote off $605 as bad debts and recorded $50 of a debt that had been
previously written off.
        An addition to the "Allowance for Bad Debts" was provided based upon ¼ of 1% on
$478,000 of sales.

12.   The balance in the "Allowance for Bad Debts" account at December 31, 2018 is   12.____
        A. $2,550   B. $2,435   C. $2,360   D. $2,240

13.   The amount of the Bad Debt expense for the calendar year 2018 is   13.____
        A. $1,195   B. $1,405   C. $1,000   D. $1,510

14.   The following ratio is based upon the 2018 financial statements of the Chino   14.____
        Corp.:
          Number of Times Bond Interest Earned: $28,000/$3,000 = 9.33 times
        Information relating to the corrections of the income data for 2018 follows:
        •   Rental payment for December 2018 at $1,200 per month had been
             recorded in January 2019. No provision has been made for this expense
             on the 2018 books.
        •   During 2018, merchandise shipped on consignment and unsold had been
             recorded as
                        Debit – Accounts Receivable $4,000
                        Credit – Sales   4,000
        (Note: The inventory of this merchandise was properly recorded.)
        If the described ratio, Number of Times Bond Interest Earned, was recomputed,
        taking into consideration the corrections listed above and ignoring tax factors in
        the calculations, the recomputed Number of Times Bond Interest Earned would
        be _____ times.
        A. 8.10   B. 7.60   C. 6.20   D. 5.10

Questions 15-16.

DIRECTIONS: Questions 15 and 16 are to be answered on the basis of the following information.

The Delancey Department Store, Inc. sells merchandise on the installment basis. The selling price of its merchandise is $500 and its cost is $325.

At the end of its fiscal year, an examination of its accounts showed the following:

Sales (Installment)	$500,000
Installment Accounts Receivable	280,000
Sales Commissions	15,000
Other Expenses	32,000

15. The net income for the fiscal year, before taxes, using the installment method of reporting income, is

    A. $30,000   B. $20,000   C. $15,000   D. $35,000

15.____

16. The balance in the Deferred Income Account at the end of the fiscal year is

    A. $110,000   B. $80,000   C. $76,000   D. $98,000

16.____

Questions 17-18.

DIRECTIONS: Questions 17 and 18 are to be answered on the basis of the following information.

The Merrimac Company sold 8,800 units of a product at $5 per unit during the calendar year 2018. In addition, it had the following transactions:

	Units	Unit Cost
Inventory – January 1, 2018	1,000	$2.80
Purchases – March	1,000	3.00
June	4,000	3.20
September	3,000	3.30
October	1,000	3.50

17. If we assume that selling and administrative expenses cost $8,800, the Net Income for the calendar year 2018, using the first-in first-out method of costing inventory, is

    A. $8,460   B. $7,360   C. $6,600   D. $4,070

17.____

18. If we assume that selling and administrative expenses cost $8,800, the Net Income for the calendar year 2018, using the last-in first-out method of costing inventory, is

    A. $4,550   B. $7,360   C. $6,600   D. $5,000

18.____

19. L. Eron and A. Pilott are partners who share income and losses in the ratio   19.____
3:2, respectively. The balance in the Profit and Loss account on December 31,
2018, prior to distribution to the partners, is $20,800. Before distributing any
profits to the partnership in the agreed ratio, L. Eron is to be given credit for
interest on his loan of $60,000, outstanding for the entire year, at 6% per
annum. A. Pilott is to receive a bonus of 10% of the net income over $5,100,
after deducting the bonus to himself and the interest to L. Eron.
Giving consideration to all the above information, the total amount of net
income to be credited to A. Pilott is
   A. $8,320   B. $2,080   C. $7,540   D. $15,700

Questions 20-21.

DIRECTIONS: Questions 20 and 21 are to be answered on the basis of the following
              information.

   Schneider and Samuels are partners with capital balances on December 31, 2018 of
$15,000 and $25,000, respectively. They share profits in a ratio of 2:1.
   Goroff is to be admitted to the partnership. He agrees to be admitted as a partner with a
cash investment to give him a one-third interest in the capital and profits of the business. All the
parties agree that the good will to be granted to Goroff should be valued at $6,000.

20. The required cash to cover Goroff's investment in a business partnership   20.____
according to the terms stated is
   A. $20,000   B. $14,000   C. $6,000   D. $25,000

21. After his cash investment, and all other initial entries, the credit to Goroff's   21.____
Capital account is
   A. $20,000   B. $14,000   C. $6,000   D. $25,000

22. The Marlin Corp. sold 7,800 units of its product at $25 per unit and suffered   22.____
a net loss for its calendar year ending December 31, 2017 of $2,000. The fixed
expenses amounted to $80,000 and the variable expenses $117,000. The
Marlin Corp. believes that by expending $20,000 in an advertising campaign, it
could increase its sales, retaining the $25 per unit selling price, to generate a
profit.
Assuming the above facts, the sales revenue for 2017 reflecting the break-even
point is
   A. $195,000   B. $217,000   C. $250,000   D. $300,000

23. The Anide Corp., which keeps its books on the accrual basis, had the following   23.____
transactions for its calendar year ending December 31, 2018.
   • April 15, 2018 – Authorized the issuance of $3,000,000 of 5.5%, 20 year bonds, dated
     May 1, 2018. Interest to be paid November 1 and May 1.
   • June 1, 2018 – Sold the entire issue at $2,965,150 plus accrued interest.
   • November 1, 2018 – Paid the interest due.
The interest expense for the calendar year ending December 31, 2018 is
   A. $85,000   B. $165,000   C. $110,000   D. $97,300

Questions 24-26.

DIRECTIONS: Questions 24 through 26 are to be answered on the basis of the following information:

The following information was taken from a worksheet that was used in the preparation of the balance sheet and the profit and loss statement of the Hott Company for 2018.

The Balance Sheet Contained	Amount
Travel Expense Unpaid	$995
Legal and Collection Fees – Prepaid in Advance	672
Interest Received in Advance	469

The Profit and Loss Statement Contained	Amount
Travel Expenses	$7,343
Legal and Collection Fees	5,461
Interest Income	3,114

The proper adjusting and closing entries were made on the books of the company by the accountant and the described information was reported on the financial statements. The books are kept on an accrual basis.

On the basis of the above facts, the balance in each of the following accounts in the trial balance, *before adjusting and closing entries were made*, was as follows:

24.   Travel Expense Account
   A. $8,338   B. $7,343   C. $6,348   D. $995

24.____

25.   Legal and Collection Fees Account
   A. $672   B. $4,789   C. $5,461   D. $6,133

25.____

26.   Interest Income Account
   A. $3,583   B. $3,114   C. $2,645   D. $469

26.____

Questions 27-28.

DIRECTIONS: Questions 27 and 28 are to be answered on the basis of the following information.

The following is the stockholder's equity section of a corporation:
   Preferred Stock (7%, cumulative, non-participating,
   $100 par value, 5,000 shares issued and outstanding) $500,000

   Common Stock ($1.00 par value, 500,000, issued and
   outstanding)   500,000
          $1,000,000

   Deficit   (40,000)
          $960,000

27. Assuming two years' dividends in arrears on the preferred stock, the book value per share of common stock is

    A. 78¢   B. 80¢   C. 63¢   D. 94¢

27.____

28. Assuming two years' dividends in arrears on the preferred stock, the book value per share of preferred stock is

    A. $130   B. $114   C. $98   D. $140

28.____

Questions 29-30.

DIRECTIONS: Questions 29 and 30 are to be answered on the basis of the following information.

Regina Corporation on December 31, 2017 had the following stockholder's equity:

Common Stock ($10 par value, 10,000 shares authorized and outstanding)	$100,000
Retained Earnings	20,000
	$120,000

On December 31, 2017, the Astro Corp. purchased 9,000 shares of the Regina Corporation's outstanding shares, paying $14 per share.

29. The entry to eliminate Astro Corp.'s investment and the Regina Corporation's stockholder's equity on consolidation would show a debit or credit to an account called "Excess of Cost Over book Value" of

    A. Credit, $18,000   B. Debit, $18,000
    C. Debit, $15,000   D. Debit, $19,000

29.____

30. If the Regina Corporation had earnings for the calendar year 2018 of $10,000 and had paid out $8,000 of these earnings as dividends, and an entry to eliminate the Astro Corp.'s investment and the Regina Corporation's stockholder's equity were made, the minority stockholder's equity would be

    A. $15,600   B. $10,100   C. $12,200   D. $14,800

30.____

KEY (CORRECT ANSWERS)

1.	B	11.	D	21.	A
2.	A	12.	B	22.	C
3.	D	13.	A	23.	D
4.	B	14.	B	24.	C
5.	A	15.	A	25.	D
6.	C	16.	D	26.	A
7.	A	17.	B	27.	A
8.	D	18.	C	28.	B
9.	C	19.	C	29.	B
10.	D	20.	B	30.	C

TEST 3

DIRECTIONS: Each question or incomplete statement is followed by several suggested answers or completions. Select the one that BEST answers the question or completes the statement. *PRINT THE LETTER OF THE CORRECT ANSWER IN THE SPACE AT THE RIGHT.*

1.   For the measurement of net income to be as realistic as possible, it is *desirable* that revenue be recognized at the point that
   A. cash is collected from customers
   B. an order for merchandise or services is received from a customer
   C. a deposit or advance payment is received from a customer
   D. goods are delivered or services are rendered to customers

1.____

2.   An accounting principle must receive substantial authoritative support to qualify as "generally accepted." Many organizations and agencies have been influential in the development of generally accepted accounting principles, but the MOST influential leadership has come from the
   A. New York Stock Exchange
   B. American Institute of Certified Public Accountants
   C. Securities and Exchange Commission
   D. American Accounting Association

2.____

3.   In which one of the following ways does the declaration and payment of a cash dividend affect corporate net income? It _____ net income.
   A. does not affect   B. reduces
   C. increases   D. capitalizes

3.____

4.   Under which one of the following headings of the corporate balance sheet should the liability for a dividend payable in stock appear?
   A. Current Liabilities   B. Long Term Liabilities
   C. Stockholders' Equity   D. Current Assets

4.____

5.   In which one of the following is "Working Capital" MOST likely to be found?
   A. Income Statement
   B. Analysis of Retained Earnings
   C. Computation of Cost of Capital
   D. Statement of Funds Provided and Applied

5.____

6.   Which of the following procedures is NOT generally mandatory in auditing a merchandising corporation?
   A. Physical observation of inventory count
   B. Written circularization of accounts receivable
   C. Confirmation of bank balance
   D. Circularization of the stockholders

6.____

7. A company purchased office supplies during 2018 in the total amount of
$1,400 and charged the entire amount to the asset account. An inventory of
supplies taken on December 31, 2018 shows the cost of unused supplies to be
$250.
The entry to record this fact, assuming the books have not been closed,
involves
   A. credit to capital
   C. credit to supplies expense
   B. debit to supplies expense
   D. debit to supplies on hand

7._____

8. A corporation's records show $600,000 (credit) in net sales, $200,000 (debit)
in year-end accounts receivable, and $2,000 (debit) in Allowance for Bad
Debts. The company's aged schedule of accounts receivable indicates a
probable future loss from failure to collect year-end receivables in the amount
of $6,000.
Of the following, the MOST correct entry to adjust the Allowance for Bad Debts
at year-end is
   A. $1,000 credit
   C. $8,000 debit
   B. $4,000 credit
   D. $8,000 credit

8._____

Questions 9-10.

DIRECTIONS: Questions 9 and 10 are to be answered on the basis of the following
information.

A company commenced business in 2018 and purchased inventory as follows:

March	100 units @	$5	$500
June	300	6	1,800
October	200	7	1,400
November	500	6	3,500
December	100	6	600
TOTAL	1,200		$7,800

**Units sold in 2018 amounted to 900

9. Under the LIFO inventory principal, the value of the remaining inventory is
   A. $1,700   B. $1,875   C. $2,145   D. $2,225

9._____

10. Under the FIFO inventory principle, the value of the remaining inventory is
   A. $1,650   B. $1,875   C. $2,000   D. $2,025

10._____

11. When doing a trial balance, assume that, as a result of a single error, the
total of the credit balances is greater than the total of the debit balances.
Which one of the following single errors could NOT be the cause of this
discrepancy?
   A. Failure to post a debit
   C. Failure to post a credit
   B. Posting a debit as a credit
   D. Posting a credit twice

11._____

Questions 12-13.

DIRECTIONS: Questions 12 and 13 are to be answered on the basis of the following information.

A and B are partners with capital balances of $20,000 and $30,000, respectively, at June 30, 2018, who share profits and losses, 40% and 60%, respectively. On July 1, 2018, C is to be admitted into the partnership under the following conditions:
- Partnership assets are to be revalued and increased by $10,000.
- C is to invest $40,000 but be credited for $30,000 while the remaining $10,000 is to be credited to A and B to compensate them for their pre-existing goodwill.

12. After C is admitt4ed and the proper entries are made, A's capital account will have a credit balance of   12.____
    A. $24,500   B. $28,000   C. $30,200   D. $36,000

13. After the admission of C to the partnership, C's share of profits and losses is agreed upon at 20%.   13.____
Assuming no other adjustments, the new percentage for profit and loss distribution to A will be
    A. 18%   B. 32%   C. 36%   D. 45%

14. A company reports as income for tax purposes $70,000 and its book income before the provision for income taxes is $100,000.   14.____
Assuming a 50% tax rate, the PROPER tax expense to be recorded following tax allocation procedures is
    A. $33,000   B. $40,000   C. $50,000   D. $60,000

15. The relationship between the total of cash and current receivables to total current liabilities is commonly referred to by accountants as the   15.____
    A. acid-test ratio   B. cross-statement ratio
    C. current ratio   D. R.O.I. ratio

16. On a statement of sources and application of funds, the depreciation expense is normally shown as a(n)   16.____
    A. addition to operating income   B. subtraction from funds provided
    C. addition to funds applied   D. reduction from operating income

17. Company A owns 100% of the capital stock of Company B and reports on a consolidated basis. During the year, Company A sold inventory to Company B at a profit of $100,000. One-half of this inventory has been sold at year-end by Company B to the public.   17.____
Which one of the following would be the MOST correct adjustment, if any, to make the consolidated retained earnings conform to generally accepted accounting principles?
    A. Decrease by $50,000   B. Increase by $50,000
    C. Increase by $100,000   D. No adjustment

18. X, Y, and Z are partners with capital of $11,000, $12,000, and $4,500. X has a
loan due from the partnership to him of $2,000. Profits and losses are shared
in the ratio of 4:5:1, respectively. The partnership has paid off all outside
liabilities, and its remaining assets consist of $9,000 in cash and $20,500 of
accounts receivable. The partners agree to disburse the $9,000 to themselves
in such a way that, even if one of the receivables is realized, no partner will
have been overpaid.
Under these conditions, which of the following MOST NEARLY represents the
amount to be paid to partner X?
A. $1,960   B. $3,200   C. $4,800   D. $5,000

18.____

19. R Company needs $2,000,000 to finance an expansion of plant facilities. The
company expects to earn a return of 15% on this investment before considering
the cost of capital or income taxes. The average income tax rate for the R
Company is 40%.
If the company raises the funds by issuing 6% bonds at face value, the
earnings available to common stockholders after the new plant facilities are in
operation may be expected to increase by
A. $65,000   B. $70,000   C. $108,000   D. $116,000

19.____

20. The budget for a given factory overhead cost was $150,000 for the year. The
actual cost for the year was $125,000.
Based on these facts, it can be said that the plant manager has done a better
job than expected in controlling this cost if the cost is a
A. semi-variable cost
B. variable cost and actual production was $83\frac{1}{3}\%$ of budgeted production
C. semi-variable cost which includes a fixed element of $25,000 per period
D. variable cost and actual production was equal to budgeted production

20.____

21. The Home Office account on the books of the City Branch shows a credit
balance of $15,000 at the end of a year and the City Branch account on the
books of the Home Office shows a debit balance of $12,000.
Of the following, the MOST likely reason for the discrepancy in the two
accounts is that
A. merchandise shipped by the Home Office to the branch has not been
recorded by the branch
B. the Home Office has not recorde4d a branch loss for the first quarter of
the year
C. the branch has just mailed a check for $3,000 to the Home Office which
has not yet been received by the Home Office
D. the Home Office has not yet recorded the branch profit for the first quarter
of the year

21.____

22. The concept of matching costs and revenues means that
A. the expenses offset against revenues should be related to the same time
period
B. revenues are at least as great as expenses on the average
C. revenues and expenses are equal
D. net income equals revenues minus expenses for the same earning period

22.____

23. If the inventory at the end of the current year is understated, and the error is not caught during the following year, the effect is to

      23.____

    A. *overstate* the income for the two-year period
    B. *overstate* income this year and understate income next year
    C. *understate* income this year and overstate income next year
    D. *understate* income this year, with no effect on the income of the next year

---

KEY (CORRECT ANSWERS)

1.	D		11.	C
2.	B		12.	B
3.	A		13.	B
4.	C		14.	C
5.	D		15.	A
6.	D		16.	A
7.	B		17.	A
8.	D		18.	C
9.	A		19.	C
10.	C		20.	D

21.	D
22.	A
23.	C

EXAMINATION SECTION
TEST 1

DIRECTIONS: Each question or incomplete statement is followed by several suggested answers or completions.Select the one that BEST answers the question or completes the statement. *PRINT THE LETTER OF THE CORRECT ANSWER IN THE SPACE AT THE RIGHT.*

1. With regard to the requirement of the auditing standard that sufficient and competent evidential matter be obtained, the term competent PRIMARILY refers to the evidence.   1._____
   A. consistency
   B. relevance
   C. measurability
   D. dependability

2. Audit working papers should NOT   2._____
   A. include any client-prepared papers or documents other than those prepared by the auditor
   B. be kept by the auditor after review and completion of the audit except for items required for the income tax return
   C. be submitted to the client to support the financial statements and to provide evidence of the audit work performed
   D. by themselves be expected to provide sufficient support for the auditor's operation

3. Mr. Jason Stone operates a small drugstore as an individual proprietor. During the past year, his books were not properly kept. He asks you, as a CPA, to give him some advice concerning the earnings of his business during the calendar year 2011. A review of his bank accounts and a diary of financial data reveal the information presented below: 3._____
   Deposits made during 2018 per bank statements totaled $226,000. Deposits include investments made by Mr. Shea as well as a loan he obtained from the bank for $25,000. Disbursements during 2018 per bank statement totaled $185,000. Included are personal withdrawals of $15,000 and payments on debt of $10,000.
   Net equity of Jason Stone at January 1, 2018 was determined to be $45,000.
   Net equity of Jason Stone at December 31, 2018 was determined to be $75,000.
   During 2018, funds invested by Jason Stone in the business amounted to $6,500.
   Based upon the *net worth* method, net income for the year ended December, 2018 was
   A. $35,000   B. $38,500   C. $40,000   D. $42,000

4. Because of past association, a senior accountant is convinced of the competence and honesty of those who prepared the financial information which he is auditing. He consequently concludes that certain verification procedures are unnecessary. This conclusion by the senior accountant is ill-advised for the proper performance of his present audit MAINLY because the   4._____
   A. members of the staff often lack the specialized skills and training without which verification in an audit cannot proceed
   B. verification procedures depend upon the materiality of the subject matter under examination and not upon the personal characteristics of the individuals involved
   C. nature of opinion expressed in the report issued by the senior accountant, at the end of his audit, is grounded on personal considerations
   D. quality of the senior accountant's independence and his objective examination of the information under review is impaired

5. Of the following statement ratios, the one that represents *a growth ratio is*   5._____
   A. working capital ratio
   B. acid-test ratio
   C. long-term debt to total capitalization
   D. dollar earnings per share

Questions-6-8.

DIRECTIONS: Questions 6 through 8 are to be answered on the basis of the information
              given below.
   During the course of an examinations of the financial statements of a wholesale
   establishment, the following facts were revealed for the year ended December 3, 2018:

   I. Although merchandise: inventory costing $3,000 was on hand and.was-included in the
      inventory count on December 31, 2018, title had passed and it was billed to the
      customer on December 31, 2018 at a sale price of $4,500.
   II. Merchandise had been billed to the customer on December 31, 2018 in the amount
      of $5,200 but had not been shipped to him. This merchandise which cost $3,500, was
      not included in the inventory at the end of the year. The goods were shipped and title
      passed on January 15, 2019.
   III. Merchandise costing $6,000 was recorded as a purchase on December 31, 2018 but
      was Not included in the inventory at that date.
   IV. Merchandise costing $5,000 was received on January 3, 2019, but was recorded on
      the books as of December 31, 2018, and included in inventory as of
      December 31, 2018. The goods were shipped on December 30, 2018 by the vendor
      F.O.B. shipping point.
   V. An examination of receiving records indicated that merchandise costing $7,000 was
      received on December 31, 2018. It was included in inventory as of that date but not
      recorded as a purchase.

6. Adjustments to correct the inventory figure will reflect a net adjustment so as to   6._____
   A. reduce it by $6,500   B. increase it by $6,500
   C. reduce it by $8,000   D. increase it by $8,000

7. Adjustments to correct the sales figure will result in a net adjustment to sales of a (n)   7._____
   A. increase by $5,200   B. decrease by $5,200
   C. increase by $6,300   D. decrease by $6,300

8. The net adjustment to purchases for the period ending December 31, 2018 will   8._____
   result in a(n)
   A. increase of $4,000   B. decrease of $7,000
   C. increase of $7,000   D. decrease of $4,000

Questions 9-10.

DIRECTIONS: Questions 9 and 10 are to be answered on the basis of the information
              given below.
   A company worth $500,000 of common capital stock, par value $100 per share with
   retained earnings of $100,000, decides to change its capitalization from a par to a no-par
   basis. It, therefore, called in its 5,000 shares of par value stock and issued in place thereof
   10,000 shares of no-par value stock.

9. The balance in the capital stock account after the change is   9._____
    A. $1,000,000   B. $500,000
    C. $,400,000   D. $200,000

10. The balance in the retained earnings account after the change is   10._____
    A. $90,000   B. $100,000   C. $125,000   D. $250,000

11. Among the assets on the December 31, 2018 balance sheet of the Wolf Corporation   11._____
was the following:
    Investment in Sheep Company
    1,000 shares @ $90 bought January 1, 2018 $90,000
The net worth section of the balance sheet of the Sheep Company on the same date
was as follows:

	NET WORTH	
Capital Stock, 1,000 shares		$100,000
Deficit January 1, 2018	$20,000	
Less Operating Profit 2018	15,000	
Deficit December 31, 2018		5,000
Total Net worth		$ 95,000

The net debit or credit to Consolidated Surplus arising from consolidation of the
Sheep Company with the parent Wolf Corporation is
    A. $3,000 credit   B. $5,000 credit
    C. $7,000 debit   D. $10,000 credit

Questions 12-15.

DIRECTIONS: Questions 12 through 15 are to be answered on the basis of the
                      Trial Balances and the Notes below.

CLIMAX CORPORATION - Trial Balances (000 Omitted)

	December 31, 2018		December 31, 2017	
	Debit	Credit	Debit	Credit
Cash	$ 178		$ 84	
Accounts Receivable	300		240	
Allowance for Bad Debts		$ 13		$ 10
Merchandise Inventory	370		400	
Building & Equipment	420		360	
Allowance for Depreciation		180		190
Accounts Payable		220		210
Mortgage Bonds		300		300
Unamortized Bond Discount	18			21
Capital Stock		357		270
Retained Earnings		125		90
Net Sales		$4,200		$4,000
Cost of Goods Sold	$2,300		$2,100	
Salaries & Wages	1,500		1,400	
Heat & Utilities	110		100	
Depreciation	20		20	
Taxes & Insurance	10		10	
Interest	16		15	
Bad Debts	20		20	
Losso on Equipment Sales (Note 1)	6		___	
Dividends Paid (Note 2)	127		300	
	$5,395	$5,395	$5,070	$5,070

NOTES: (1) In 2018 equipment costing $40,000 and having a net bookvalue of $10,000 was sold for $4,000.
   (2) Dividends paid in 2018 include a stock dividend of $27,000.

12. The net change in working capital from 2017 to 2018 is   12._____
   A. $111,000   B. $130,000   C. $260,000   D. $333,000

13. The amount of funds provided from net income for the year ended December 31, 2018 is   13._____
   A. $214,000   B. $244,000   C. $254,000   D. $284,000

14. The amount of funds applied to dividends during the year 2018 is   14._____
   A. $100,000   B. $125,000   C. $175,000   D. $202,350

15. The amount of funds applied to building and equipment during the year 2018 is   15._____
   A. $100,000   B. $70,000   C. $50,000   D. $30,000

Questions 16-17.

DIRECTIONS: Questions 16 and 17 are to be answered on the basis of the information given below.
   The Natural Sales Company issues gift certificates in denominations of $5, $10 and $25. They are redeemable in merchandise having a markup of 30% of Selling Price.

   During December, $35,000 of gift certificates was sold and $20,000 was redeemed. It is estimated that 5% of the certificates issued will never be redeemed.

16. The PROPER entry to reflect the current liability with respect to these certificates is   16._____
   A. $13,250   B. $14,250   C. $15,250   D. $16,250

17. The cost of the merchandise issued to meet the redeemed certificates is   17._____
   A. $11,000   B. $13,000   C. $14,000   D. $17,000

Questions 18-19.

DIRECTIONS: Questions 18 and 19 are to be answered on the basis of the information given below.
   Arthur Evans commenced business in 2017 but did not maintain a complete set of proper records. He relied on the bank statements in order to compute his income. All his receipts Are deposited, and all his expenditures are made by check.
   His bank statements and other records reflected the following:

Bank balance per bank 12/31/2017	$ 14,735
Bank balance per bank 12/31/2018	18,380
Deposits for 2018 per bank statement	209,450
Deposits in transit 12/31/2017	3,590
Deposits in transit 12/31/2018	4,150

   Checks returned with the January 2018 bank statement showed a total of $4,770 checks issued in 2018.
   2018 checks not returned by the bank at December 31, 2018 amounted to $5,150.
   $6,430 of checks were issued in 2018 in payment of purchases made in 2017.
   $9,425 of deposits was made by Mr. Evans in 2018 representing 2017 sales.

   Unpaid bills for 2018 amounted to $2,150 on December 31, 2018.

Accounts Receivable for 2018 on December 31, 2018 were $10,930.
Merchandise inventory figures on the following dates were:

December 31, 2017 $13,000
December 31, 2018   17,580

On July 1, 2018, machinery costing $8,000 was purchased. The estimated life was 5 years with a salvage value of $500.

18. The balance of the cash in the bank according to the books on December 31, 2018 was   18._____
    A. $18,380   B. $17,380   C. $16,380   D.$15,380

19. The Sales Revenue for 2018 was   19._____
    A. $211,515   B.$209,515   C. $208,515   D.$207,515

Questions 20-21.

DIRECTIONS: Questions 20 and 21 are to be answered on the basis of the information given below.

In the examination of an imprest petty cash fund of $600, you were presented with the following fund composition shown below. The date of examining the petty cash fund was the balance sheet date.

Currency - bills	$310.00
Cash - coins	3.15
Postage stamps	50.00
Sales returns memos for cash refunded to customers	15.50
Check of one employee dated one month in advance	75.00
Vouchers for miscellaneous office expenses	100.85
Sales slip of an employee who purchased company merchandise; the money in payment was taken from the fund, entered as cash sale, and the sales slip inserted in the fund	45.50

20. The corrected balance of petty cash for balance sheet purposes is   20._____
    A. $313.15   B. $319.32   C. $347.53   D. $409.27

21. A correcting journal entry to establish the correct fund balance would increase   21._____
expenses by
    A. $100.85   B. $212.31   C. $28.28   D. $139.50

22. The PRIMARY objective of an audit, as generally understood in accounting practice,   22._____
is to
    A. assert a series of claims for management as to the financial condition of the company
    B. establish the reliability or unreliability as to the financial statements and supporting accounting records of the company
    C. install special procedures involved in the periodic closing of the accounts prior to the preparation of financial statements of the company
    D. summarize accounts and financial transactions to determine the costs of processes or units of production for the company

Questions 23-25.

DIRECTIONS: Questions 23 through 25 are to be answered on the basis of the information given below.

The following data related to the business operations for the calendar years 2016, 2017, and 2018 of the Wholly Corporation.

	2016	2017	2018
Net income per books	$170,000	$190,000	$140,000
Dividends	15,000	20,000	10,000
Purchases made in year 2017 recorded as purchased in 2018 but recorded in inventory in 2017		25,000	
Inventory value December 31, 2018 underestimated			5,000
Depreciation omitted - applicable to 2016	3,000		
applicable to 2017		4,500	
applicable to 2018			6,000
Overstatement of prepaid advertising as of January 1, 2017		1,500	
Salaries - earned during 2016 paid during 2017 - no accruals	18,000		
Payroll taxes on salarie	1,440		

23. The net profit for 2016 after adjusting for the facts given above is
    A. $146,060   B. $150,050   C. $164,200   D. $192,835
23.____

24. The net profit for 2017 after adjusting for facts given
    A. $152,400   B. $165,700   C. $173,145   D. $181,440
24.____

25. If the balance of the retained earnings account was $265,000 on January 1, 2016, the balance of the retainedearnings account on December 31, 2018 after corrections is
    A. $711,500   B. $525,000   C. $424,360   D. $307,420
25.____

Questions 26-30.

DIRECTIONS: Each question numbered 26 through 30 consists of a description of a transaction that indicates a two fold change on the balance sheet. Each of these transactions may be classified under one of the following categories. Examine each question carefully. In the correspondingly numbered space at the right, mark the appropriate space for the letter preceding the category below which BEST represents the charges that should be made on the balance sheet, as of December 31, 2017.

A. Current Assets are *overstated* and Retained Earnings are *overstated*
B. Current Assets are *understated* and Retained Earnings are *understated*
C. Current Liabilities are *overstated* and Retained Earnings are *overstated*
D. Current Liabilities are *understated* and Retained Earnings are *overstated*

26. Goods shipped on consignment out were not included in the final inventory although the entries were properly madefor such consignments.

26._____

27. A number of cash sales made subsequent to the balance sheet date were recorded as sales in the prior periodbefore the balance sheet date. The merchandise was included in inventories.

27._____

28. A cash dividend declared December 21, 2017, payable on January 15, 2018 to stockholders of record as of December 28, 2017, had not been recorded as of December 31, 2017.

28._____

29. The provision for the allowance for doubtful accounts receivable for the current period that should have been made had not been recorded.

29._____

30. Merchandise received by December 31, 2017, and properly included in inventory on that date, was not entered as a purchase until January 2018.

30._____

Questions 31-33.

DIRECTIONS: Questions 31 through 33 are to be answered on the basis of the information given below.

Ten men work as a group on a particular manufacturing operation. When the weekly production of the group exceeds a standard number of pieces per hour, each man in the group is paid a bonus for the excess production; the bonus is in addition to his wages at the hourly rate. The amount of the bonus is computed by first determining the percentage by which the groups production exceeds the standard. One-half of this percentage is then applied to a wage rate of $1.25 to determine an hourly bonus rate. Each man in the group is paid, as a bonus, the bonus rate applied to his total hours worked during the week. The standard rate of production before a bonus can be earned is two hundred pieces per hour.

The production record for a given week was: Hours Worked Production

Days	Hours worked	Production
Monday	72	17,680
Tuesday	72	17,348
Wednesday	72	18,800
Thuresday	72	18,560
Friday	71.5	17,888
Saturday	40	9,600
	399.5	99,076

31. The rate of the bonus for the week is_____ %.
    A. 24   B. 20   C. 18   D. 12

31._____

32. The bonus paid to the ten-man group for the week is
    A. $59.93   B. $69.39   C. $95.00   D. $225.00

32._____

33. The total wages of one employee who worked 40 hours at a base rate of $1.00 per hour are
    A. $46   B. $50   C. $54   D. $58

33._____

34. A junior accountant reported to his senior that he had performed the operations listed below.
Which one of the following statements about these operations CORRECTLY describes the operation?
    A. Vouchered the amount of petty cash
    B. Vouchered.the receivables ledger accounts with the sales register
    C. Analyzed the fixed assets account
    D. Checked all entries in the general journal to original evidence

34._____

35. Sales during July 2018 for the Major Company were $267,500, of which $170,000 was on account. The sales figure presented to you includes the total sales tax charged to retail customers (assume a sales tax rate of 7%).
The sales tax liability that should be shown at the end of July 2018 is
    A. $8,300
    B. $9,400
    C. $17,500
    D. $18,750

35._____

Questions 36-37.

DIRECTIONS: Questions 36 and 37 are to be answered on the basis of the information given below.

During the audit of records of the Short Corporation for the year ended December 31, 2018, the auditor was presented with the following information:

The finished goods inventory consisted of 22,000 units carried at a cost of $17,600 at December 31, 2018. The finished goods inventory at the beginning of the year (January 1, 2018) consisted of 24,000 units, priced at a cost of $16,800. During the year, 4,000 units were manufactured at a cost of $3,600 and 6,000 units were sold.

36. To PROPERLY reflect the cost of the finished goods inventory at December 31, 2018, if the FIFO method was used, assuming there was no work-in-process inventory, would require an adjustment of
    A. $1,400 credit   B. $1,400 debit   C.$1,600 credit   D. $1,600 debit

36._____

37. To PROPERLY reflect the cost of the finished goods inventory at December 31, 2018 if the LIFO method was used, assuming there was no work-in-process Inventory, would require an adjustment of
    A. $2,200 debit   B. $2,200 credit   C. $4,200 credit   D. $4,200 debit

37._____

38. Within the general field of auditing, there are internal auditors and independent auditors who differ significantly one from the other in that the latter group:

    A. is responsible for a more complete, detailed examination of accounting data
    B. conduct standard audits established by custom and usage for a particular trade or industry
    C. direct their investigations primarily to matters of fraud and criminal'misrepresentation
    D. issue reports for the benefit of other interests, such as shareholders and creditors

38._____

39. Moreland Corporation sells merchandise at a gross profit of 25% of sales. Fire on the premises of this Corporation on July 16, 2018 resulted in the destruction of the merchandise. The Corporation's merchandise is insured against fire by a $150,000 insurance policy with an 80% co-insurance clause. The Corporation's records show the following:

Sales -- January 1, 2018 to July 16, 2018	$400,000
Inventory -- January 1, 2018	$ 65,000
Purchases -- January 1, 2018 to July 16, 2018	$460,000
Merchandise salvaged	$ 25,000

39._____

The amount of inventory destroyed by fire is
   A. $150,000   B. $200,000   C. $225,000   D. $300,000

40. Below are the totals of the cash receipts and disbursement books of the Small Corporation for the calendar year 2018
   Receipts $392,369.72
   Disbursements $331,477.87
The bank balance on January 1, 2018 was $38,610.21. The bank balance on December 31, 2018 was $101,918.34. No checks were outstanding on January 1, 2018. Checks out standing on December 31, 2018 amounted to $5,416.28. Undeposited checks on hand December 31, 2018 were $3,000 which are included in the December cash receipts. Bank deposits for the year total $387,643.72.
The total SHORTAGE in cash is
   A. $1,726   B. $2,416.28   C. $3,000   D. $3,452

40._____

41. A state corporation, all of whose business is done within the city, showed the following for 2018:

Entire net income	$ 1,000
Salaries to Officers deducted in determining entire net income	$ 40,000
Average capital	$ 450,000

41._____

The corporation's city business tax payable (assuming a 7% rate on income and a .001 rate on capital) is
   A. $546   B. $450   C. $70   D. $25

42. Sales revenue serves as the basis for determining _____ taxes.
   A. estate   B. excise   C. payroll   D. property.

42._____

43. ABC Corporation operates in the city and would be subjected to the following taxes:
   I. Federal Corporation Income Tax – Surtax 26% and
      Normal Tax 22%
   II. State Franchise Tax - 72%
If income before taxes for 2018 was $370,000 per the federal tax return (after establishing estimate), assuming the rates as noted above, the tax liabilities that should be set up are Federal and State.
   A. $180,000; $25,800   B. $177,600; $29,700
   C. $165,500; $20,000   D. $171,100; $30,000

43._____

44. In the examination of a manufacturing company where inventory values are of a   44._____
    material amount, the client has restricted the extent of the independent CPA's audit
    examination of his records by not permitting the CPA to observe the taking of inventory
    at the close of the company's fiscal year. In such a case, which of the following opinions
    with regard to the audit report would be APPROPRIATE?_____opinion.
    A. Unqualified   B. Qualified
    C. Adverse   D. Disclaimer of

45. Accounting data are subject to error from a variety of sources and for a variety of   45._____
    reasons. Of the following, the MOST efficient way to lessen this problem is to
    A. identify'and classify errors as to type and kind as soon as they are detected
    B. provide for machine calculation of accounting datawherever possible
    C. confirm accounting data by independent third parties
    D. designate an individual to be responsible for the accuracy of accounting data

46. Normally, an auditor does NOT rely upon his study and testing of a system of internal   46._____
    control to
    A. evaluate the reliability of the system
    B. uncover embezzlements of the client's system
    C. help determine the scope of other auditing procedures to be followed
    D. gain support for his opinion as to the accuracy and fairness of the financial
       statements

Questions 47-50.

DIRECTIONS: Questions 47 through 50 are to be answered on the basis of the
             information given below.
         An office clerk who was not familiar with proper accounting procedures prepared the
following financial report for the Dunrite Corporation as of June 30, 2018. In addition to the
errors in presentation, additional data below were not considered in the preparationof the
report. Restate this balance sheet in proper form, giving recognition to the additional data
so that you will be able to determine the required information to answer these questions.

DUNRITE CORPORATION

June 30, 2018

CURRENT ASSETS		
Cash		$155,000
Marketable securities		82,400
Investment in affiliated company.		175,000
Treasury stock	$ 25,500	
Less reserve for trea	25,500	
Accounts receivable	$ 277,800	
Accounts payable	135,000	142,800
Total current assets		$ 555,200
PLANT ASSETS		
Equipment		$ 450,000
Building	$400,000	
Reserve for plant expansion	100,000	300,000
Land.		50,000
Goodwill		35,000
Prepaid expenses		12,000
		847,000
Total Assets		$1,402,200

LIABILITIES

Cash dividend payable		$25,000
Stock dividend payable		15,000
Accrued liabilities		15,700
Bonds payable	$400,000	
Sinking fund	325,000	75,000
Total Current Liabilities		$ 130,700

STOCKHOLDERS' EQUITY

Paid-in capital			
Common stock		$550,000	
Retained earnings and reserves			
Premium common stock	$74,000		
Reserve - doubtful accounts	7,500		
Reserve - depreciation of equipment	140,000		
Reserve - depreciation building	170,000		
Reserve - income-taxes	50,000		
Retained earnings	280,000	$721,500	
Total Liabilities and Equity			$1,402,200

ADDITIONAL DATA:
A. The reserve for income taxes represents the balance due on the estimated liability for taxes on income of the current fiscal year.
B. Marketable securities are recorded at cost and have a market value at June 30, 2018 of $81,000. They represent temporary investments.
C. The investment in the affiliated company is a minority interest carried at cost.
D. Bonds payable are due 10 years from the balance-sheet date.
E. The stock dividend payable was declared on June 30, 2018.

47. After restatement of the balance sheet in proper form, and giving recognition to The additional data, the Total Current Assets would be
   A. $509,200   B. $519,700   C. $610,000   D. $735,000

47._____

48. After restatement of the balance sheet in proper form, and giving recognition to the Additional data, the Total Current Liabilities would be
   A. $225,700   B. $325,200   C. $352,700   D. $480,000

48._____

49. After restatement of the balance sheet in proper form, and giving recognition to the additional data, the Stockholders' Equity shows a total of
   A. $730,100   B. $819,000   C. $910,000   D. $1,019,000

49._____

50. After restatement of the balance sheet in proper form, and giving recognition to the additional data, the net book value of the total plant equipment would be
   A. $440,000   B. $590,000   C. $750,000   D. $850,000

50._____

KEY (CORRECT ANSWERS)

1.	D	26.	B
2.	C	27.	A
3.	B	28.	D
4.	D	29.	A
5.	D	30.	D
6.	B	31.	D
7.	B	32.	A
8.	C	33.	A
9.	B	34.	C
10.	B	35.	C
11.	D	36.	A
12.	A	37.	B
13.	B	38.	D
14.	A	39.	B
15.	A	40.	A
16.	A	41.	A
17.	C	42.	B
18.	B	43.	D
19.	A	44.	D
20.	A	45.	C
21.	A	46.	B
22.	B	47.	B
23.	A	48.	A
24.	D	49.	D
25.	A	50.	B

TEST 2

DIRECTIONS: Each question or incomplete statement is followed by several suggested answers or completions.Select the one that BEST answers the question or completes the statement. *PRINT THE LETTER OF THE CORRECT ANSWER IN THE SPACE AT THE RIGHT.*

Question 1.

DIRECTIONS: Question 1 is based on the following portion of an income tax withholding table. In answering this question, assume that this table was in effect for the full year.

If the payroll period with respect to an employee is daily:

And the wages are		And the number of witholding exemptions claimed is				
At least	But less than	0	1	2	3	4
		The amount of income tax to be withheld shall be				
$172	$176	$24.40	$20.80	$17.20	$13.60	$10.00
176	180	24.90	21.30	17.70	14.20	10.60
180	184	25.50	18.30	18.30	14.70	11.10

1. K received a daily wage of $176.40 the first 7 pay periods and $182.50 the last 19 pay periods. He claimed 3 exemptions the first 9 pay periods and 4 the rest of the year. Total income tax withheld during the year was   1._____
    A. $288.10   B. $295.30
    C. $316.50   D. $317.50
    E. none of the above

2. A voucher contained the following items: 2._____
      6 desks @89.20 $525.20
      8 chairs @32.50   260.00
                     Total   885.20
The terms were given on the voucher as 3%, 10 days; net, 30 days. Verify the computations, which may be incorrect, and calculate the correct amount to be paid. If payment is made within the discount period, the amount to be paid is
    A. $761.64   B. $771.34
    C. $795.20   D. $858.64
    E. none of the above

3. Under the income tax law in effect for last year, an individual who is blind on the last day   3._____
of the taxable year is entitled to claim an exemption of $600 because of such blindness, in addition to any other exemptions to which he may be entitled.
Richard Roe, who files his income tax returns on the calendar year basis, became permanently blind on December 15 of last year.
In filing his income tax return for last year, Mr. Roe may claim an exemption for blindness of
    A. $300   B. $550
    C. $574   D. $600
    E. none of the above

4. The Jones Company had a merchandise inventory of $24,625 on January 1 of last year. 4._____
During that year, purchases made by the company amounted to $60,000, sales to $85,065, and cost of goo ds sold to $28,060.
The inventory on December 31 of last year was
   A. $25,065
                    B. $28,500
   C. $49,690
                    D. $57,005
   E. none of the above

――――

KEY (CORRECT ANSWERS)

1. D
2. B
3. D
4. E

――――

ACCOUNTING

EXAMINATION SECTION
TEST 1

DIRECTIONS : Each question or incomplete statement is followed by several suggested
answers or completions. Select the one that *BEST* answers the question or
completes the statement. *PRINT THE LETTER OF THE CORRECT ANSWER
IN THE SPACE AT THE RIGHT.*

Questions 1-5.

DIRECTIONS: Assume that you are requested to verify certain financial data with respect to
the various business entities described below. This information is required to
verify that tax returns and/or other financial reports submitted to your agency
are correct.

In an auditing review of the income statements of several business firms (Companies X,
Y, and Z), you find the financial information given below. Based upon the account balances
shown, select the correct answer for the statement information requested.

Company X -
Sales	$ 160,000
Opening Inventory	$ 70,000
Purchases	$ 80,000
Purchase Returns	$ 1,200
Cost of Goods Sold	$ 127,000

1. The ending inventory based upon the data above is   1._____

    A. $21,800   B. $23,000   C. $24,200   D. $33,000

Company Y -
Opening Inventory	$ 50,000
Purchases	$ 145,000
Ending Inventory	$ 28,500
Gross Profit	$ 56,000
Sales and Administrative Expenses	$ 64,000

2. Sales for the period based upon the data above are   2._____

    A. $110,500   B. $166,500   C. $222,500   D. $286,500

Company Z -
Sales for the period	$ 200,000
Net Profit	7% of Sales
Purchases	$ 180,000
Ending Inventory	$ 70,000
Gross Profit	$ 60,000

3. Cost of Goods sold for Company Z is   3._____

    A. $110,000   B. $140,000   C. $180,000   D. $250,000

4. The opening inventory of Company Z would be   4._____

    A. $10,000   B. $20,000   C. $30,000   D. $80,000

5. The operating expenses for Company Z would be   5._____

    A. $10,000   B. $14,000   C. $20,000   D. $46,000

Questions 6-8.

DIRECTIONS: The following information is taken from the books and records of a business firm:

Sales for the calendar year 2018:	$52,000
Based upon FIFO Inventory:	
Good available for Sale	$46,900
Inventory at December 31, 2018	$12,700
Based upon LIFO Inventory:	
Goods available for Sale	$46,900
Inventory at December 31, 2018	$10,400

6. If FIFO Inventory valuation is used, the Gross Profit will be   6.____

A. $5,100   B. $15,500   C. $17,800   D. $34,200

7. If LIFO Inventory valuation method is used, the Gross Profit will be   7.____

A. $2,300   B. $15,500   C. $17,800   D. $36,500

8. If LIFO Inventory method is used, compared with the FIFO method, the cost of goods sold will be   8.____

A. more by $2,300
C. more by $10,400
B. less by $2,300
D. less by $12,700

9. Which one of the following would NOT properly be classified as an asset on the balance sheet of a business firm?   9.____

A. Investment in stock of another firm
B. Premium cost of a three-year fire insurance policy
C. Cash surrender value of life insurance on life of corporate officer. Policy is owned by the company and the company is the beneficiary
D. Amounts owing to employees for services rendered

10. Which one of the following would NOT properly be classified as a current asset?   10.____

A. Travel advances to salespeople
B. Postage in a postage meter
C. Cash surrender value of life insurance policy on an officer, which policy names the corporation as the beneficiary
D. Installment notes receivable due over 18 months in accordance with normal trade practice

11. Able, Baker and Carr formed a partnership. Able contributed $10,000, Baker contributed $5,000, and Carr contributed an automobile with a fair market value of $5,000. They have no partnership agreement. The first year the partnership earned $18,000. The partners will share the profits as follows: 11.____

A. Able, $9,000; Baker, $4,500; Carr, $4,500
B. Able, $6,000; Baker, $6,000; Carr, $6,000
C. Able, $12,000; Baker, $6,000; Carr, No share
D. Able, $8,000; Baker, $5,000; Carr, $5,000

Questions 12-13.

DIRECTIONS: Answer Questions 12 through 13 based on the information below.

The XYZ partnership had the following balance sheet as of December 31, 2018.

Cash	$ 5,000	Liabilities	$ 12,000
Other assets	40,000	X Capital	20,000
Total	$45,000	Y Capital	10,000
		Z Capital	3,000
		Total	$45,000

The partners shared profits equally. They decided to liquidate the partnership at December 31, 2018.

12. If the other assets were sold for $52,000, each partner will be entitled to a final cash distribution of   12._____

    A. X, $15,000; Y, $15,000; Z, $15,000
    B. X, $24,000; Y, $14,000; Z, $ 7,000
    C. X, $20,000; Y, $10,000; Z, $ 3,000
    D. X, $23,000; Y, $13,000; Z, $ 6,000

13. If the other assets were sold for $31,000, each partner will be entitled to a final cash distribution of   13._____

    A. X, $14,000; Y, $ 5,000; Z, $5,000
    B. X, $ 8,000; Y, R 8,000; Z, $8,000
    C. X, $15,000; Y, $15,000; Z, $15,000
    D. X, $17,000; Y, $ 7,000; Z, No cash share

14. Items selling for $40 for which there were 10% selling costs were purchased for inventory   14._____
at $20 each. Selling prices and costs remained steady but at the date of the financial
statement the market price had dropped to $16. The inventory remaining from the original purchase was written down to $16.
Of the following, it is correct to state that the

    A. cost of sales of the subsequent year will be overstated
    B. current year's income is overstated
    C. income of the following year will be overstated
    D. closing inventory of the current year is overstated

15. Dividends in arrears on a cumulative preferred stock should be reported on the balance   15._____
sheet as

    A. an accrued liability
    B. restricted retained earnings
    C. an explanatory note
    D. a deduction from preferred stock

16. The effect of recording the payment of a 10% dividend paid in stock would be to   16._____

    A. *increase* the current ratio
    B. *decrease* the amount of working capital
    C. *increase* the total stockholder equity
    D. *decrease* the book value per share of stock outstanding

17. The owner of a truck which originally had cost $12,000 but now has a book value of $1,500 was offered $3,000 for it by a used truck dealer. However, the owner traded it in for a new truck listed at $19,000 and received a trade-in allowance of $4,000. The cost basis for the new truck, following the Federal income tax rules, *properly* amounts to

   A. $15,000   B. $16,000   C. $16,500   D. $17,500

17.____

18. In planning for purchases to be made during the next month, the following information is to be used:

   Budgeted sales for the month   73,000 units
   Inventory at beginning of the month   19,000 units
   Planned inventory at end of the month   14,000 units

From the above information, the number of units to be purchased is

   A. 40,000   B. 59,000   C. 68,000   D. 78,000

18.____

19. A branch office of a company has the following plan:

   Cash balance at beginning of the month $ 10,000
   Planned cash balance at end of the month $ 15,000
   Expected receipts for the month $ 180,000
   Expected disbursements for the month $ 205,000

In order to comply with this plan, the accountant should recommend that the branch obtain an additional allocation of

   A. $20,000   B. $25,000   C. $30,000   D. $50,000

19.____

20. A company uses the reserve method of bad debt expense and sets up a Bad Debt account at 2% of sales. The sales were $500,000. The company wrote off $7,500 in accounts receivable.
The effect of these entries on net income for the period is a(n)

   A. $2,500 increase   B. $7,500 decrease
   C. $8,000 decrease   D. $10,000 decrease

20.____

KEY (CORRECT ANSWERS)

1.	A	11.	B
2.	C	12.	B
3.	B	13.	D
4.	C	14.	C
5.	D	15.	C
6.	C	16.	D
7.	B	17.	C
8.	A	18.	C
9.	D	19.	C
10.	C	20.	D

TEST 2

DIRECTIONS : Each question or incomplete statement is followed by several suggested answers or completions. Select the one that *BEST* answers the question or completes the statement. *PRINT THE LETTER OF THE CORRECT ANSWER IN THE SPACE AT THE RIGHT.*

1. The Delox Corporation has applied to their bank for a $50,000 loan which they will need for 90 days. The bank grants the loan, which will be discounted at 7% interest. The Delox Corporation will receive credit in their account at the bank for (based on a 360-day year):   1.____

    A. $46,500   B. $49,125   C. $50,000   D. $50,875

Questions 2-5.

DIRECTIONS: Answer Questions 2 through 5 based on the information below.

Assume that you are reviewing some accounts of a company and find the following: The Machinery Account and the Accumulated Depreciation - Machinery Account.

MACHINERY				
Jan. 1, 2015	Machine #1	20,000	July 1, 2016	6,000
Jan. 1, 2016	Machine #2	16,000		
July 1, 2016	Machine #3	12,000		
Jan. 1, 2018	Machine #4	20,000		

ACCUMULATED DEPRECIATION - MACHINERY		
	Dec. 31, 2015	5,000
	Dec. 31, 2016	10,500

Machines are depreciated based upon a four-year life and using the straight-line method. Assume no salvage values.

On July 1, 2016, Machine #1, purchased on January 1, 2015, was sold for $6,000 cash. The bookkeeper debited Cash and credited Machinery for $6,000.

On January 1, 2018, Machine #2 was traded in for a newer model. The new Machine had a list price of $34,000. A trade-in value of $10,000 was granted. $20,000 was paid in cash and the bookkeeper debited Machinery and credited Cash for $20,000. Income-tax rules should have been applied making this entry.

If any errors were made in recording the machine values or depreciation, you are asked to correct them and determine the corrected asset values and proper accumulated depreciation.

2. As of December 31, 2015, you determine that these two accounts   2.____

    A. are correct
    B. are incorrect
    C. overstate asset book values
    D. understate asset book values

3. As of December 31, 2016, you determine that, to correct the Machinery Account Balance, you should leave it   3.____

    A. unchanged   B. increased by $6,000
    C. decreased by $14,000   D. decreased by $5,500

4. As of December 31, 2016, you determine that, to reflect the proper balance, the Accumulated Depreciation - Machinery account should

    A. remain unchanged   B. be increased by $10,000
    C. be decreased by $10,000   D. be decreased by $ 5,500

    4.____

5. After the January 1, 2018 entry, you determine that the Machinery Account should, *properly,*

    A. remain unchanged
    B. reflect a corrected balance of $52,000
    C. reflect a corrected balance of $40,000
    D. reflect a corrected balance of $56,000

    5.____

Questions 6-9.

DIRECTIONS: Answer Questions 6 through 9 based on the information below.

Assume that you are assigned to prepare an Audit Report Summary on the L Company. The L Company uses the accrual method and has an accounting year ending December 31. The bookkeeper of the company has made the following errors:
1. A $1,500 collection from a customer was received on December 29, 2017, but not recorded until the date of its deposit in the bank, January 4, 2018
2. A supplier's $1,900 invoice for inventory items received December 2017 was not recorded until January 2018 (Inventories at December 31, 2017 and 2018 were stated correctly, based on physical count)
3. Depreciation for 2017 was understated by $700
4. In September 2017, a $350 invoice for office supplies was charged to the Utilities Expense account. Office supplies are expensed as purchased
5. December 31, 2017, sales on account of $2,500 were recorded in January 2018, although the merchandise had been shipped and was not in the inventory

Assume that no other errors have occurred and that no correcting entries have been made. Ignore all income taxes.

6. After correcting the errors reported above, the corrected Net Income for 2017 was

    A. overstated by $100
    B. understated by $800
    C. understated by $1,800
    D. neither understated nor overstated

    6.____

7. Working Capital on December 31, 2017 was

    A. understated by $600
    B. understated by $2,300
    C. understated by $1,200
    D. neither understated nor overstated

    7.____

8. Total Assets on December 31, 2018 were

    A. overstated by $1,100
    B. overstated by $1,800

    8.____

C. understated by $850
D. neither understated nor overstated

9. The cash balance was 9._____

    A. correct as stated originally   B. overstated by $1,500
    C. understated by $2,500   D. understated by $1,500

Questions 10-13.

DIRECTIONS: Answer Questions 10 through 13 based on the information below.

    Salary expense was listed as a total of $27,600 for the month of June 2018. Withholding taxes were determined to be $7,250 for Income taxes and $1,170 for FICA taxes withheld from employees. Payroll deductions for employee pension fund contribution amounted to $2,500.
    Assume the employer's FICA tax share is equal to the employees' and that the employer's share of pension costs is double that of the employees and the employer also pays a 3% Unemployment Insurance Tax based upon $20,000 of the wages paid. The employer pays $1,500 for health insurance plans.

10. The amount of cash that must be obtained to meet this net payroll to pay employees is 10._____

    A. $16,680   B. $19,180   C. $20,350   D. $27,600

11. The total payroll tax expense for this payroll period is 11._____

    A. $1,170   B. $1,760   C. $2,340   D. $2,940

12. The total liability for withholding and payroll taxes payable is 12._____

    A. $2,340   B. $7,250   C. $8,420   D. $10,190

13. The expense of the employer for pension and health-care fringe benefits is 13._____

    A. $1,500   B. $2,500   C. $5,000   D. $6,500

14. Currently preferred terminology for statements to be presented limits the use of the term "reserve" to 14._____

    A. an actual liability of a known amount
    B. estimated liabilities
    C. appropriations of retained earnings
    D. valuation (contra) accounts

Questions 15-16.

DIRECTIONS: Answer Questions 15 through 16 based on the following.

    The Victory Corporation provides an incentive plan whereby its president receives a bonus equal to 10% of the corporate income in excess of $150,000. The bonus is based upon income before income taxes but after calculating the bonus.

15. If the income for the calendar year 2018, before income taxes and before the bonus were $480,000 and the effective tax rate is 40%, the amount of the bonus would be 15._____

A. $15,000   B. $30,000   C. $33,000   D. $48,000

16. The income tax expense for calendar year 2012 would be   16._____

    A. $60,000   B. $132,000   C. $180,000   D. $192,000

Questions 17-18.

DIRECTIONS: Answer Questions 17 through 18 based on the information below.

A contract has been awarded to the low bidder. This contractor will then commence construction of a building for the total contract price of $30,000,000. The expected cost of construction is $27,510,000. You are given the additional facts:

	2016	2017	2018
Contract Price as above	$ 30,000,000	$ 30,000,000	$ 30,000,000
Actual Cost to date	$ 9,170,000	$ 13,755,000	$ 27,510,000
Estimated Cost to complete	18,340,000	13,755,000	
Estimated Total Cost	$ 27,510,000	$ 27,510,000	$ 27,510,000
Estimated Total Income	$ 2,490,000	$	$
Billings	$ 9,000,000	$ 9,000,000	$ 9,000,000

17. For 2016, the income to be recognized on a percentage-of-completion basis would be   17._____

    A. $830,000   B. $2,490,000
    C. $3,000,000   D. $9,000,000

18. For 2017, the income to be recognized by the contractor on a percentage-of-completion   18._____
basis would be

    A. $415,000   B. $424,500   C. $830,000   D. $1,245,000

19. If the city borrows the $9,000,000 to pay the first billing for the contract above at 10%   19._____
interest for two years, and the second $9,000,000 at 7% interest for one year, then the
interest costs related to this building are, approximately,

    A. $630,000   B. $1,800,000
    C. $2,430,000   D. $3,000,000

20. The books of the Monmouth Corporation show the following: 20._____

Average earnings for	2018	2017	2016
prior 3 years	$70,000	$75,000	$78,000
Net tangible assets	$40,000	$42,000	$50,000

If it is expected that 15% would be normal earnings on net tangible assets, then the
average excess earnings are

    A. $7,120   B. $8,333   C. $9,800   D. $10,800

21. A business showed the following figures in its accounts for the year 2018:   21._____
    Sales - $346,000
    Inventory, December 31, 2018 - $58,000
    Inventory, December 31, 2017 - $52,000
    Purchases - $274,000
    Operating Expenses - $36,000
The gross profit earned by this concern is

    A. $72,000   B. $42,000   C. $66,000   D. $78,000

22. A business firm buys an article for $320, less 40% and 10%, terms 2/10 n/30, on March 18. If it pays the bill on March 27, it should pay

    A. $169.34   B. $172.80   C. $160.00   D. $156.80

22.____

23. In the partnership of Danvers and Edwards, Danvers has a capital of $10,000 and Edwards has a capital of $15,000. If Furgal wishes to invest $11,000 and thereby receive a 1/4 interest in the business, the goodwill in the business has been computed to be worth

    A. $19,000   B. $33,000   C. $14,000   D. $8,000

23.____

24. George Bailey's capital at the beginning of the year was $14,000. At the end of the year his assets were $62,000 and his liabilities were $39,000. His drawings for the year amounted to $6,000.
His profit for the year was

    A. $15,000   B. $3,000   C. $9,000   D. $17,000

24.____

25. George Wilson's check book shows the following:

Balance at the beginning of the month   -$3,517.42
Deposits during the month   -$1,923.98
Checks drawn during the month   -$2,144.36

In going over his bank statement, he finds that a deposit of $455.64 made by him has not yet been credited by the bank and that the bank has charged him $9.40 for services rendered. He also finds that he has outstanding checks totaling $268.19.
His bank statement balance should be printed as

    A. $3,100.19   B. $3,118.99   C. $2,563.81   D. $4,011.47

25.____

KEY (CORRECT ANSWERS)

1. B	11. B		
2. A	12. D		
3. C	13. D		
4. C	14. C		
5. C	15. B		
6. A	16. C		
7. A	17. A		
8. B	18. A		
9. D	19. C		
10. A	20. B		

21. D
22. A
23. D
24. A
25. A

ACCOUNTING
EXAMINATION SECTION
TEST 1

DIRECTIONS : Each question or incomplete statement is followed by several suggested answers or completions. Select the one that *BEST* answers the question or completes the statement. *PRINT THE LETTER OF THE CORRECT ANSWER IN THE SPACE AT THE RIGHT.*

Questions 1-5.

DIRECTIONS: Answer Questions 1 through 5 based on the information below.

When balance sheets are analyzed, working capital always receives close attention. Adequate working capital enables a company to carry sufficient inventories, meet current debts, take advantage of cash discounts and extend favorable terms to customers. A company that is deficient in working capital and unable to do these things is in a poor competitive position.
Below is a Trial Balance as of June 30, 2015, in alphabetical order, of the Worth Corporation:

	Debits	Credits
Accounts Payable		$ 50,000
Accounts Receivable	$ 40,000	
Accrued Expenses Payable		10,000
Capital Stock		10,000
Cash	20,000	
Depreciation Expense	5,000	
Inventory	60,000	
Plant & Equipment (net)	30,000	
Retained Earnings		20,000
Salary Expense	35,000	
Sales		100,000
	$190,000	$190,000

1. The Worth Corporation's Working Capital, based on the data above, is   1.____

   A. $50,000   B. $55,000   C. $60,000   D. $65,000

2. Which one of the following transactions increases Working Capital?   2.____

   A. Collecting outstanding accounts receivable
   B. Borrowing money from the bank based upon a 90-day interest-bearing note payable
   C. Paying off a 60-day note payable to the bank
   D. Selling merchandise at a profit

3. The Worth Corporation's Current Ratio, based on the above data, is   3.____

   A.   1.7 to 1   B.   2 to 1   C.   2.5 to 1   D.   4 to 3

4. Which one of the following transactions decreases the Current Ratio?   4.____

    A. Collecting an account receivable
    B. Borrowing money from the bank giving a 90-day interest-bearing note payable
    C. Paying off a 60-day note payable to the bank
    D. Selling merchandise at a profit

5. The payment of a current liability, such as Payroll Taxes Payable, will   5.____

    A. *increase* the current ratio but have no effect on the working capital
    B. *increase* the Working Capital, but have no effect on the current ratio
    C. *decrease* both the current ratio and working capital
    D. *increase* both the current ratio and working capital

6. During the year 2015, the Ramp Equipment Co. made sales to customers totaling   6.____
$100,000 that were subject to sales taxes of $8,000. Net cash collections totaled
$92,000. Discounts of $3,000 were allowed. During the year 2015, uncollectible accounts
in the sum of $2,000 were written off the books.
The net change in accounts receivable during the year 2015 was

    A. $10,500   B. $11,000   C. $13,000   D. $13,500

7. The Grable Co. received a $6,000, 8%, 60-day note dated May 1, 2015 from a customer.   7.____
On May 16, 2015, the Grable Co. discounted the note at 6% at the bank.
The net proceeds from the discounting of the note amounted to

    A. $5,954.40   B. $6,034.40   C. $6,064.80   D. $6,080.00

Question 8.

DIRECTIONS: Answer Question 8 based on the information below.

In reviewing the customers' accounts in the Accounts Receivable Ledger for the entire
year 2014, the following errors are discovered
    1. A sale in the amount of $500 to the J. Brown Co. was erroneously posted to the K.
       Brown Co.
    2. A sales return of $100 from the Gale Co. was debited to their account
    3. A check was received from a customer, M. White and Co. in payment of a sale of
       $500 less 2% discount. The check was entered properly in the cash receipts book
       but was posted to the M. White and Co. account in the amount of $490

8. The difference between the controlling account and its related accounts receivable   8.____
schedule amounts to

    A. $90   B. $110   C. $190   D. $210

9. Assume that you are called upon to audit a cash fund. You find in the cash drawer post-   9.____
age stamps and I.O.U.'s signed by employees, totaling together $425.
In preparing a financial report, the $425 should be reported as

    A. petty cash   B. investments
    C. supplies and receivables   D. cash

10. On December 31, 2014, before adjustment, Accounts Receivable had a debit balance of $60,000 and the Allowance for Uncollectible Accounts had a debit balance of $1,000. If credit losses are estimated at 5% of Accounts Receivable and the estimated method of reporting bad debts is used, then bad debts expense for the year 2014 would be reported as

    10._____

    A. $1,000   B. $2,000   C. $3,000   D. $4,000

Questions 11-12.

DIRECTIONS: Answer Questions 11 through 12 based on the information below.

Accrued salaries payable on $7,500 had not been recorded on December 31, 2014. Office supplies on hand of $2,500 at December 31, 2014 were erroneously treated as expense instead of inventory. Neither of these errors was discovered or corrected.

11. These two errors would cause the income for 2014 to be

    11._____

    A. *understated* by $5,000   B. *overstated* by $5,000
    C. *understated* by $10,000   D. *overstated* by $10,000

12. The effect of these errors on the retained earnings at December 31, 2014 would be

    12._____

    A. *understated* by $2,500   B. *overstated* by $2,500
    C. *understated* by $5,000   D. *overstated* by $5,000

Questions 13-14.

DIRECTIONS: Answer Questions 13 through 14 based on the information below.

Albano, Borrone, and Colluci operate a retail store under the trade name of ABC. Their partnership agreement provides for equally sharing profits and losses after salaries of $5,000 to Albano, $10,000 to Borrone, and $15,000 to Colluci.

13. If the net income of the partnership (prior to salaries to partners) is $21,000, then Albano's share of the profits, considering all aspects of the agreement, is determined to be

    13._____

    A. $2,000   B. $3,000   C. $5,000   D. $7,000

14. The share of the profits that apply to Borrone, similarly, is determined to be

    14._____

    A. $2,000   B. $3,000   C. $5,000   D. $7,000

Questions 15-17.

DIRECTIONS: Answer Questions 15 through 17 based on the information below.

The Kay Company currently uses FIFO for inventory valuation. Their records for the year ended June 30, 2015 reflect the following:

July 1, 2014 inventory   100,000 units @ $7.50
Purchases during year   400,000 units @ $8.00
Sales during year   350,000 units @ $15.00
Expenses exclusive of income taxes $1,290,000
Cash Balance on June 30, 2014 $250,000
Income Tax Rate   45%
Assume the July 1, 2014 inventory will be the LIFO Base Inventory.

15. If the company should change to the LIFO as of June 30, 2015, then their income before taxes for the year-ended June 30, 2015, as compared with the income FIFO method, will be   15.____

     A.   *increased b $50,000*
     B.   *decreased by $50,000*
     C.   *increased by $100,000*
     D.   *decreased by $100,000*

16. Assuming the given tax rate (45%), the use of the LIFO method will result in an approximate tax expense for fiscal 2015 of   16.____

     A. $45,000   B. $50,000   C. $72,000   D. $94,500

17. Assuming the given tax rate (45%), the use of the LIFO inventory method compared with the FIFO method, will result in a change in the approximate income tax expense for fiscal 2015 as follows: 17.____

     A.   *Increase of $22,500*
     B.   *Decrease of $22,500*
     C.   *Increase of $45,000*
     D.   *Decrease of $45,000*

18. An accountant in an agency, in addition to his regular duties, has been assigned to train a newly appointed assistant accountant. The latter believes that he is not being given the training that he needs in order to perform his duties.
Accordingly, the most appropriate FIRST step for the assistant accountant to take in order to secure the needed training is to   18.____

     A.   register for the appropriate courses at the local college as soon as possible
     B.   advise the accountant in a formal memo that his apparent lack of interest in the training is impeding his progress
     C.   discuss the matter with the accountant privately and try to discover what seems to be the problem
     D.   secure such training informally from more sympathetic accountants in the agency

19. You have worked very hard and successfully helped complete a difficult audit of a large corporation doing business with your agency. Your supervisor gives you a brief nod of approval when you expected a more substantial degree of recognition. You are angry and feel unappreciated. Of the following, the *most appropriate* course of action for you to take would be to   19.____

     A.   voice your displeasure to your fellow workers at being taken for granted by an unappreciative supervisor
     B.   say nothing now and assume that your supervisor's nod of approval may be his customary acknowledgment of efforts well done
     C.   let your supervisor know that he owes you something by repeatedly stressing the outstanding job you've done
     D.   ease off on your work quality and productivity until your efforts are finally appreciated

20. You have been assisting in an audit of the books and records of businesses as a member   20.____
of a team. The accountant in charge of your group tells you to start preliminary work
independently on a new audit. This audit is to take place at the offices of the business.
The business officers have been duly notified of the audit date. Upon arrival at their
offices, you find that their records and files are in disarray and that their personnel are
antagonistic and uncooperative. Of the following, the *most desirable* action for you to
take is to

    A. advise the business officers that serious consequences may follow unless immedi-
ate cooperation is secured
    B. accept whatever may be shown or told you on the grounds that it would be unwise
to further antagonize uncooperative personnel
    C. inform your supervisor of the situation and request instructions
    D. leave immediately and return later in the expectation of encountering a more coop-
erative attitude.

KEY (CORRECT ANSWERS)

1.	C	11.	C
2.	D	12.	A
3.	B	13.	A
4.	B	14.	D
5.	A	15.	B
6.	B	16.	C
7.	B	17.	B
8.	D	18.	C
9.	C	19.	B
10.	D	20.	C

TEST 2

DIRECTIONS : Each question or incomplete statement is followed by several suggested answers or completions. Select the one that *BEST* answers the question or completes the statement. *PRINT THE LETTER OF THE CORRECT ANSWER IN THE SPACE AT THE RIGHT.*

Questions 1-3.

DIRECTIONS: Answer Questions 1 through 3 based on the following.

The city is planning to borrow money with a 5-year, 7% bond issue totaling $10,000,000 on principal when other municipal issues are paying 8%.
  Present value of $ 1 - 8% - 5 years - .68058
  Present value of annual interest payments - annuity 8% - 5 years -3.99271

1. The funds obtained from this bond issue (ignoring any costs related to issuance) would be, approximately,

    A. $9,515,390   B. $10,000,000
    C. $10,484,610   D. $10,800,000

1._____

2. At the date of maturity, the bonds will be redeemed at

    A. $9,515,390   B. $10,000,000
    C. $10,484,610   D. $10,800,000

2._____

3. As a result of this issue, the *actual* interest costs each year as related to the 7% interest payments will

    A. be the same as paid ($700,000)
    B. be more than $700,000
    C. be less than $700,000
    D. fluctuate depending on the market conditions

3._____

4. Following the usual governmental accounting concepts, the activities of a municipal employee retirement plan, which is financed by equal employer and employee contributions, should be accounted for in a(n)

    A. agency fund
    B. intragovernmental service fund
    C. special assessment fund
    D. trust fund

4._____

Questions 5-7.

DIRECTIONS: Answer Questions 5 through 7 based on the following.

The Balance Sheet of the JLA Corp. is as follows:

Current assets	$50,000	Current liabilities	$20,000
Other assets	75,000	Common stock	75,000
Total	$125,000	Retained earnings	30,000
		Total	$125,000

5. The working capital of the JLA Corp. is   5._____

    A. $30,000   B. $50,000   C. $105,000   D. $125,000

6. The operating ratio of the JLA Corp. is   6._____

    A.   2 to 1   B. $2\frac{1}{2}$ to 1   C.   1 to 2   D.   1 to $2\frac{1}{2}$

7. The stockholders' equity is   7._____

    A. $30,000   B. $75,000   C. $105,000   D. $125,000

Question 8.

DIRECTIONS: Answer Question 8 based on the following figures taken from a set of books for the year ending June 30, 2015.

	Trial Balance Before Adjustments	Trial Balance After Adjustments
Commissions Payable	cr ---	cr $ 1,550
Office Salaries	dr $9,500	dr $10,680
Rental Income	cr $4,300	cr $ 4,900
Accumulated Depreciation	cr $7,000	cr $ 9,700
Supplies Expense	dr $1,760	dr $ 1,200

8. As a result of the adjustments reflected in the adjusted trial balance, the net income of the company before taxes will be   8._____

    A. *increased* by $4,270   B. *decreased* by $4,270
    C. *increased* by $5,430   D. *decreased* by $5,430

Question 9.

DIRECTIONS: Answer Question 9 based on the following facts concerning the operations of a manufacturer of office desks.

Jan. 1, 2014	Goods in Process Inventory	4,260 units	40% complete
Dec. 31, 2014	Goods in Process Inventory	3,776 units	25% complete
Jan. 1, 2014	Finished Goods Inventory	2,630 units	
Dec. 31, 2014	Finished Goods Inventory	3,180 units	

Sales consummated during the year-127,460 units

9. Assuming that all the desks are the same style, the number of equivalent complete units, manufactured during the year 2008 is: 9._____

    A. 127,250   B. 127,460   C. 128,010   D. 131,510

Questions 10-11.

DIRECTIONS: Answer Questions 10 through 11 based on the following.

On January 1, 2015, the Lenox Corporation was organized with a cash investment of $50,000 by the shareholders. Some of the corporate records were destroyed. However you were able to discover the following facts from various sources:

Accounts Payable at December 31, 2015 (arising from merchandise purchased)	$16,000
Accounts Receivable at December 31, 2015 (arising from the sales of merchandise)	18,000
Sales for the calendar year 2015	94,000
Inventory, December 31, 2015	20,000
Cost of Goods Sold is 60% of the selling price	
Bank loan outstanding - December 31, 2015	15,000
Expenses paid in cash during the year	35,000
Expenses incurred but unpaid as of December 31, 2015	4,000
Dividend paid	25,000

10. The *correct* cash balance is   10.____

   A. $5,600   B. $20,600   C. $38,600   D. $40,600

11. The stockholders' equity on December 31, 2015 is   11.____

   A. $23,600   B. Deficit of $26,400
   C. $27,600   D. $42,400

Questions 12-13.

DIRECTIONS: Answer Questions 12 and 13 based on the following facts developed from the records of a company that sells its merchandise on the installment plan.

Sales	Calendar Year 2014	Calendar Year 2015
Total volume of sales	$80,000	$100,000
Cost of Goods Sold	60,000	40,000
Gross Profit	$20,000	$ 60,000
Cash Collections		
From 2014 Sales	$18,000	$36,000
From 2015 Sales		22,000
Total Cash Collections	$18,000	$58,000

12. Using the deferred profit method of determining the income from installment sales, the   12.____
    gross profit on sales for the calendar year 2014 was

   A. $4,500   B. $18,000   C. $20,000   D. None

13. Using the deferred profit method of determining the income from installment sales, the   13.____
    gross profit on sales for the calendar year 2015 was

   A. $22,000   B. $22,200   C. $60,000   D. None

Questions 14-15.

DIRECTIONS: Answer Questions 14 through 15 based on the following data developed from an examination of the records of Ralston, Inc. for the month of April 2015.
   Beginning inventory: 10,000 units @ $4.00 each

	Purchases		sales	
April	10	20,000 units @ $5 each	April 13	15,000 units @ $8 each
	17	60,000 units @ $6 each	21	50,000 units @ $9 each
	26	40,000 units @ $7 each	27	50,000 units @ $10 each

14. The gross profit on sales for the month of April, 2015, assuming that inventory is priced   14.____
    on the FIFO basis, is

    A. $330,000   B. $355,000   C. $395,000   D. $435,000

15. The gross profit on sales for the month of April, 2015, assuming that inventory is priced   15.____
    on the LIFO basis, is

    A. $330,000   B. $355,000   C. $395,000   D. $435,000

Question 16.

DIRECTIONS: Answer Question 16 based on the data presented for June 30, 2015.

Balance per Bank Statement	$24,019.00
Balance per General Ledger	20,592.64
Proceeds of note collected by the bank which had	
not been recorded in the Cash account	4,000.00
Interest on note collected by the bank (no book entries	
made)	39.40
Debit memo for Bank charges for the month of May	23.50
Deposit in Transit (June 30, 2015)	2,144.00
Customer's check returned by the bank due to lack of funds	150.00
Outstanding checks - June 30, 2015	1,631.46
Error in recording check made by our bookkeeper - check	
cleared in the amount of $463.00 but entered in the bank	
book for $436.00	

16. If we wish to reconcile the bank and book balance so that the bank balance and the book   16.____
    balance are reconciled to a corrected balance, the corrected balance should be

    A. $20,592.64   B. $24,019.00   C. $24,531.54   D. $26,163.00

17. The Ateb Company has issued a $500,000 bond issue on January 1, 2014, at 8% inter-   17.____
    est, payable semi-annually, sold at par, with interest payable on June 30 and December
    31.
    On September 30, 2014, at the close of the fiscal year of the Ateb Company, the inter-
    est expense accrual should reflect interest payable of, approximately,

    A. $10,000   B. $20,000   C. $40,000   D. $50,000

18. Assume that a new procedure requires that a particular and unvarying sequence of steps   18.____
    be followed in order to yield the desired data. You are assigned to be in charge of subor-
    dinates working with this procedure.
    Which one of the following is *most likely* to impress subordinates with the importance
    of following the sequence of steps exactly as given?

    A. *Explain* the consequences of error if the procedure is not followed
    B. *Suggest* how rewarding would be the feeling of finding errors before the supervisor
        catches them
    C. *Indicate* that independent verification of their work will be done by other staff mem-
        bers
    D. *Advise* that upward career mobility usually results from following instructions
        exactly

19. It is essential for an experienced accountant to know approximately how long it will take him to complete a particular assignment because

    19.____

    A. his supervisors will need to obtain this information only from someone planning to perform the assignment
    B. he must arrange his schedule to insure proper completion of the assignment consistent with agency objectives
    C. he must measure whether he is keeping pace with others performing similar assignments
    D. he must determine what assignments are essential and have the greatest priority within his agency

20. There are circumstances which call for special and emergency efforts by employees. You must assign your staff to make this type of effort.
Of the following, this special type of assignment is *most likely* to succeed if the

    20.____

    A. time schedule required to complete the assignment is precisely stated but is not adhered to
    B. employees are individually free to determine the work schedule
    C. assignment is clearly defined
    D. employees are individually free to use any procedure or method available to them

_____

KEY (CORRECT ANSWERS)

1.	A		11.	A
2.	B		12.	A
3.	B		13.	B
4.	D		14.	C
5.	A		15.	B
6.	B		16.	C
7.	C		17.	A
8.	B		18.	A
9.	A		19.	B
10.	B		20.	C

_____

ACCOUNTING
EXAMINATION SECTION
TEST 1

DIRECTIONS : Each question or incomplete statement is followed by several suggested answers or completions. Select the one that *BEST* answers the question or completes the statement. *PRINT THE LETTER OF THE CORRECT ANSWER IN THE SPACE AT THE RIGHT.*

Questions 1-5.

DIRECTIONS: Answer Questions 1 through 5 based on the information below.

When balance sheets are analyzed, working capital always receives close attention. Adequate working capital enables a company to carry sufficient inventories, meet current debts, take advantage of cash discounts and extend favorable terms to customers. A company that is deficient in working capital and unable to do these things is in a poor competitive position.

Below is a Trial Balance as of June 30, 2015, in alphabetical order, of the Worth Corporation:

	Debits	Credits
Accounts Payable		$ 50,000
Accounts Receivable	$ 40,000	
Accrued Expenses Payable		10,000
Capital Stock		10,000
Cash	20,000	
Depreciation Expense	5,000	
Inventory	60,000	
Plant & Equipment (net)	30,000	
Retained Earnings		20,000
Salary Expense	35,000	
Sales		100,000
	$190,000	$190,000

1.   The Worth Corporation's Working Capital, based on the data above, is   1.____

   A. $50,000   B. $55,000   C. $60,000   D. $65,000

2.   Which one of the following transactions increases Working Capital?   2.____

   A. Collecting outstanding accounts receivable
   B. Borrowing money from the bank based upon a 90-day interest-bearing note payable
   C. Paying off a 60-day note payable to the bank
   D. Selling merchandise at a profit

3.   The Worth Corporation's Current Ratio, based on the above data, is   3.____

   A. 1.7 to 1   B. 2 to 1   C. 2.5 to 1   D. 4 to 3

4. Which one of the following transactions decreases the Current Ratio?   4._____

    A. Collecting an account receivable
    B. Borrowing money from the bank giving a 90-day interest-bearing note payable
    C. Paying off a 60-day note payable to the bank
    D. Selling merchandise at a profit

5. The payment of a current liability, such as Payroll Taxes Payable, will   5._____

    A. *increase* the current ratio but have no effect on the working capital
    B. *increase* the Working Capital, but have no effect on the current ratio
    C. *decrease* both the current ratio and working capital
    D. *increase* both the current ratio and working capital

6. During the year 2015, the Ramp Equipment Co. made sales to customers totaling   6._____
$100,000 that were subject to sales taxes of $8,000. Net cash collections totaled
$92,000. Discounts of $3,000 were allowed. During the year 2015, uncollectible accounts
in the sum of $2,000 were written off the books.
The net change in accounts receivable during the year 2015 was

    A. $10,500   B. $11,000   C. $13,000   D. $13,500

7. The Grable Co. received a $6,000, 8%, 60-day note dated May 1, 2015 from a customer.   7._____
On May 16, 2015, the Grable Co. discounted the note at 6% at the bank.
The net proceeds from the discounting of the note amounted to

    A. $5,954.40   B. $6,034.40   C. $6,064.80   D. $6,080.00

Question 8.

DIRECTIONS: Answer Question 8 based on the information below.

    In reviewing the customers' accounts in the Accounts Receivable Ledger for the entire year 2014, the following errors are discovered
    1. A sale in the amount of $500 to the J. Brown Co. was erroneously posted to the K. Brown Co.
    2. A sales return of $100 from the Gale Co. was debited to their account
    3. A check was received from a customer, M. White and Co. in payment of a sale of $500 less 2% discount. The check was entered properly in the cash receipts book but was posted to the M. White and Co. account in the amount of $490

8. The difference between the controlling account and its related accounts receivable   8._____
schedule amounts to

    A. $90   B. $110   C. $190   D. $210

9. Assume that you are called upon to audit a cash fund. You find in the cash drawer post-   9._____
age stamps and I.O.U.'s signed by employees, totaling together $425.
In preparing a financial report, the $425 should be reported as

    A. petty cash   B. investments
    C. supplies and receivables   D. cash

10. On December 31, 2014, before adjustment, Accounts Receivable had a debit balance of 10.____
$60,000 and the Allowance for Uncollectible Accounts had a debit balance of $1,000. If
credit losses are estimated at 5% of Accounts Receivable and the estimated method of
reporting bad debts is used, then bad debts expense for the year 2014 would be reported
as

   A. $1,000   B. $2,000   C. $3,000   D. $4,000

Questions 11-12.

DIRECTIONS: Answer Questions 11 through 12 based on the information below.

   Accrued salaries payable on $7,500 had not been recorded on December 31, 2014.
Office supplies on hand of $2,500 at December 31, 2014 were erroneously treated as
expense instead of inventory. Neither of these errors was discovered or corrected.

11. These two errors would cause the income for 2014 to be   11.____

   A. *understated* by $5,000   B. *overstated* by $5,000
   C. *understated* by $10,000   D. *overstated* by $10,000

12. The effect of these errors on the retained earnings at December 31, 2014 would be   12.____

   A. *understated* by $2,500   B. *overstated* by $2,500
   C. *understated* by $5,000   D. *overstated* by $5,000

Questions 13-14.

DIRECTIONS: Answer Questions 13 through 14 based on the information below.

   Albano, Borrone, and Colluci operate a retail store under the trade name of ABC. Their
partnership agreement provides for equally sharing profits and losses after salaries of $5,000
to Albano, $10,000 to Borrone, and $15,000 to Colluci.

13. If the net income of the partnership (prior to salaries to partners) is $21,000, then   13.____
Albano's share of the profits, considering all aspects of the agreement, is determined to
be

   A. $2,000   B. $3,000   C. $5,000   D. $7,000

14. The share of the profits that apply to Borrone, similarly, is determined to be   14.____

   A. $2,000   B. $3,000   C. $5,000   D. $7,000

Questions 15-17.

DIRECTIONS: Answer Questions 15 through 17 based on the information below.

   The Kay Company currently uses FIFO for inventory valuation. Their records for the year
ended June 30, 2015 reflect the following:

```
July 1, 2014 inventory                    100,000 units @ $7.50
Purchases during year                     400,000 units @ $8.00
Sales during year                         350,000 units @ $15.00
Expenses exclusive of income taxes        $1,290,000
Cash Balance on June 30, 2014             $250,000
Income Tax Rate                           45%
Assume the July 1, 2014 inventory will be the LIFO Base Inventory.
```

15. If the company should change to the LIFO as of June 30, 2015, then their income before taxes for the year-ended June 30, 2015, as compared with the income FIFO method, will be

    A. *increased* b $50,000   B. *decreased* by $50,000
    C. *increased* by $100,000   D. *decreased* by $100,000

15.____

16. Assuming the given tax rate (45%), the use of the LIFO method will result in an approximate tax expense for fiscal 2015 of

    A. $45,000   B. $50,000   C. $72,000   D. $94,500

16.____

17. Assuming the given tax rate (45%), the use of the LIFO inventory method compared with the FIFO method, will result in a change in the approximate income tax expense for fiscal 2015 as follows:

    A. *Increase* of $22,500   B. *Decrease* of $22,500
    C. *Increase* of $45,000   D. *Decrease* of $45,000

17.____

18. An accountant in an agency, in addition to his regular duties, has been assigned to train a newly appointed assistant accountant. The latter believes that he is not being given the training that he needs in order to perform his duties.
Accordingly, the most appropriate FIRST step for the assistant accountant to take in order to secure the needed training is to

    A. register for the appropriate courses at the local college as soon as possible
    B. advise the accountant in a formal memo that his apparent lack of interest in the training is impeding his progress
    C. discuss the matter with the accountant privately and try to discover what seems to be the problem
    D. secure such training informally from more sympathetic accountants in the agency

18.____

19. You have worked very hard and successfully helped complete a difficult audit of a large corporation doing business with your agency. Your supervisor gives you a brief nod of approval when you expected a more substantial degree of recognition. You are angry and feel unappreciated. Of the following, the *most appropriate* course of action for you to take would be to

    A. voice your displeasure to your fellow workers at being taken for granted by an unappreciative supervisor
    B. say nothing now and assume that your supervisor's nod of approval may be his customary acknowledgment of efforts well done
    C. let your supervisor know that he owes you something by repeatedly stressing the outstanding job you've done
    D. ease off on your work quality and productivity until your efforts are finally appreciated

19.____

20. You have been assisting in an audit of the books and records of businesses as a member
of a team. The accountant in charge of your group tells you to start preliminary work
independently on a new audit. This audit is to take place at the offices of the business.
The business officers have been duly notified of the audit date. Upon arrival at their
offices, you find that their records and files are in disarray and that their personnel are
antagonistic and uncooperative. Of the following, the *most desirable* action for you to
take is to

    A. advise the business officers that serious consequences may follow unless immedi-
ate cooperation is secured
    B. accept whatever may be shown or told you on the grounds that it would be unwise
to further antagonize uncooperative personnel
    C. inform your supervisor of the situation and request instructions
    D. leave immediately and return later in the expectation of encountering a more coop-
erative attitude.

20._____

KEY (CORRECT ANSWERS)

1.	C	11.	C
2.	D	12.	A
3.	B	13.	A
4.	B	14.	D
5.	A	15.	B
6.	B	16.	C
7.	B	17.	B
8.	D	18.	C
9.	C	19.	B
10.	D	20.	C

TEST 2

DIRECTIONS : Each question or incomplete statement is followed by several suggested answers or completions. Select the one that *BEST* answers the question or completes the statement. *PRINT THE LETTER OF THE CORRECT ANSWER IN THE SPACE AT THE RIGHT.*

Questions 1-3.

DIRECTIONS: Answer Questions 1 through 3 based on the following.

The city is planning to borrow money with a 5-year, 7% bond issue totaling $10,000,000 on principal when other municipal issues are paying 8%.
  Present value of $ 1 - 8% - 5 years - .68058
  Present value of annual interest payments - annuity 8% - 5 years -3.99271

1. The funds obtained from this bond issue (ignoring any costs related to issuance) would be, approximately,

   A. $9,515,390   B. $10,000,000
   C. $10,484,610   D. $10,800,000

2. At the date of maturity, the bonds will be redeemed at

   A. $9,515,390   B. $10,000,000
   C. $10,484,610   D. $10,800,000

3. As a result of this issue, the *actual* interest costs each year as related to the 7% interest payments will

   A. be the same as paid ($700,000)
   B. be more than $700,000
   C. be less than $700,000
   D. fluctuate depending on the market conditions

4. Following the usual governmental accounting concepts, the activities of a municipal employee retirement plan, which is financed by equal employer and employee contributions, should be accounted for in a(n)

   A. agency fund
   B. intragovernmental service fund
   C. special assessment fund
   D. trust fund

Questions 5-7.

DIRECTIONS: Answer Questions 5 through 7 based on the following.

The Balance Sheet of the JLA Corp. is as follows:

Current assets	$50,000	Current liabilities	$20,000
Other assets	75,000	Common stock	75,000
Total	$125,000	Retained earnings	30,000
		Total	$125,000

1.____

2.____

3.____

4.____

5. The working capital of the JLA Corp. is

   A. $30,000   B. $50,000   C. $105,000   D. $125,000

5.____

6. The operating ratio of the JLA Corp. is

   A. 2 to 1   B. $2\frac{1}{2}$ to 1   C. 1 to 2   D. 1 to $2\frac{1}{2}$

6.____

7. The stockholders' equity is

   A. $30,000   B. $75,000   C. $105,000   D. $125,000

7.____

Question 8.

DIRECTIONS: Answer Question 8 based on the following figures taken from a set of books for the year ending June 30, 2015.

	Trial Balance Before Adjustments	Trial Balance After Adjustments
Commissions Payable	cr ---	cr $ 1,550
Office Salaries	dr $9,500	dr $10,680
Rental Income	cr $4,300	cr $ 4,900
Accumulated Depreciation	cr $7,000	cr $ 9,700
Supplies Expense	dr $1,760	dr $ 1,200

8. As a result of the adjustments reflected in the adjusted trial balance, the net income of the company before taxes will be

   A. *increased* by $4,270   B. *decreased* by $4,270
   C. *increased* by $5,430   D. *decreased* by $5,430

8.____

Question 9.

DIRECTIONS: Answer Question 9 based on the following facts concerning the operations of a manufacturer of office desks.

Jan. 1, 2014	Goods in Process Inventory	4,260 units	40% complete
Dec. 31, 2014	Goods in Process Inventory	3,776 units	25% complete
Jan. 1, 2014	Finished Goods Inventory	2,630 units	
Dec. 31, 2014	Finished Goods Inventory	3,180 units	

Sales consummated during the year-127,460 units

9. Assuming that all the desks are the same style, the number of equivalent complete units, manufactured during the year 2008 is:

   A. 127,250   B. 127,460   C. 128,010   D. 131,510

9.____

Questions 10-11.

DIRECTIONS: Answer Questions 10 through 11 based on the following.

   On January 1, 2015, the Lenox Corporation was organized with a cash investment of $50,000 by the shareholders. Some of the corporate records were destroyed. However you were able to discover the following facts from various sources:

3 (#2)

Accounts Payable at December 31, 2015	$16,000
(arising from merchandise purchased)	
Accounts Receivable at December 31, 2015	18,000
(arising from the sales of merchandise)	
Sales for the calendar year 2015	94,000
Inventory, December 31, 2015	20,000
Cost of Goods Sold is 60% of the selling price	
Bank loan outstanding - December 31, 2015	15,000
Expenses paid in cash during the year	35,000
Expenses incurred but unpaid as of December 31, 2015	4,000
Dividend paid	25,000

10. The *correct* cash balance is   10.____

    A. $5,600   B. $20,600   C. $38,600   D. $40,600

11. The stockholders' equity on December 31, 2015 is   11.____

    A. $23,600   B. Deficit of $26,400
    C. $27,600   D. $42,400

Questions 12-13.

DIRECTIONS: Answer Questions 12 and 13 based on the following facts developed from the records of a company that sells its merchandise on the installment plan.

Sales	Calendar Year 2014	Calendar Year 2015
Total volume of sales	$80,000	$100,000
Cost of Goods Sold	60,000	40,000
Gross Profit	$20,000	$ 60,000
Cash Collections		
From 2014 Sales	$18,000	$36,000
From 2015 Sales		22,000
Total Cash Collections	$18,000	$58,000

12. Using the deferred profit method of determining the income from installment sales, the gross profit on sales for the calendar year 2014 was   12.____

    A. $4,500   B. $18,000   C. $20,000   D. None

13. Using the deferred profit method of determining the income from installment sales, the gross profit on sales for the calendar year 2015 was   13.____

    A. $22,000   B. $22,200   C. $60,000   D. None

Questions 14-15.

DIRECTIONS: Answer Questions 14 through 15 based on the following data developed from an examination of the records of Ralston, Inc. for the month of April 2015.
Beginning inventory: 10,000 units @ $4.00 each

Purchases				sales			
April	10	20,000 units @ $5 each	April	13	15,000	units	@ $8 each
	17	60,000 units @ $6 each		21	50,000	units	@ $9 each
	26	40,000 units @ $7 each		27	50,000	units	@ $10 each

14. The gross profit on sales for the month of April, 2015, assuming that inventory is priced   14._____
on the FIFO basis, is

    A. $330,000   B. $355,000   C. $395,000   D. $435,000'

15. The gross profit on sales for the month of April, 2015, assuming that inventory is priced   15._____
on the LIFO basis, is

    A. $330,000   B. $355,000   C. $395,000   D. $435,000

Question 16.

DIRECTIONS: Answer Question 16 based on the data presented for June 30, 2015.

Balance per Bank Statement	$24,019.00
Balance per General Ledger	20,592.64
Proceeds of note collected by the bank which had not been recorded in the Cash account	4,000.00
Interest on note collected by the bank (no book entries made)	39.40
Debit memo for Bank charges for the month of May	23.50
Deposit in Transit (June 30, 2015)	2,144.00
Customer's check returned by the bank due to lack of funds	150.00
Outstanding checks - June 30, 2015	1,631.46
Error in recording check made by our bookkeeper - check cleared in the amount of $463.00 but entered in the bank book for $436.00	

16. If we wish to reconcile the bank and book balance so that the bank balance and the book   16._____
balance are reconciled to a corrected balance, the corrected balance should be

    A. $20,592.64   B. $24,019.00   C. $24,531.54   D. $26,163.00

17. The Ateb Company has issued a $500,000 bond issue on January 1, 2014, at 8% inter-   17._____
est, payable semi-annually, sold at par, with interest payable on June 30 and December
31.
On September 30, 2014, at the close of the fiscal year of the Ateb Company, the interest expense accrual should reflect interest payable of, approximately,

    A. $10,000   B. $20,000   C. $40,000   D. $50,000

18. Assume that a new procedure requires that a particular and unvarying sequence of steps   18._____
be followed in order to yield the desired data. You are assigned to be in charge of subordinates working with this procedure.
Which one of the following is *most likely* to impress subordinates with the importance
of following the sequence of steps exactly as given?

    A. *Explain* the consequences of error if the procedure is not followed
    B. *Suggest* how rewarding would be the feeling of finding errors before the supervisor
       catches them
    C. *Indicate* that independent verification of their work will be done by other staff mem-
       bers
    D. *Advise* that upward career mobility usually results from following instructions
       exactly

19. It is essential for an experienced accountant to know approximately how long it will take him to complete a particular assignment because

   A. his supervisors will need to obtain this information only from someone planning to perform the assignment
   B. he must arrange his schedule to insure proper completion of the assignment consistent with agency objectives
   C. he must measure whether he is keeping pace with others performing similar assignments
   D. he must determine what assignments are essential and have the greatest priority within his agency

19._____

20. There are circumstances which call for special and emergency efforts by employees. You must assign your staff to make this type of effort.
Of the following, this special type of assignment is *most likely* to succeed if the

   A. time schedule required to complete the assignment is precisely stated but is not adhered to
   B. employees are individually free to determine the work schedule
   C. assignment is clearly defined
   D. employees are individually free to use any procedure or method available to them

20._____

KEY (CORRECT ANSWERS)

1.	A	11.	A
2.	B	12.	A
3.	B	13.	B
4.	D	14.	C
5.	A	15.	B
6.	B	16.	C
7.	C	17.	A
8.	B	18.	A
9.	A	19.	B
10.	B	20.	C

EXAMINATION SECTION
TEST 1

DIRECTIONS: Each question or incomplete statement is followed by several suggested answers or completions. Select the one that BEST answers the question or completes the statement. *PRINT THE LETTER OF THE CORRECT ANSWER IN THE SPACE AT THE RIGHT.*

1. Which of the following is NOT usually performed by the accountant in a review engagement of a nonpublic entity? 1.____

   A. Writing an engagement letter to establish an understanding regarding the services to be performed.
   B. Issuing a report stating that the review was performed in accordance with standards established by the AICPA.
   C. Communicating any material weaknesses discovered during the study and evaluation of internal accounting control.
   D. Reading the financial statements to consider whether they conform with generally accepted accounting principles.

2. When the financial statements are prepared on the going concern basis but the auditor concludes there is substantial doubt whether the client can continue in existence and also believes there are uncertainties about the recoverability of recorded asset amounts on the financial statements, the auditor may issue a(n) 2.____

   A. adverse opinion
   B. *except for* qualified opinion
   C. *subject to* qualified opinion
   D. unqualified opinion with an explanatory separate paragraph

3. A small client recently put its cash disbursements system on a microcomputer. About which of the following internal accounting control features would an auditor MOST likely be concerned? 3.____

   A. Programming of this microcomputer is in BASIC, although COBOL is the dominant, standard language for business processing.
   B. This microcomputer is operated by employees who have other, non-data-processing job responsibilities.
   C. The microcomputer terminal is physically close to the computer and directly connected to it.
   D. There are restrictions on the amount of data that can be stored and on the length of time that data can be stored.

4. When an independent accountant issues a comfort letter to an underwriter containing comments on data that have not been audited, the underwriter MOST likely will receive 4.____

   A. a disclaimer on prospective financial statements
   B. a limited opinion on *pro forma* financial statements
   C. positive assurance on supplementary disclosures
   D. negative assurance on capsule information

5. When an auditor conducts an examination in accordance with generally accepted auditing standards and concludes that the financial statements are fairly presented in accordance with a comprehensive basis of accounting other than generally accepted accounting principles such as the cash basis of accounting, the auditor should issue a   5.____

    A. disclaimer of opinion   B. review report
    C. qualified opinion   D. special report

6. A limitation on the scope of the auditor's examination sufficient to preclude an unqualified opinion will ALWAYS result when management   6.____

    A. asks the auditor to report on the balance sheet and not on the other basic financial statements
    B. refuses to permit its lawyer to respond to the letter of audit inquiry
    C. discloses material related party transactions in the footnotes to the financial statements
    D. knows that confirmation of accounts receivable is not feasible

7. Which of the following audit procedures would an auditor be LEAST likely to perform using a generalized computer audit program?   7.____

    A. Searching records of accounts receivable balances for credit balances
    B. Investigating inventory balances for possible obsolescence
    C. Selecting accounts receivable for positive and negative confirmation
    D. Listing of unusually large inventory balances

8. An auditor evaluates the existing system of internal accounting control PRIMARILY to   8.____

    A. ascertain whether employees adhere to managerial policies
    B. determine the extent of substantive tests that must be performed
    C. determine whether procedures and records concerning the safeguarding of assets are reliable
    D. establish a basis for deciding which compliance tests are necessary

9. When an independent CPA is associated with the financial statements of a publicly held entity but has not audited or reviewed such statements, the appropriate form of report to be issued must include a(n)   9.____

    A. disclaimer of opinion
    B. compilation report
    C. adverse opinion
    D. unaudited association report

10. An auditor includes a separate paragraph in an otherwise unqualified report to emphasize that the entity being reported upon had significant transactions with related parties. The inclusion of this separate paragraph   10.____

    A. violates generally accepted auditing standards if this information is already disclosed in footnotes to the financial statements
    B. necessitates a revision of the opinion paragraph to include the phrase *with the foregoing explanation*
    C. is appropriate and would not negate the unqualified opinion
    D. is considered an *except for* qualification of the report

11. Which of the following requires recognition in the auditor's opinion as to consistency?   11.____

    A. The correction of an error in the prior year's financial statements resulting from a mathematical mistake in capitalizing interest
    B. The change from the cost method to the equity method of accounting for investments in common stock
    C. A change in the estimate of provisions for warranty costs
    D. A change in depreciation method which has no effect on current year's financial statements but is certain to affect future years

12. The auditor who intends to express a qualified opinion should disclose all the substantive   12.____
reasons in a separate explanatory paragraph of the report EXCEPT when the opinion paragraph

    A. makes reference to a contingent liability
    B. describes a limitation on the scope of the examination
    C. describes the use of an accounting principle at variance with generally accepted accounting principles
    D. makes reference to a change in accounting principle

13. When an examination is made in accordance with generally accepted auditing standards, the auditor should ALWAYS   13.____

    A. document the auditor's understanding of the client's internal accounting control system
    B. employ analytical review procedures
    C. obtain certain written representations from management
    D. observe the taking of physical inventory on the balance sheet date

14. Which of the following flowchart symbols represents online storage?   14.____

    A.   B.

    C.   D.

15. What is the continuing auditor's obligation concerning the discovery at an interim date of   15.____
a material weakness in the internal accounting control of a client if this same weakness had been communicated to the client during the prior year's audit?
The auditor

    A. should communicate this weakness to the client immediately because the discovery of such weaknesses in internal accounting control is the purpose of a review of interim financial information
    B. need not communicate this weakness to the client because it had already been communicated the prior year

C. should communicate this weakness to the client following completion of the examination unless the auditor decides to communicate it to the client at the interim date

D. should extend the audit procedures to investigate whether this weakness had any effect on the prior year's financial statements

16. To achieve good internal accounting control, which department should perform the activities of matching shipping documents with sales orders and preparing daily sales summaries?

16.____

A. Billing   B. Shipping
C. Credit   D. Sales order

17. A PRIMARY advantage of using generalized audit software packages in auditing the financial statements of a client that uses an EDP system is that the auditor may

17.____

A. substantiate the accuracy of data through self-checking digits and hash totals
B. access information stored on computer files without a complete understanding of the client's hardware and software features
C. reduce the level of required compliance testing to a relatively small amount
D. gather and permanently store large quantities of supportive evidential matter in machine readable form

18. An auditor is concerned with completing various phases of the examination after the balance sheet date.
This subsequent period extends to the date of the

18.____

A. auditor's report
B. final review of the audit working papers
C. public issuance of the financial statements
D. delivery of the auditor's report to the client

19. The permanent file section of the working papers that is kept for each audit client MOST likely contains

19.____

A. review notes pertaining to questions and comments regarding the audit work performed
B. a schedule of time spent on the engagement by each individual auditor
C. correspondence with the client's legal counsel concerning pending litigation
D. narrative descriptions of the client's accounting procedures and internal accounting controls

20. If, after completing the review of the design of internal accounting controls, the auditor plans to rely on internal accounting control procedures pertaining to plant asset transactions, the auditor should NEXT

20.____

A. make extensive substantive tests of plant asset balances
B. establish the physical existence of current year additions
C. complete the plant asset section of the internal accounting control questionnaire
D. perform compliance tests of the controls expected to be relied upon

21. Sound internal accounting control procedures dictate that defective merchandise returned by customers should be presented to the _____ clerk.   21._____

    A. purchasing
    C. inventory control
    B. receiving
    D. sales

22. In a properly designed accounts payable system, a voucher is prepared after the invoice, purchase order, requisition, and receiving report are verified.   22._____
The NEXT step in the system is to

    A. cancel the supporting documents
    B. enter the check amount in the check register
    C. approve the voucher for payment
    D. post the voucher amount to the expense ledger

23. Alpha Company uses its sales invoices for posting perpetual inventory records. Inadequate internal accounting controls over the invoicing function allow goods to be shipped that are not invoiced.   23._____
The inadequate controls could cause an

    A. understatement of revenues, receivables, and inventory
    B. overstatement of revenues and receivables, and an understatement of inventory
    C. understatement of revenues and receivables, and an overstatement of inventory
    D. overstatement of revenues, receivables, and inventory

24. After an auditor had been engaged to perform the first audit for a nonpublic entity, the client requested to change the engagement to a review.   24._____
In which of the following situations would there be a reasonable basis to comply with the client's request?

    A. The client's bank required an audit before committing to a loan, but the client subsequently acquired alternative financing.
    B. The auditor was prohibited by the client from corresponding with the client's legal counsel.
    C. Management refused to sign the client representation letter.
    D. The auditing procedures were substantially complete and the auditor determined that an unqualified opinion was warranted, but there was a disagreement concerning the audit fee.

25. Which of the following statements BEST describe the auditor's responsibility regarding the detection of material irregularities?   25._____

    A. Because of the inherent limitations of an audit, the auditor is not responsible for the failure to detect material irregularities.
    B. The auditor is responsible for the failure to detect material irregularities when such failure results from nonperformance of audit procedures specifically described in the engagement letter.
    C. The auditor should extend auditing procedures to actively search for evidence of material irregularities where the examination indicates that material irregularities may exist.
    D. The auditor is responsible for the failure to detect material irregularities when the auditor's evaluation of internal accounting control indicates that there is no basis for any reliance thereon.

26. Comparative financial statements include the financial statements of a prior period which were examined by a predecessor auditor whose report is not presented.
If the predecessor auditor's report was qualified, the successor auditor MUST

    A. obtain written approval from the predecessor auditor to include the prior year's financial statements
    B. issue a standard comparative audit report indicating the division of responsibility
    C. express an opinion on the current year statements alone and make no reference to the prior year statements
    D. disclose the reasons for any qualification in the predecessor auditor's opinion

26.____

27. The auditor may conclude that depreciation charges are insufficient by noting

    A. large amounts of fully depreciated assets
    B. continuous trade-ins of relatively new assets
    C. excessive recurring losses on assets retired
    D. insured values greatly in excess of book values

27.____

28. An auditor compares yearly revenues and expenses with those of the prior year and investigates all changes exceeding 10%.
By this procedure, the auditor would be MOST likely to learn that

    A. fourth quarter payroll taxes were not paid
    B. the client changed its capitalization policy for small tools for the year
    C. an increase in property tax rates has not been recognized in the client's accrual
    D. the yearly provision for uncollectible accounts is inadequate because of worsening economic conditions

28.____

29. The development of constructive suggestions to clients for improvements in internal accounting control is

    A. a requirement of the auditor's study and evaluation of internal accounting control
    B. a desirable by-product of an audit engagement
    C. addressed by the auditor only during a special engagement
    D. as important as establishing a basis for reliance upon the internal accounting control system

29.____

30. Of the following statements about an internal accounting control system, which one is CORRECT?

    A. The maintenance of the system of internal accounting control is an important responsibility of the internal auditor.
    B. Administrative controls relate directly to the safeguarding of assets and the systems of authorization and approval.
    C. Because of the cost/benefit relationship, internal accounting control procedures may be applied on a test basis in some circumstances.
    D. Internal accounting control procedures reasonably ensure that collusion among employees cannot occur.

30.____

KEY (CORRECT ANSWERS)

1.	C	16.	A
2.	C	17.	B
3.	B	18.	A
4.	D	19.	D
5.	D	20.	D
6.	B	21.	B
7.	B	22.	C
8.	B	23.	C
9.	A	24.	A
10.	C	25.	C
11.	B	26.	D
12.	D	27.	C
13.	C	28.	B
14.	A	29.	B
15.	C	30.	C

TEST 2

DIRECTIONS: Each question or incomplete statement is followed by several suggested answers or completions. Select the one that BEST answers the question or completes the statement. *PRINT THE LETTER OF THE CORRECT ANSWER IN THE SPACE AT THE RIGHT.*

1. Which of the following statistical sampling methods is MOST useful to auditors when testing for compliance?

   1.____

   A. Ratio estimation
   C. Difference estimation
   B. Variable sampling
   D. Discovery sampling

2. If after completing the preliminary phase of the review of the internal accounting control system the auditor plans to rely on the system, the auditor should NEXT

   2.____

   A. trace several transactions through the related documents and records to observe the related internal accounting control procedures in operation
   B. perform compliance tests to provide reasonable assurance that the accounting control procedures are being applied as prescribed
   C. complete the review of the system to determine whether the accounting control procedures are suitably designed
   D. design substantive tests that contemplate reliance on the system of internal accounting control

3. The form of communication with a client in a management advisory service consultation should be

   3.____

   A. either oral or written
   B. oral with appropriate documentation in the workpapers
   C. written and copies should be sent to both management and the board of directors
   D. written and a copy should be sent to management alone

4. Which of the following control procedures may prevent the failure to bill customers for some shipments?

   4.____

   A. Each shipment should be supported by a prenumbered sales invoice that is accounted for.
   B. Each sales order should be approved by authorized personnel.
   C. Sales journal entries should be reconciled to daily sales summaries.
   D. Each sales invoice should be supported by a shipping document.

5. A part of the auditor's planning of an audit engagement should be a plan to search for

   5.____

   A. errors or irregularities that would have a material or immaterial effect on the financial statements
   B. errors or irregularities that would have a material effect on the financial statements
   C. errors that would have a material effect on the financial statements, but the auditor need not plan to search for irregularities
   D. irregularities that would have a material effect on the financial statements, but the auditor need not plan to search for errors

6. In a study and evaluation of the system of internal accounting control, the completion of a questionnaire is MOST closely associated with which of the following?   6._____

    A. Tests of compliance
    B. Substantive tests
    C. Preliminary evaluation of the system
    D. Review of the system design

7. The audit work performed by each assistant should be reviewed to determine whether it was adequately performed and to evaluate whether   7._____

    A. there has been a thorough documentation of the internal accounting controls
    B. the auditor's system of quality control has been maintained at a high level
    C. the assistants' preliminary judgments about materiality differ from the materiality levels of the persons who will rely on the financial statements
    D. the results are consistent with the conclusions to be presented in the auditor's report

8. During a review of the financial statements of a nonpublic entity, the CPA finds that the financial statements contain a material departure from generally accepted accounting principles.   8._____
    If management refuses to correct the financial statement presentations, the CPA should

    A. attach a footnote explaining the effects of the departure
    B. disclose the departure in a separate paragraph of the report
    C. issue a compilation report
    D. issue an adverse opinion

9. The profession's ethical standards would MOST likely be considered to have been violated when the CPA represents that specific consulting services will be performed for a stated fee and it is apparent at the time of the representation that the   9._____

    A. CPA would not be independent
    B. fee was a competitive bid
    C. actual fee would be substantially higher
    D. actual fee would be substantially lower than the fees charged by other CPAs for comparable services

10. After the preliminary phase of the review of a client's EDP controls, an auditor may decide not to perform compliance tests related to the control procedures within the EDP portion of the client's internal accounting control system.   10._____
    Which of the following would NOT be a valid reason for choosing to omit compliance tests?

    A. The controls appear adequate.
    B. The controls duplicate operative controls existing elsewhere in the system.
    C. There appear to be major weaknesses that would preclude reliance on the stated procedure.
    D. The time and dollar costs of testing exceed the time and dollar savings in substantive testing if the compliance tests show the controls to be operative.

11. Before applying principal substantive tests to the details of asset and liability accounts at an interim date, the auditor should

    11.____

    A. assess the difficulty in controlling incremental audit risk
    B. investigate significant fluctuations that have occurred in the asset and liability accounts since the previous balance sheet date
    C. select only those accounts which can effectively be sampled during year-end audit work
    D. consider the compliance tests that must be applied at the balance sheet date to extend the audit conclusions reached at the interim date

12. A violation of the profession's ethical standards would MOST likely occur when a CPA who

    12.____

    A. is also admitted to the Bar represents on letterhead to be both an attorney and a CPA
    B. writes a newsletter on financial management also permits a publishing company to solicit subscriptions by direct mail
    C. is controller of a bank permits the bank to use the controller's CPA title in the listing of officers in its publications
    D. is the sole shareholder in a professional accountancy corporation that uses the designation *and company* in the firm title

13. After beginning an audit of a new client, Larkin, CPA, discovers that the professional competence necessary for the engagement is lacking. Larkin informs management of the situation and recommends another CPA, and management engages the other CPA. Under these circumstances,

    13.____

    A. Larkin's lack of competence should be construed to be a violation of generally accepted auditing standards
    B. Larkin may request compensation from the client for any professional services rendered to it in connection with the audit
    C. Larkin's request for a commission from the other CPA is permitted because a more competent audit can now be performed
    D. Larkin may be indebted to the other CPA since the other CPA can collect from the client only the amount the client originally agreed to pay Larkin

14. Which of the following BEST describes what is meant by generally accepted auditing standards?

    14.____

    A. Pronouncements issued by the Auditing Standards Board
    B. Procedures to be used to gather evidence to support financial statements
    C. Rules acknowledged by the accounting profession because of their universal compliance
    D. Measures of the quality of the auditor's performance

15. A CPA purchased stock in a client corporation and placed it in a trust as an educational fund for the CPA's minor child. The trust securities were not material to the CPA but were material to the child's personal net worth. Would the independence of the CPA be considered to be impaired with respect to the client?

    15.____

    A. *Yes,* because the stock would be considered a direct financial interest and, consequently, materiality is not a factor

B. *Yes,* because the stock would be considered an indirect financial interest that is material to the CPA's child

C. *No,* because the CPA would not be considered to have a direct financial interest in the client

D. *No,* because the CPA would not be considered to have a material indirect financial interest in the client

16. The auditor concludes that there is a material inconsistency in the other information in an annual report to shareholders containing audited financial statements.
If the client refuses to revise or eliminate the material inconsistency, the auditor should

    16.____

    A. revise the auditor's report to include a separate explanatory paragraph describing the material inconsistency

    B. consult with a party whose advice might influence the client, such as the client's legal counsel

    C. issue a qualified opinion after discussing the matter with the client's board of directors

    D. consider the matter closed since the other information is not in the audited financial statements

17. One of the major problems in an EDP system is that incompatible functions may be performed by the same individual. One compensating control for this is the use of

    17.____

    A. a self-checking digit system
    B. echo checks
    C. a computer log
    D. computer-generated hash totals

18. An auditor plans to examine a sample of 20 purchase orders for proper approvals as prescribed by the client's internal accounting control procedures. One of the purchase orders in the chosen sample of 20 cannot be found, and the auditor is unable to use alternative procedures to test whether that purchase order was properly approved. The auditor should

    18.____

    A. choose another purchase order to replace the missing purchase order in the sample

    B. consider this compliance test invalid and proceed with substantive tests since internal accounting control cannot be relied upon

    C. treat the missing purchase order as a deviation for the purpose of evaluating the sample

    D. select a completely new set of 20 purchase orders

19. Where computer processing is used in significant accounting applications, internal accounting control procedures may be defined by classifying control procedures into two types: general and

    19.____

    A. administrative   B. specific
    C. application   D. authorization

20. The principal auditor is satisfied with the independence and professional reputation of   20.____
the other auditor who has audited a subsidiary.
To indicate the division of responsibility, the principal auditor should modify

    A. both the scope and opinion paragraphs of the report
    B. only the scope paragraph of the report
    C. only the opinion paragraph of the report
    D. only the opinion paragraph of the report and include an explanatory middle paragraph

21. When the auditor is unable to determine the amounts associated with the illegal acts of   21.____
client personnel because of an inability to obtain adequate evidence, the auditor should
issue a(n)

    A. *subject to* qualified opinion
    B. disclaimer of opinion
    C. adverse opinion
    D. unqualified opinion with a separate explanatory paragraph

22. An auditor would be MOST likely to consider expressing a qualified opinion if the client's   22.____
financial statements include a footnote on related party transactions that

    A. lists the amounts due from related parties including the terms and manner of settlement
    B. discloses compensating balance arrangements maintained for the benefit of related parties
    C. represents that certain transactions with related parties were consummated on terms equally as favorable as would have been obtained in transactions with unrelated parties
    D. presents the dollar volume of related party transactions and the effects of any change in the method of establishing terms from that of the prior period

23. After issuance of the auditor's report, the auditor has no obligation to make any further   23.____
inquiries with respect to audited financial statements covered by that report unless

    A. a final resolution of a contingency that had resulted in a qualification of the auditor's report is made
    B. a development occurs that may affect the client's ability to continue as a going concern
    C. an investigation of the auditor's practice by a peer review committee ensues
    D. new information is discovered concerning undisclosed related party transactions of the previously audited period

24. The accountant's report expressing an opinion on an entity's system of internal accounting control would NOT include a   24.____

    A. brief explanation of the broad objectives and inherent limitations of internal accounting control
    B. specific date that the report covers, rather than a period of time
    C. statement that the entity's system of internal accounting control is consistent with that of the prior year after giving effect to subsequent changes
    D. description of the scope of the engagement

25. Which of the following legal situations would be considered to impair the auditor's independence?   25.____

    A. An expressed intention by the present management to commence litigation against the auditor alleging deficiencies in audit work for the client, although the auditor considers that there is only a remote possibility that such a claim will be filed

    B. Actual litigation by the auditor against the client for an amount not material to the auditor or to the financial statements of the client arising out of disputes as to billings for management advisory services

    C. Actual litigation by the auditor against the present management alleging management fraud or deceit

    D. Actual litigation by the client against the auditor for an amount not material to the auditor or to the financial statements of the client arising out of disputes as to billings for tax services

26. The PRIMARY reason an auditor requests letters of inquiry be sent to a client's attorneys is to provide the auditor with   26.____

    A. a description and evaluation of litigation, claims, and assessments that existed at the date of the balance sheet

    B. an expert opinion as to whether a loss is possible, probable, or remote

    C. the opportunity to examine the documentation concerning litigation, claims, and assessments

    D. corroboration of the information furnished by management concerning litigation, claims, and assessments

27. In connection with the element of professional development, a CPA firm's system of quality control should ordinarily provide that all personnel   27.____

    A. have the knowledge required to enable them to fulfill responsibilities assigned

    B. possess judgment, motivation, and adequate experience

    C. seek assistance from persons having appropriate levels of knowledge, judgment, and authority

    D. demonstrate compliance with peer review directives

28. Edwards Corp. uses the last-in, first-out method of costing for half of its inventory and the first-in, first-out method of costing for the other half of its inventory.   28.____
Because of these recording and reporting methods, the auditor should issue a(n) _____ opinion.

    A. unqualified   B. disclaimer of

    C. *except for* qualified   D. *subject to* qualified

29. Purchase cutoff procedures should be designed to test whether or not all inventory   29.____

    A. purchased and received before the end of the year was paid for

    B. ordered before the end of the year was received

    C. purchased and received before the end of the year was recorded

    D. owned by the company is in the possession of the company at the end of the year

30. Matthews Corp. has changed from a system of recording time worked on clock cards to a computerized payroll system in which employees record time in and out with magnetic cards. The EDP system automatically updates all payroll records.
Because of this change,

    A. a generalized computer audit program must be used
    B. part of the audit trail is altered
    C. the potential for payroll related fraud is diminished
    D. transactions must be processed in batches

30.____

KEY (CORRECT ANSWERS)

1.	D		16.	A
2.	C		17.	C
3.	A		18.	C
4.	A		19.	C
5.	B		20.	A
6.	D		21.	B
7.	D		22.	C
8.	B		23.	D
9.	C		24.	C
10.	A		25.	C
11.	A		26.	D
12.	D		27.	A
13.	B		28.	A
14.	D		29.	C
15.	A		30.	B

EXAMINATION SECTION
TEST 1

DIRECTIONS: Each question or incomplete statement is followed by several suggested answers or completions. Select the one that BEST answers the question or completes the statement. *PRINT THE LETTER OF THE CORRECT ANSWER IN THE SPACE AT THE RIGHT.*

1. If an auditor believes there is minimal likelihood that resolution of an uncertainty will have a material effect on the financial statements, the auditor should issue a(n) _____ opinion.

   A. unqualified
   B. disclaimer of
   C. *except for* qualified
   D. *subject to* qualified

   1._____

2. Which of the following BEST describes the auditor's reporting responsibility concerning information accompanying the basic financial statements in an auditor-submitted document?
   The auditor should report on

   A. all the information included in the document
   B. the basic financial statements but may not issue a report covering the accompanying information
   C. the information accompanying the basic financial statements only if the auditor participated in the preparation of the accompanying information
   D. the information accompanying the basic financial statements only if the document is being distributed to public shareholders

   2._____

3. Which of the following are prospective financial statements upon which an accountant may appropriately report for general use?

   A. Pro forma financial statements
   B. Financial projections
   C. Partial presentations
   D. Financial forecasts

   3._____

4. Given one or more hypothetical assumptions, a responsible party may prepare, to the best of its knowledge and belief, an entity's expected financial position, results of operations, and changes in financial position.
   Such prospective financial statements are known as

   A. Pro forma financial statements
   B. Financial projections
   C. Partial presentations
   D. Financial forecasts

   4._____

5. Subsequent to the issuance of the auditor's report, the auditor became aware of facts existing at the report date that would have affected the report had the auditor then been aware of such facts.
   After determining that the information is reliable, the auditor should NEXT

   5._____

A. notify the board of directors that the auditor's report must no longer be associated with the financial statements

B. determine whether there are persons relying or likely to rely on the financial statements who would attach importance to the information

C. request that management disclose the effects of the newly discovered information by adding a footnote to subsequently issued financial statements

D. issue revised pro forma financial statements taking into consideration the newly discovered information

6. When an auditor reports on financial statements prepared on an entity's income tax basis, the auditor's report should

6._____

A. disclose that the statements are not intended to conform with generally accepted accounting principles

B. disclaim an opinion on whether the statements were examined in accordance with generally accepted auditing standards

C. not express an opinion on whether the statements are presented in conformity with the comprehensive basis of accounting used

D. include an explanation of how the results of operations differ from the cash receipts and disbursements basis of accounting

7. When reporting on comparative financial statements where the financial statements of the prior period have been examined by a predecessor auditor whose report is not presented, the successor auditor should indicate in the scope paragraph

7._____

A. the reasons why the predecessor auditor's report is not presented

B. the identity of the predecessor auditor who examined the financial statements of the prior year

C. whether the predecessor auditor's review of the current year's financial statements revealed any matters that might have a material effect on the successor auditor's opinion

D. the type of opinion expressed by the predecessor auditor

8. The auditor would MOST likely issue a disclaimer of opinion because of

8._____

A. the client's failure to present supplementary information required by the FASB

B. inadequate disclosure of material information

C. a client imposed scope limitation

D. the qualification of an opinion by the other auditor of a subsidiary where there is a division of responsibility

9. The principal auditor is satisfied with the independence and professional reputation of the other auditor who has audited a subsidiary but wants to indicate the division of responsibility.
The principal auditor should

9._____

A. modify only the scope paragraph of the report

B. modify only the opinion paragraph of the report

C. modify both the scope and opinion paragraphs of the report

D. not modify the report except for inclusion of a separate explanatory paragraph

10. The management of a client company believes that the statement of changes in financial   10.____
position (statement of cash flows) is not a useful document and refuses to include one in
the annual report to stockholders.
As a result of this circumstance, the auditor's opinion should be

   A. adverse
   B. unqualified
   C. qualified due to inadequate disclosure
   D. qualified due to a scope limitation

11. When an auditor qualifies an opinion because of a scope limitation, which paragraph(s)   11.____
of the auditor's report should indicate that the qualification pertains to the possible effects
on the financial statements and not to the scope limitation itself?

   A. The scope paragraph and the separate explanatory paragraph
   B. The separate explanatory paragraph and the opinion paragraph
   C. The scope paragraph *only*
   D. The opinion paragraph *only*

12. When an independent accountant's report based on a review of interim financial informa-   12.____
tion is incorporated by reference in a registration statement, the Securities and Exchange
Commission requires that the prospectus clarify that the accountant's report is NOT

   A. a part of the registration statement within the meaning of the Securities Act of 1933
   B. subject to the Statements on Standards for Accounting and Review Services
   C. to be relied upon due to the limited nature of the procedures applied
   D. included in the company's quarterly report on Form 10-Q

13. A client acquired 25% of its outstanding capital stock after year-end and prior to comple-   13.____
tion of the auditor's field work.
The auditor should

   A. advise management to adjust the balance sheet to reflect the acquisition
   B. issue pro forma financial statements giving effect to the acquisition as if it had
      occurred at year-end
   C. advise management to disclose the acquisition in the notes to the financial state-
      ments
   D. disclose the acquisition in the opinion paragraph of the auditor's report

14. An auditor concludes that an audit procedure considered necessary at the time of the   14.____
examination had been omitted. The auditor should assess the importance of the omitted
procedure to the ability to support the previously expressed opinion.
Which of the following would be LEAST helpful in making that assessment?

   A. A discussion with the client about whether there are persons relying on the audi-
      tor's report
   B. A reevaluation of the overall scope of the examination
   C. A discussion of the circumstances with engagement personnel
   D. A review of the other audit procedures that were applied that might compensate for
      the one omitted

15. Which of the following statements concerning the auditor's use of the work of a specialist   15.____
is CORRECT?

    A. If the specialist is related to the client, the auditor is not permitted to use the specialist's findings as corroborative evidence.
    B. The specialist may be identified in the auditor's report only when the auditor issues a qualified opinion.
    C. The specialist should have an understanding of the auditor's corroborative use of the specialist's findings.
    D. If the auditor believes that the determinations made by the specialist are unreasonable, only an adverse opinion may be issued.

16. When using a computer to gather evidence, the auditor need not have working knowledge of the client's programming language.   16.____
However, it is necessary that the auditor understand the

    A. audit specifications
    B. programming techniques
    C. database retrieval system
    D. manual testing techniques

17. Which of the following is NOT a major reason why an accounting audit trail should be   17.____
maintained for a computer system?

    A. Query answering
    B. Deterrent to irregularities
    C. Monitoring purposes
    D. Analytical review

18. Working papers that record the procedures used by the auditor to gather evidence   18.____
should be

    A. considered the primary support for the financial statements being examined
    B. viewed as the connecting link between the books of account and the financial statements
    C. designed to meet the circumstances of the particular engagement
    D. destroyed when the audited entity ceases to be a client

19. If the financial statements, including accompanying notes, fail to disclose information that   19.____
is required by generally accepted accounting principles, the auditor should express either a(n)

    A. *except for* qualified opinion or an adverse opinion
    B. adverse opinion or a *subject to* qualified opinion
    C. *subject to* qualified opinion or an unqualified opinion with a separate explanatory paragraph
    D. unqualified opinion with a separate explanatory paragraph or an *except for* qualified opinion

20. If there were no changes during the reporting period in the application of accounting principles, which of the following types of opinions should omit any reference to consistency?   20.____
_____ opinion.

    A. *except for* qualified   B. unqualified
    C. *subject to* qualified   D. adverse

21. A limitation on the scope of the auditor's examination sufficient to preclude an unqualified opinion will ALWAYS result when management   21.____

    A. prevents the auditor from reviewing the working papers of the predecessor auditor
    B. engages the auditor after the year-end physical inventory count is completed
    C. fails to correct a material internal accounting control weakness that had been identified during the prior year's audit
    D. refuses to furnish a management representation letter to the auditor

22. Operational auditing is PRIMARILY oriented toward   22.____

    A. future improvements to accomplish the goals of management
    B. the accuracy of data reflected in management's financial records
    C. the verification that a company's financial statements are fairly presented
    D. past protection provided by existing internal accounting control

23. Which of the following is the BEST audit procedure for determining the existence of unrecorded liabilities at year-end?
Examine   23.____

    A. a sample of invoices dated a few days prior to and subsequent to year-end to ascertain whether they have been properly recorded
    B. a sample of cash disbursements in the period subsequent to year-end
    C. confirmation requests returned by creditors whose accounts appear on a subsidiary trial balance of accounts payable
    D. unusual relationships between monthly accounts payable balances and recorded purchases

24. An auditor ordinarily should send a standard confirmation request to all banks with which the client has done business during the year under audit, regardless of the year-end balance, because this procedure   24.____

    A. provides for confirmation regarding compensating balance arrangements
    B. detects kiting activities that may otherwise not be discovered
    C. seeks information about indebtedness to the bank
    D. verifies securities held by the bank in safekeeping

25. On receiving the bank cutoff statement, the auditor should trace   25.____

    A. deposits in transit on the year-end bank reconciliation to deposits in the cash receipts journal
    B. checks dated prior to year-end to the outstanding checks listed on the year-end bank reconciliation
    C. deposits listed on the cutoff statement to deposits in the cash receipts journal
    D. checks dated subsequent to year-end to the outstanding checks listed on the year-end bank reconciliations

26. Which of the following would the accountant MOST likely investigate during the review of financial statements of a nonpublic entity if accounts receivable did not conform to a predictable pattern during the year?   26.____

    A. Sales returns and allowances   B. Credit sales
    C. Sales of consigned goods   D. Cash sales

27. Prior to commencing the compilation of financial statements of a nonpublic entity, the accountant should

27.____

    A. perform analytical review procedures sufficient to determine whether fluctuations among account balances appear reasonable
    B. complete the preliminary phase of the study and evaluation of the entity's internal accounting control
    C. verify that the financial information supplied by the entity agrees with the books of original entry
    D. acquire a knowledge of any specialized accounting principles and practices used in the entity's industry

28. After discovering that a related party transaction exists, the auditor should be aware that the

28.____

    A. substance of the transaction could be significantly different from its form
    B. adequacy of disclosure of the transaction is secondary to its legal form
    C. transaction is assumed to be outside the ordinary course of business
    D. financial statements should recognize the legal form of the transaction rather than its substance

29. Which of the following auditing procedures is ordinarily performed LAST?

29.____

    A. Obtaining a management representation letter
    B. Testing the purchasing function
    C. Reading the minutes of directors' meetings
    D. Confirming accounts payable

30. Which of the following is the MOST effective audit procedure for verification of dividends earned on investments in marketable equity securities?

30.____

    A. Tracing deposit of dividend checks to the cash receipts book
    B. Reconciling amounts received with published dividend records
    C. Comparing the amounts received with preceding year dividends received
    D. Recomputing selected extensions and footings of dividend schedules and comparing totals to the general ledger

KEY (CORRECT ANSWERS)

1.	A	16.	A
2.	A	17.	D
3.	D	18.	C
4.	B	19.	A
5.	B	20.	D
6.	A	21.	D
7.	D	22.	A
8.	C	23.	B
9.	C	24.	C
10.	C	25.	B
11.	D	26.	B
12.	A	27.	D
13.	C	28.	A
14.	A	29.	A
15.	C	30.	B

———

TEST 2

DIRECTIONS: Each question or incomplete statement is followed by several suggested answers or completions. Select the one that BEST answers the question or completes the statement. *PRINT THE LETTER OF THE CORRECT ANSWER IN THE SPACE AT THE RIGHT.*

1. When auditing merchandise inventory at year-end, the auditor performs a purchase cut-off test to obtain evidence that   1.____

    A. all goods purchased before year-end are received before the physical inventory count
    B. no goods held on consignment for customers are included in the inventory balance
    C. no goods observed during the physical count are pledged or sold
    D. all goods owned at year-end are included in the inventory balance

2. Without the consent of the client, a CPA should NOT disclose confidential client information contained in working papers to a   2.____

    A. voluntary quality control review board
    B. CPA firm that has purchased the CPA's accounting practice
    C. federal court that has issued a valid subpoena
    D. disciplinary body created under state statute

3. An example of an analytical review procedure is the comparison of   3.____

    A. financial information with similar information regarding the industry in which the entity operates
    B. recorded amounts of major disbursements with appropriate invoices
    C. results of a statistical sample with the expected characteristics of the actual population
    D. EDP generated data with similar data generated by a manual accounting system

4. Audit evidence can come in different forms with different degrees of persuasiveness. Which of the following is the LEAST persuasive type of evidence?   4.____

    A. Bank statement obtained from the client
    B. Computations made by the auditor
    C. Prenumbered client sales invoices
    D. Vendor's invoice

Questions 5-7.

DIRECTIONS: Questions 5 through 7 are to be answered on the basis of the following section of a system flowchart for a payroll application.

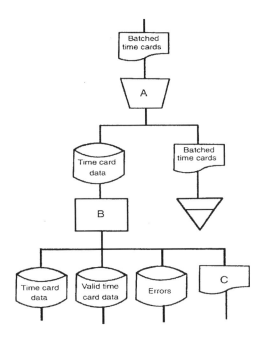

5. Symbol C could represent   5.____

    A. batched time cards
    B. unclaimed payroll checks
    C. erroneous time cards
    D. an error report

6. Symbol B could represent   6.____

    A. computation of net pay
    B. separation of erroneous time cards
    C. validation of payroll data
    D. preparation of the payroll register

7. Symbol A could represent   7.____

    A. computation of gross pay
    B. input of payroll data
    C. preparation of paychecks
    D. verification of payrates

8. When there are a large number of relatively small account balances, negative confirma-   8.____
   tion of accounts receivable is feasible if internal accounting control is _____ and the
   individuals receiving the confirmation requests are _____ to give them adequate consideration.

    A. strong; unlikely   B. weak; likely
    C. weak; unlikely   D. strong; likely

9. When there are few property and equipment transactions during the year, the continuing auditor USUALLY makes a

    9.____

    A.   complete review of the related internal accounting controls and performs compliance tests of those controls being relied upon
    B.   complete review of the related internal accounting controls and performs analytical review tests to verify current year additions to property and equipment
    C.   preliminary review of the related internal accounting controls and performs a thorough examination of the balances at the beginning of the year
    D.   preliminary review of the related internal accounting controls and performs extensive tests of current year property and equipment transactions

10. A weakness in internal accounting control over recording retirements of equipment may cause the auditor to

    10.____

    A.   inspect certain items of equipment in the plant and trace those items to the accounting records
    B.   review the subsidiary ledger to ascertain whether depreciation was taken on each item of equipment during the year
    C.   trace additions to the *other assets* account to search for equipment that is still on hand but no longer being used
    D.   select certain items of equipment from the accounting records and locate them in the plant

11. The auditor may observe the distribution of paychecks to ascertain whether

    11.____

    A.   payrate authorization is properly separated from the operating function
    B.   deductions from gross pay are calculated correctly and are properly authorized
    C.   employees of record actually exist and are employed by the client
    D.   paychecks agree with the payroll register and the time cards

12. The auditor's communication of material weaknesses in internal accounting control is

    12.____

    A.   required to enable the auditor to state that the examination has been made in accordance with generally accepted auditing standards
    B.   the principal reason for studying and evaluating the system of internal accounting controls
    C.   incident to the auditor's objective of forming an opinion as to the fair presentation of the financial statements
    D.   required to be documented in a written report to the board of directors or the board's audit committee

13. The purpose of segregating the duties of hiring personnel and distributing payroll checks is to separate the

    13.____

    A.   operational responsibility from the record keeping responsibility
    B.   responsibilities of recording a transaction at its origin from the ultimate posting in the general ledger
    C.   authorization of transactions from the custody of related assets
    D.   human resources function from the controllership function

14. Which of the following internal accounting control procedures could BEST prevent direct   14.____
labor from being charged to manufacturing overhead?

    A. Reconciliation of work in process inventory with cost records
    B. Comparison of daily journal entries with factory labor summary
    C. Comparison of periodic cost budgets and time cards
    D. Reconciliation of unfinished job summary and production cost records

15. Instead of taking a physical inventory count on the balance-sheet date, the client may   15.____
take physical counts prior to the year-end if internal accounting controls are adequate
and

    A. computerized records of perpetual inventory are maintained
    B. inventory is slow-moving
    C. EDP error reports are generated for missing pre-numbered inventory tickets
    D. obsolete inventory items are segregated and excluded

16. In a properly designed internal accounting control system, the same employee may be   16.____
permitted to

    A. receive and deposit checks, and also approve writeoffs of customer accounts
    B. approve vouchers for payment, and also sign checks
    C. reconcile the bank statements, and also receive and deposit cash
    D. sign checks, and also cancel supporting documents

17. An internal accounting control questionnaire indicates that an approved receiving report   17.____
is required to accompany every check request for payment of merchandise.
Which of the following procedures provides the GREATEST assurance that this control
is operating effectively?
Select and examine

    A. cancelled checks and ascertain that the related receiving reports are dated no ear-
       lier than the checks
    B. cancelled checks and ascertain that the related receiving reports are dated no later
       than the checks
    C. receiving reports and ascertain that the related cancelled checks are dated no ear-
       lier than the receiving reports
    D. receiving reports and ascertain that the related cancelled checks are dated no later
       than the receiving reports

18. The completeness of EDP-generated sales figures can be tested by comparing the num-   18.____
ber of items listed on the daily sales report with the number of items billed on the actual
invoices.
This process uses

    A. check digits   B. control totals
    C. validity tests   D. process tracing data

19. For effective internal accounting control, employees maintaining the accounts receivable   19.____
subsidiary ledger should NOT also approve

    A. employee overtime wages
    B. credit granted to customers
    C. write-offs of customer accounts
    D. cash disbursements

20. Based on a study and evaluation completed at an interim date, the auditor concludes that 20.____
no significant internal accounting control weaknesses exist.
The records and procedures would MOST likely be tested again at year-end if

    A. compliance tests were not performed by the internal auditor during the remaining period
    B. the internal accounting control system provides a basis for reliance in reducing the extent of substantive testing
    C. the auditor used nonstatistical sampling during the interim period compliance testing
    D. inquiries and observations lead the auditor to believe that conditions have changed

21. After completing the preliminary phase of the review of internal accounting control, the 21.____
auditor decides not to rely on the system to restrict substantive tests. Documentation
may be limited to the auditor's

    A. understanding of the internal accounting control system
    B. reasons for deciding not to extend the review
    C. basis for concluding that errors and irregularities will be prevented
    D. completed internal accounting control questionnaire

Question 22.

DIRECTIONS: Question 22 is to be answered on the basis of the following diagram, which depicts the auditor's estimated deviation rate compared with the tolerable rate, and also depicts the true population deviation rate compared with the tolerable rate.

Auditor's Estimate Based on Sample Results	True State of Population	
	Deviation Rate Exceeds Tolerable Rate	Deviation Rate is Less Than Tolerable Rate
Deviation Rate Exceeds Tolerable Rate	I.	III.
Deviation Rate is Less Than Tolerable Rate	II.	IV.

22. As a result of compliance testing, the auditor underrelies on internal accounting control 22.____
and thereby increases substantive testing.
This is illustrated by situation

    A. I   B. II   C. III   D. IV

23. Which of the following MOST likely constitutes a weakness in the internal accounting 23.____
control of an EDP system?
The

    A. control clerk establishes control over data received by the EDP department and reconciles control totals after processing
    B. application programmer identifies programs required by the systems design and flowcharts the logic of these programs

6 (#2)

C. systems analyst reviews output and controls the distribution of output from the EDP department
D. accounts payable clerk prepares data for computer processing and enters the data into the computer

24. Which of the following is LEAST likely to be evidence the auditor examines to determine whether operations are in compliance with the internal accounting control system?   24._____

   A. Records documenting usage of EDP programs
   B. Cancelled supporting documents
   C. Confirmations of accounts receivable
   D. Signatures on authorization forms

25. The PRIMARY purpose of a management advisory services engagement is to help the client   25._____

   A. become more profitable by relying upon the CPA's existing personal knowledge about the client's business
   B. improve the use of its capabilities and resources to achieve its objectives
   C. document and quantify its future plans without impairing the CPA's objectivity or allowing the CPA to assume the role of management
   D. obtain benefits that are guaranteed implicitly by the CPA

26. When unable to obtain sufficient competent evidential matter to determine whether certain client acts are illegal, the auditor would MOST likely issue   26._____

   A. an unqualified opinion with a separate explanatory paragraph
   B. either a qualified opinion or an adverse opinion
   C. either a disclaimer or opinion or a qualified opinion,
   D. either an adverse opinion or a disclaimer of opinion

27. Which of the following statements BEST describes the auditor's responsibility regarding the detection of material errors and irregularities?   27._____

   A. The auditor is responsible for the failure to detect material errors and irregularities only when such failure results from the nonapplication of generally accepted accounting principles.
   B. Extended auditing procedures are required to detect material errors and irregularities if the auditor's examination indicates that they may exist.
   C. The auditor is responsible for the failure to detect material errors and irregularities only when the auditor fails to confirm receivables or observe inventories.
   D. Extended auditing procedures are required to detect unrecorded transactions even if there is no evidence that material errors and irregularities may exist.

28. An abnormal fluctuation in gross profit that might suggest the need for extended audit procedures for sales and inventories would MOST likely be identified in the planning phase of the audit by the use of   28._____

   A. tests of transactions and balances
   B. a preliminary review of internal accounting control
   C. specialized audit programs
   D. analytical review procedures

115

29. When considering internal control, an auditor should be aware of the concept of reasonable assurance, which recognizes that the

    29.____

    A. segregation of incompatible functions is necessary to ascertain that internal control is effective
    B. employment of competent personnel provides assurance that the objectives of internal control will be achieved
    C. establishment and maintenance of a system of internal control is an important responsibility of the management and not of the auditor
    D. cost of internal control should not exceed the benefits expected to be derived from internal control

30. When performing an audit of a city that is subject to the requirements of the Uniform Single Audit Act of 1984, an auditor should adhere to

    30.____

    A. Governmental Accounting Standards Board GENERAL STANDARDS
    B. Governmental Finance Officers Association GOVERNMENTAL ACCOUNTING, AUDITING, AND FINANCIAL REPORTING PRINCIPLES
    C. General Accounting Office STANDARDS FOR AUDIT OF GOVERNMENTAL ORGANIZATIONS, PROGRAMS, ACTIVITIES, AND FUNCTIONS
    D. Securities and Exchange Commission REGULATION S-X

KEY (CORRECT ANSWERS)

1.	D		16.	D
2.	B		17.	B
3.	A		18.	B
4.	C		19.	C
5.	D		20.	D
6.	C		21.	B
7.	B		22.	C
8.	D		23.	C
9.	D		24.	C
10.	D		25.	B
11.	C		26.	C
12.	C		27.	B
13.	C		28.	D
14.	B		29.	D
15.	A		30.	C

EXAMINATION SECTION
TEST 1

DIRECTIONS: Each question is followed by several suggested answers or completions.
Select the one that *BEST* answers the question or completes the statement.
*PRINT THE LETTER OF THE CORRECT ANSWER IN THE SPACE AT THE
RIGHT.*

1. The current funds group of a not-for-private university includes which of the following?   1._____

	Agency funds	Plant funds
A.	No	No
B.	No	Yes
C.	Yes	Yes
D.	Yes	No

2. A local governmental unit could use which of the following types of funds?   2._____

	Fiduciary	Proprietary
A.	Yes	No
B.	Yes	Yes
C.	No	Yes
D.	No	No

3. A comprehensive annual financial report (CAFR) of a governmental unit should contain a   3._____
combined statement of revenue, expenditures, and changes in fund balances for

	Account groups	Proprietary funds
A.	Yes	No
B.	Yes	Yes
C.	No	Yes
D.	No	No

4. Which of the following not-for-profit organizations would use plant funds to account for   4._____
land, buildings, equipment, and other capital assets?

	Colleges and universities	Voluntary health and welfare organizations
A.	Yes	Yes
B.	Yes	No
C.	No	No
D.	No	Yes

5. Which of the following funds of a governmental unit uses the same basis of accounting   5._____
as an enterprise fund?

   A. Special revenue
   B. Expendable trust
   C. Capital projects
   D. Internal service

6. The debt service fund of a governmental unit is used to account for the accumulation of   6._____
resources to pay, and the payment of, general long-term debt

	Principal	Interest
A.	Yes	Yes
B.	Yes	No
C.	No	No
D.	No	Yes

7. Which of the following funds of a governmental unit recognizes revenues in the account-   7._____
   ing period in which they become available and measurable?

   A. Nonexpendable trust
   B. General
   C. Enterprise
   D. Internal service

8. Which of the following accounts of a governmental unit is debited when a purchase order   8._____
   is approved?

   A. Appropriations control
   B. Vouchers payable
   C. Fund balance reserved for encumbrances
   D. Encumbrances control

9. The estimated revenues control account of a governmental unit is debited when   9._____

   A. the budget is closed at the end of the year
   B. the budget is recorded
   C. actual revenues are recorded
   D. actual revenues are collected

10. Under which basis of accounting for a governmental unit should revenues be recognized   10._____
    in the accounting period in which they become available and measurable?

	Accrual basis	*Modified accrual basis*
A.	Yes	No
B.	Yes	Yes
C.	No	Yes
D.	No	No

11. A company is considering exchanging an old asset for a new asset. Ignoring income tax   11._____
    considerations, which of the following is (are) economically relevant to the decision?

	Carrying amount of old asset	*Disposal value of old asset*
A.	No	No
B.	No	Yes
C.	Yes	Yes
D.	Yes	No

12. The capital budgeting technique known as accounting rate of return uses   12._____

	Depreciation expense	*Time value of money*
A.	No	No
B.	No	Yes
C.	Yes	Yes
D.	Yes	No

13. In using cost-volume-profit analysis to calculate expected unit sales, which of the follow-   13._____
    ing should be added to fixed costs in the numerator?

    A. Predicted operating loss
    B. Predicted operating profit
    C. Unit contribution margin
    D. Variable costs

14. When production levels are expected to decline within a relevant range, and a flexible budget is used, what effects would be anticipated with respect to each of the following? 14.____

	Fixed costs per unit	Variable costs per unit
A.	Increase	No change
B.	Increase	Increase
C.	No change	No change
D.	No change	Increase

15. In an income statement prepared as an internal report using the variable costing method, which of the following terms should appear? 15.____

	Gross profit (margin)	Operating income
A.	Yes	Yes
B.	Yes	No
C.	No	No
D.	No	Yes

16. Direct materials cost is a 16.____

	Period cost	Product cost
A.	Yes	No
B.	No	No
C.	No	Yes
D.	Yes	Yes

17. Residual income is the 17.____

   A. contribution margin of an investment center, less the imputed interest on the invested capital used by the center
   B. contribution margin of an investment center, plus the imputed interest on the invested capital used by the center
   C. income of an investment center, less the imputed interest on the invested capital used by the center
   D. income of an investment center, plus the imputed interest on the invested capital used by the center

18. Actual sales values at the split-off point for joint products Y and Z are not known. For purposes of allocating joint costs to products Y and Z, the relative sales value at split-off method is used. An increase in the costs beyond split-off occurs for product Z, while those of product Y remain constant. If the selling prices of finished products Y and Z remain constant, the percentage of the total joint costs allocated to Product Y and Product Z would 18.____

   A. decrease for Product Y and Product Z
   B. decrease for Product Y and increase for Product Z
   C. increase for Product Y and Product Z
   D. increase for Product Y and decrease for Product Z

19. Under the three-variance method for analyzing factory overhead, which of the following is used in the computation of the spending variance?   19.____

	Actual factory overhead	Budget allowance based on actual hours
A.	No	Yes
B.	No	No
C.	Yes	No
D.	Yes	Yes

20. In a job order cost system using predetermined factory overhead rates, indirect materials usually are recorded initially as an increase in   20.____

    A. work in process control
    B. factory overhead applied
    C. factory overhead control
    D. stores control

21. When combined financial statements are prepared for a group of related companies, intercompany transactions an intercompany profits or losses should be eliminated when the group is composed of   21.____

	Commonly controlled companies	Unconsolidated subsidiaries
A.	No	No
B.	No	Yes
C.	Yes	Yes
D.	Yes	No

22. Personal financial Personal statements should include a   22.____

	Statement of financial condition	Statement of changes in financial position
A.	No	Yes
B.	No	No
C.	Yes	No
D.	Yes	Yes

23. How are trade receivables used in the calculation of each of the following?   23.____

	Acid test (quick) ratio	Receivable turnover
A.	Denominator	Denominator
B.	Not used	Numerator
C.	Numerator	Numerator
D.	Numerator	Denominator

24. For a compensatory stock option plan for which the date of grant and the measurement date are different, the stock options outstanding account should be reduced at the   24.____

    A. adoption date of the plan
    B. date of grant
    C. measurement date
    D. exercise date

25. An employer sponsoring a defined benefit pension plan should   25.____

    A. disclose the projected benefit obligation, identifying the accumulated benefit obligation and the vested benefit obligation
    B. disclose the projected benefit obligation, identifying the accumulated benefit obligation but not the vested benefit obligation
    C. disclose the projected benefit obligation, identifying the vested benefit obligation but not the accumulated benefit obligation
    D. not disclose the projected benefit obligation

26. A loss on the sale of machinery in the ordinary course of business should be presented in a statement of changes in financial position prepared on a cash basis (indirect method) as a (an)   26.____

    A. deduction from income from continuing operations
    B. addition to income from continuing operations
    C. inflow and outflow of cash
    D. outflow of cash

27. A decrease in net accounts receivable should be presented in a statement of changes in financial position prepared on a cash basis (indirect method) as a (an)   27.____

    A. inflow and outflow of cash
    B. outflow of cash
    C. deduction from income from continuing operations
    D. addition to income from continuing operations

28. The if-converted method of computing earnings per share data assumes conversion of convertible securities as of the   28.____

    A. beginning of the earliest period reported (or at time of issuance, if later)
    B. beginning of the earliest period reported (regardless of time of issuance)
    C. middle of the earliest period reported (regardless of time of issuance)
    D. ending of the earliest period reported (regardless of time of issuance)

29. In financial reporting for segments of a business enterprise, which of the following should be taken into account in computing the amount of industry segment's identifiable assets?   29.____

	Accumulated depreciation	Allowance for doubtful accounts
A.	No	No
B.	No	Yes
C.	Yes	Yes
D.	Yes	No

30. When the occurrence of a gain contingency is probable and its amount can be reasonably estimated, the gain contingency should be   30.____

    A. recognized in the income statement and disclosed
    B. classified as an appropriation of retained earnings
    C. disclosed, but **not** recognized in the income statement
    D. neither recognized in the income statement nor disclosed

KEY (CORRECT ANSWERS)

1.	A	16.	C
2.	B	17.	C
3.	D	18.	D
4.	A	19.	D
5.	D	20.	D
6.	A	21.	C
7.	B	22.	C
8.	D	23.	D
9.	B	24.	D
10.	C	25.	A
11.	B	26.	B
12.	D	27.	D
13.	B	28.	A
14.	A	29.	C
15.	D	30.	C

TEST 2

DIRECTIONS: Each question is followed by several suggested answers or completions. Select the one that *BEST* answers the question or completes the statement. *PRINT THE LETTER OF THE CORRECT ANSWER IN THE SPACE AT THE RIGHT.*

1. Rent may be accrued or deferred to provide an appropriate cost in each period for   1.____

	Interim financial reporting	Year-end financial reporting
A.	No	No
B.	No	Yes
C.	Yes	Yes
D.	Yes	No

2. A business combination occurs in the middle of the year. Results of operations for the year of combination would include the combined results of operations of the separate companies for the entire year if the business combination is a   2.____

	Pooling of interests	Purchase
A.	Yes	No
B.	Yes	Yes
C.	No	Yes
D.	No	No

3. A business combination is accounted for properly as a pooling of interests. Which of the following expenses related to effecting the business combination should enter into the determination of net income of the combined corporation for the period in which the expenses are incurred?   3.____

	Fees of finders and consultants	Registration fees
A.	No	Yes
B.	No	No
C.	Yes	No
D.	Yes	Yes

4. Company N donated computer equipment to a university (a nonreciprocal transfer). The fair value of the computer equipment was determinable. The difference between the fair value of the nonmonetary asset transferred and its recorded amount at the date of donation should be recognized in Company N's income statement when the difference results in a   4.____

	Gain	Loss
A.	Yes	No
B.	Yes	Yes
C.	No	Yes
D.	No	No

5. The effect of a change in accounting principle which is inseparable from the effect of a change in accounting estimate should be reported   5.____

   A. in the period of change and future periods if the change affects both
   B. by restating the financial statements of all prior periods presented
   C. by showing the pro forma effects of retroactive application
   D. as a correction of an error

6. Which of the following should be disclosed in the summary of significant accounting policies?

	Composition of inventories	Depreciation expense
A.	No	No
B.	No	Yes
C.	Yes	Yes
D.	Yes	No

7. A segment of a business has been discontinued during the year. The loss on disposal should

   A. include operating losses of the current period up to the measurement date
   B. include employee relocation costs associated with the decision to dispose
   C. exclude severance pay associated with the decision to dispose
   D. exclude operating losses during the phase-out period

8. The cumulative effect on prior years' earnings of a change in accounting principle should be reported separately as a component of income after income from continuing operations, for a change from

   A. completed-contract method of accounting for long-term construction-type contracts to the percentage-of-completion method
   B. percentage-of-completion method of accounting for long-term construction-type contracts to the completed-contract method
   C. FIFO method of inventory pricing to the weighted-average method
   D. LIFO method of inventory pricing to the weighted-average method

9. Which of the following should be used for inter-period tax allocation?

	Comprehensive allocation	Partial allocation
A.	No	No
B.	Yes	No
C.	Yes	Yes
D.	No	Yes

10. An employer offered for a short period of time special termination benefits to some employees. The employees accepted the offer, which provided for immediate lump-sum payments and future payments at the end of the next two years. The amounts can be reasonably estimated. The amount of expense recognized this year should include

   A. one third of the lump-sum payments and one third of the present value of the future payments
   B. only the lump-sum payments
   C. the lump-sum payments and the total of the future payments
   D. the lump-sum payments and the present value of the future payments

11. A research and development activity for which the cost would be expensed as incurred is

   A. modification of the design of a product
   B. trouble-shooting in connection with breakdowns during commercial production
   C. routine design of tools
   D. engineering follow-through in an early phase of commercial production

12. A company issued for no consideration rights to its existing shareholders to purchase, for $30 per share, unissued shares of $15 par value common stock.
The common stock account will be

    A. credited when the rights are exercised.
    B. credited when the rights are issued.
    C. debited when the rights are exercised.
    D. debited when the rights lapse.

12.____

13. The effect of a material transaction that is infrequent in occurrence but **not** unusual in nature should be presented separately as a component of income from continuing operations when the transaction results in a

	Gain	Loss
A.	No	Yes
B.	No	No
C.	Yes	No
D.	Yes	Yes

13.____

14. A foreign subsidiary's functional currency is its local currency, which has not experienced significant inflation. The weighted average exchange rate for the current year would be the appropriate exchange rate for translating

	Wages expense	Sales to customers
A.	Yes	No
B.	Yes	Yes
C.	No	Yes
D.	No	No

14.____

15. When should an anticipated loss on a long-term contract be recognized under the percentage-of-completion method and the completed-contract method, respectively?

	Percentage of Completion	Completed Contract
A.	Over life of project	Contract complete
B.	Immediately	Contract complete
C.	Over life of project	Immediately
D.	Immediately	Immediately

15.____

16. How would the declaration of a liquidating dividend by a corporation affect each of the following?

	Contributed capital	Total stockholders' equity
A.	No effect	Decrease
B.	Decrease	Decrease
C.	Decrease	No effect
D.	No effect	No effect

16.____

17. A company changes from an accounting principle that is not generally accepted to one that is generally accepted. The effect of the change should be reported, net of applicable income taxes, in the current

    A. income statement after income from continuing operations and before extraordinary items
    B. income statement after extraordinary items
    C. retained earnings statement as an adjustment of the opening balance
    D. retained earnings statement after net income but before dividends

17.____

18. The partnership agreement for the partnership of Somer and Primrose provided for inter-   18.____
    est on each partner's average capital investment. Somer's average capital investment
    was more than Primrose's average capital investment. Profit in excess of interest was
    allocated equally. If during the year the partnership had profits in excess of the interest
    on each partner's average capital investment, the amount of Somer's partnership capital
    would

    A. increase the same as Primrose's
    B. increase more than Primrose's
    C. decrease the same as Primrose's
    D. decrease more than Primrose's

19. Treasury stock was acquired for cash at a price in excess of its par value. The treasury   19.____
    stock was subsequently reissued for cash at a price in excess of its acquisition price.
    Assuming that the cost method of accounting for treasury stock transactions is used,
    what is the effect on retained earnings?

	Acquisition of treasury stock	Reissuance of treasury stock
A.	No effect	Decrease
B.	No effect	No effect
C.	Increase	Decrease
D.	Decrease	Increase

20. For a capital lease, the amount recorded initially by the lessee as a liability should   20.____

    A. exceed the present value at the beginning of the lease term of minimum lease pay-
        ments during the lease term
    B. exceed the total of the minimum lease payments during the lease term
    C. not exceed the fair value of the leased property at the inception of the lease
    D. equal the total of the minimum lease payments during the lease term

21. In a sale-leaseback transaction, the seller-lessee retains the right to substantially all of   21.____
    the remaining use of the equipment sold. The profit on the sale should be deferred and
    subsequently amortized by the lessee when the lease is classified as a (an)

	Capital lease	Operating lease
A.	No	Yes
B.	No	No
C.	Yes	No
D.	Yes	Yes

22. Legal fees incurred by a company in defending its patent rights should be capitalized   22.____
    when the outcome of the litigation is

	Successful	Unsuccessful
A.	Yes	Yes
B.	Yes	No
C.	No	No
D.	No	Yes

23. According to the FASB conceptual framework, comprehensive income includes which of the following?

23._____

	Gross margin	Operating income
A.	No	No
B.	No	Yes
C.	Yes	Yes
D.	Yes	No

24. A company using the group depreciation method for its delivery trucks retired one of its delivery trucks after the average service life of the group was reached. Cash proceeds were received from a salvage company. The net carrying amount of these group asset accounts would be decreased by the

24._____

   A. original cost of the truck
   B. original cost of the truck less the cash proceeds
   C. cash proceeds received
   D. cash proceeds received and original cost of the truck

25. A lessee incurred costs to construct walkways to improve leased property. The estimated useful life of the walkways is fifteen years. The remaining term of the nonrenewable lease is twenty years. The walkway costs should be

25._____

   A. capitalized as leasehold improvements and depreciated over twenty years
   B. capitalized as leasehold improvements and depreciated over fifteen years
   C. capitalized as leasehold improvements and expensed in the year in which the lease expires
   D. expensed as incurred

26. A depreciable asset has an estimated 15% salvage value. At the end of its estimated useful life, the accumulated depreciation would equal the original cost of the asset under which of the following depreciation methods?

26._____

	Productive output	Sum of the years' digits
A.	Yes	No
B.	No	No
C.	No	Yes
D.	Yes	Yes

27. A company is constructing an asset for its own use. Construction began in 2000. The asset is being financed entirely with a specific new borrowing. Construction expenditures were made in 2000 and 2001 at the end of each quarter. The total amount of interest cost capitalized in 2001 should be determined by applying the interest rate on the specific new borrowing to the

27._____

   A. total accumulated expenditures for the asset in 2000 and 2001
   B. average accumulated expenditures for the asset in 2000 and 2001
   C. average expenditures for the asset in 2001
   D. total expenditures for the asset in 2001

28. The original cost of an inventory item is above the replacement cost. The replacement cost is above the net realizable value. Under the lower of cost or market method, the inventory item should be reported at its

    A. original cost
    B. replacement cost
    C. net realizable value
    D. net realizable value less the normal profit margin

28._____

29. During periods of rising prices, when the FIFO inventory cost flow method is used, a perpetual inventory system would

    A. not be permitted
    B. result in a higher ending inventory than a periodic inventory system
    C. result in the same ending inventory as a periodic inventory system
    D. result in a lower ending inventory than a periodic inventory system

29._____

30. A company records inventory at the gross invoice price. Theoretically, how should the following affect the costs in inventory?

30._____

	Warehousing costs	Cash discounts available
A.	Increase	Decrease
B.	No effect	Decrease
C.	No effect	No effect
D.	Increase	No effect

KEY (CORRECT ANSWERS)

1.	C		16.	B
2.	A		17.	C
3.	D		18.	B
4.	B		19.	B
5.	A		20.	C
6.	A		21.	D
7.	B		22.	B
8.	C		23.	C
9.	B		24.	C
10.	D		25.	B
11.	A		26.	B
12.	A		27.	B
13.	D		28.	C
14.	B		29.	C
15.	D		30.	A

EXAMINATION SECTION
TEST 1

DIRECTIONS: Each question or incomplete statement is followed by several suggested answers or completions. Select the one that BEST answers the question or completes the statement. *PRINT THE LETTER OF THE CORRECT ANSWER IN THE SPACE AT THE RIGHT.*

1. When a supervisor in a large office introduces a change in the regular office procedure, it is USUAL to expect   1._____

   A. immediate acceptance by office staff, unless the change is unnecessary
   B. an immediate production increase, since new procedures are more stimulating than old ones
   C. a temporary production loss, even if the change is really an overall improvement
   D. resistance to the change only if it has been put into writing

2. A supervisor evaluates the performance of subordinates and then applies measures, where needed, which result in bringing performance up to desired standards. Which of the following functions of management might he BEST be described as performing?   2._____

   A. Organizing   B. Controlling   C. Directing   D. Planning

3. Assume that, as a supervisor, you have been assigned responsibility for a new and complex project which entails collection and analysis of data. You have prepared general written instructions which explain the project and procedures to be followed by several statisticians.
   Which of the procedures below would be MOST advisable for you, as the supervisor, to follow?   3._____

   A. Distribute the instructions to your subordinates to come to you with any important questions
   B. Distribute the instructions and advise subordinates to come to you with any important questions
   C. Meet with subordinates as a group and explain the project using the written instructions as a handout
   D. Delegate responsibility for further explanation of the project to an immediate qualified subordinate to free you for concentration on research design

4. Supervisors have an obligation to make careful and thorough appraisals and reports of probationary employees. Of the following, the MOST important justification for this statement is that the probationary period   4._____

   A. should be used for positive development of the employee's understanding of the organization
   B. is the most effective period for changing a new employee's knowledges, skills, and attitudes
   C. insures that the employee will meet work standard requirements on future assignments
   D. should be considered as the final step in the selection process

5. Many studies of management indicate that a principal reason for failure of supervisors lies in their ability to delegate duties effectively.
    Which one of the following practices by a supervisor would NOT be a block to successful delegation?

    A. Instructing the delegatee to follow a set procedure in carrying out the assignment
    B. Maintaining point by point control over the process delegated
    C. Transferring ultimate responsibility for the duties assigned to the delegatee
    D. Requiring the delegatee to keep the delegator informed of his progress

6. Crosswise communication occurs between personnel at lower or middle levels of different organizational units. It often speeds information and improves understanding, but has certain dangers.
    Of the following proposed policies, which would NOT be important as a safeguard in crosswise communication?

    A. Supervisors should agree as to how crosswise communication should occur.
    B. Crosswise relationships must exist only between employees of equal status.
    C. Subordinates must keep their superiors informed about their interdepartmental communications.
    D. Subordinates must refrain from making commitments beyond their authority.

7. *Systems* theory has given us certain principles which are as applicable to organizational and social activities as they are to those of science. With regard to the training of employees in an organization, which of the following is likely to be most consistent with the modern *systems* approach?
    Training can be effective ONLY when it is

    A. related to the individual abilities of the employees
    B. done on all levels of the organizational hierarchy
    C. evaluated on the basis of experimental and control groups
    D. provided on the job by the immediate supervisor

8. The management of a large agency, before making a decision as to whether or not to computerize its operations, should have a feasibility study made.
    Of the following, the one which is LEAST important to include in such a study is

    A. the current abilities of management and staff to use a computer
    B. projected workloads and changes in objectives of functional units in the agency
    C. the contributions expected of each organizational unit towards achievement of agency objectives
    D. the decision-making activity and informational needs of each management function

9. Managing information covers the creation, collection, processing, storage and transmission of information that appears in a variety of forms. A supervisor responsible for a statistical unit can be considered, in many respects, an information manager.
    Of the following, which would be considered the LEAST important aspect of the information manager's job?

    A. Establishing better information standards and formats
    B. Reducing the amount of unnecessary paper work performed
    C. Producing progressively greater numbers of informational reports
    D. Developing a greater appreciation for information among management members

5._____

6._____

7._____

8._____

9._____

10. Because of the need for improvement in information systems throughout industry and government, various techniques for improving these systems have been developed. Of these, *systems simulation* is a technique for improving systems which

    A. creates new ideas and concepts through the use of a computer
    B. deals with time controlling of interrelated systems which make up an overall project
    C. permits experimentation with various ideas to see what results might be obtained
    D. does not rely on assumptions which condition the value of the results

10.____

11. The one of the following which it is NOT advisable for a supervisor to do when dealing with individual employees is to

    A. recognize a person's outstanding service as well as his mistakes
    B. help an employee satisfy his need to excel
    C. encourage an efficient employee to seek better opportunities even if this action may cause the supervisor to lose a good worker
    D. take public notice of an employee's mistakes so that fewer errors will be made in the future

11.____

12. Suppose that you are in a department where you are given the responsibility for teaching seven new assistants a number of routine procedures that all assistants should know. Of the following, the BEST method for you to follow in teaching these procedures is to

    A. separate the slower learners from the faster learners and adapt your presentation to their level of ability
    B. instruct all the new employees in a group without attempting to assess differences in learning rates
    C. restrict your approach to giving them detailed written instructions in order to save time
    D. avoid giving the employees written instructions in order to force them to memorize job procedures quickly

12.____

13. Suppose that you are a supervisor to whom several assistants must hand in work for review. You notice that one of the assistants gets very upset whenever you discover an error in his work, although all the assistants make mistakes from time to time. Of the following, it would be BEST for you to

    A. arrange discreetly for the employee's work to be reviewed by another supervisor
    B. ignore his reaction since giving attention to such behavior increases its intensity
    C. suggest that the employee seek medical help since he has such great difficulty in accepting normal criticism
    D. try to build the employee's self-confidence by emphasizing those parts of his work that are done well

13.____

14. Suppose you are a supervisor responsible for supervising a number of assistants in an agency where each assistant receives a manual of policies and procedures when he first reports for work. You have been asked to teach your subordinates a new procedure which requires knowledge of several items of policy and procedure found in the manual. The one of the following techniques which it would be BEST for you to employ is to

    A. give verbal instructions which include a review of the appropriate standard procedures as well as an explanation of new tasks
    B. give individual instruction restricted to the new procedure to each assistant as the need arises
    C. provide written instructions for new procedural elements and refer employees to their manuals for explanation of standard procedures
    D. ask employees to review appropriate sections of their manual and then explain those aspects of the new procedure which the manual did not cover

14.____

15. Suppose that you are a supervisor in charge of a unit in which changes in work procedures are about to be instituted. The one of the following which you, as the supervisor, should anticipate as being MOST likely to occur during the changeover is

    A. a temporary rise in production because of interest in the new procedures
    B. uniform acceptance of these procedures on the part of your staff
    C. varying interpretations of the new procedures by your staff
    D. general agreement among staff members that the new procedures are advantageous

15.____

16. Suppose that a supervisor and one of the assistants under his supervision are known to be friends who play golf together on weekends.
The maintenance of such a friendship on the part of the supervisor is GENERALLY

    A. *acceptable* as long as this assistant continues to perform his duties satisfactorily
    B. *unacceptable* since the supervisor will find it difficult to treat the assistant as a subordinate
    C. *acceptable* if the supervisor does not favor this assistant above other employees
    D. *unacceptable* because the other assistants will resent the friendship regardless of the supervisor's behavior on the job

16.____

17. Suppose that you are a supervisor assigned to review the financial records of an agency which has recently undergone a major reorganization.
Which of the following would it be best for you to do FIRST?

    A. Interview the individual in charge of agency financial operations to determine whether the organizational changes affect the system of financial review
    B. Discuss the nature of the reorganization with your own supervisor to anticipate and plan a new financial review procedure.
    C. Carry out the financial review as usual, and adjust your methods to any problems arising from the reorganization.
    D. Request a written report from the agency head explaining the nature of the reorganization and recommending changes in the system of financial review.

17.____

18. Suppose that a newly assigned supervisor finds that he must delegate some of his duties to subordinates in order to get the work done.
Which one of the following would NOT be a block to his delegating these duties effectively?

    A. Inability to give proper directions as to what he wants done
    B. Reluctance to take calculated risks
    C. Lack of trust in his subordinates
    D. Retaining ultimate responsibility for the delegated work

18.____

19. A supervisor sometimes performs the staff function of preparing and circulating reports among bureau chiefs. Which of the following is LEAST important as an objective in designing and writing such reports?

    A. Providing relevant information on past, present, and future actions
    B. Modifying his language in order to insure goodwill among the bureau chiefs
    C. Helping the readers of the report to make appropriate decisions
    D. Summarizing important information to help readers see trends or outstanding points.

19.____

20. Suppose you are a supervisor assigned to prepare a report to be read by all bureau chiefs in your agency.
The MOST important reason for avoiding highly technical accounting terminology in writing this report is to

    A. ensure the accuracy and relevancy of the text .
    B. insure winning the readers' cooperation
    C. make the report more interesting to the readers
    D. make it easier for the readers to understand

20.____

21. Which of the following conditions is MOST likely to cause low morale in an office?

    A. Different standards of performance for individuals in the same title
    B. A requirement that employees perform at full capacity
    C. Standards of performance that vary with titles of employees
    D. Careful attention to the image of the division or department

21.____

22. A wise supervisor or representative of management realizes that, in the relationship between supervisor and subordinates, all power is not on the side of management, and that subordinates do sometimes react to restrictive authority in such a manner as to seriously retard management's objectives. A wise supervisor does not stimulate such reactions.
In the subordinate's attempt to retaliate against an unusually authoritative management style, which of the following actions would generally be LEAST successful for the subordinate? He

    A. joins with other employees in organizations to deal with management
    B. obviously delays in carrying out instructions which are given in an arrogant or incisive manner
    C. performs assignments exactly as instructed even when he recognizes errors in instructions
    D. holds back the flow of feedback information to superiors

22.____

23. Which of the following is the MOST likely and costly effect of vague and indefinite instruc-   23.____
tions given to subordinates by a supervisor?

 A. Misunderstanding and ineffective work on the part of the subordinates
 B. A necessity for the supervisor to report identical instructions with each assignment
 C. A failure of the supervisor to adequately keep the attention of subordinates
 D. Inability of subordinates to assist each other in the absence of the supervisor

24. At the professional level, there is a kind of informal authority which exercises itself even   24.____
though no delegation of authority has taken place from higher management. It occurs
within the context of knowledge required and professional competence in a special area.
An example of the kind of authority described in this statement is MOST clearly exem-
plified in the situation where a senior supervisor influences associates and subordinates by virtue of the

 A. salary level fixed for his particular set of duties
 B. amount of college training he possesses
 C. technical position he has gained and holds on the work team
 D. initiative and judgment he has demonstrated to his supervisor

25. An assistant under your supervision attempts to conceal the fact that he has made an   25.____
error.
Under this circumstance, it would be BEST for you, as the supervisor, to proceed on
the assumption that

 A. this evasion indicates something wrong in the fundamental relationship between
    you and the assistant
 B. this evasion is not deliberate, if the error is subsequently corrected by the assistant
 C. this evasion should be overlooked if the error is not significant
 D. detection and correction of errors will come about as an automatic consequence of
    internal control procedures

KEY (CORRECT ANSWERS)

1.	C		11.	D
2.	B		12.	B
3.	C		13.	D
4.	D		14.	A
5.	D		15.	C
6.	B		16.	C
7.	B		17.	A
8.	A		18.	D
9.	C		19.	B
10.	C		20.	D

21.	A
22.	B
23.	A
24.	C
25.	A

TEST 2

DIRECTIONS: Each question or incomplete statement is followed by several suggested answers or completions. Select the one that BEST answers the question or completes the statement. *PRINT THE LETTER OF THE CORRECT ANSWER IN THE SPACE AT THE RIGHT.*

1. The unit which you supervise has a number of attorneys, accountants, examiners, statis- 1.____
ticians, and clerks who prepare some of the routine papers required to be filed.
In order to be certain that nothing goes out of your office that is improper, you have
instituted a system that requires that you review and initial all moving papers, memoranda of law and briefs that are prepared. As a result, you put in a great deal of overtime and even must take work home with you frequently.
A situation such as this is

   A. inevitable if you are to keep proper controls over the quality of the office work product
   B. indicative of the fact that the agency must provide an additional position within your
office for an assistant supervisor who would do all the reviewing, leaving you free
for other pressing administrative work and to handle the most difficult work in your
unit
   C. the logical result of an ever-increasing case load
   D. symptomatic of poor supervision and management

2. Your unit has been assigned a new employee who has never worked for the city. 2.____
To orient him to his job in your unit, of the following, the BEST procedure is first to

   A. assign him to another employee to whatever work that employee gives him so that
he can become familiar with your work and at the same time be productive
   B. give him copies of the charter and code provisions affecting your operations plus
any in-office memoranda or instructions that are available and have him read them
   C. assign him to work on a relatively simple problem and then, after he has finished it,
tell him politely what he did wrong
   D. explain to him the duties of his position and the functions of the office

3. A bureau chief who supervises other supervisors makes it a practice to assign them 3.____
more cases than they can possibly handle.
This approach is

   A. *right,* because it results in getting more work done than would otherwise be the
case
   B. *right,* because it relieves the bureau chief making the assignments of the responsibility of getting the work done
   C. *wrong,* because it builds resistance on the part of those called upon to handle the
case load
   D. *wrong,* because superiors lose track of cases

4. Assume you are a supervisor and are expected to exercise *authority* over subordinates. 4.____
Which of the following BEST defines *authority?* The

   A. ability to control the nature of the contribution a subordinate is desirous of making
   B. innate inability to get others to do for you what you want to get done irrespective of
their own wishes
   C. legal right conferred by the agency to control the actions of others
   D. power to determine a subordinate's attitude toward his agency and his superiors

5. Paternalistic leadership stresses a paternal or fatherly influence in the relationships   5.____
   between the leader and the group and is manifest in a watchful care for the comfort and
   welfare of the followers.
   Which one of the following statements regarding paternalistic leadership is MOST
   accurate?

   A. Employees who work well under paternalistic leadership come to expect such lead-
      ership even when the paternal leader has left the organization.
   B. Most disputes arising out of supervisor-subordinate relationships develop because
      group leaders do not understand the principles of paternalistic leadership.
   C. Paternalistic leadership frequently destroys office relationships because most
      employees are turned into non-thinking dependent robots.
   D. Paternalistic leadership is rarely, if ever, successful because employees resent
      paternalistic leadership which they equate with weakness.

6. Employees who have extensive dealings with members of the public should have, as   6.____
   much as possible, *real acceptance* of all people and a willingness to serve everyone
   impartially and objectively.
   Assuming that this statement is correct, the one of the following which would be the
   BEST demonstration of *real acceptance* is

   A. condoning antisocial behavior
   B. giving the appearance of agreeing with everyone encountered
   C. refusing to give opinions on anyone's behavior
   D. understanding the feelings expressed through a person's behavior

7. Assume that the agency chief has requested you to help plan a public relations program   7.____
   because of recent complaints from citizens about the unbecoming conduct and language
   of various groups of city employees who have dealings with the public.
   In carrying out this assignment, the one of the following steps which should be under-
   taken FIRST is to

   A. study the characteristics of the public clientele dealt with by employees in your
      agency
   B. arrange to have employees attend several seminars on human relations
   C. develop several procedures for dealing with the public and allow the staff to choose
      the one which is best
   D. find out whether the employees in your agency may oppose any plan proposed by
      you

8. The one of the following statements which BEST expresses the relationship between the   8.____
   morale of government employees and the public relations aspects of their work is:

   A. There is little relationship between employee morale and public relations, chiefly
      because public opinion is shaped primarily by response to departmental policy for-
      mulation.
   B. Employee morale is closely related to public relations, chiefly because the
      employee's morale will largely determine the manner in which he deals with the
      public.
   C. There is little relationship between employee morale and public relations, chiefly
      because public relations is primarily a function of the agency's public relations
      department.
   D. Employee morale is closely related to public relations, chiefly because employee
      morale indicates the attitude of the agency's top officials toward the public.

9. As a supervisor, you are required to deal extensively with the public. The agency chief has indicated that he is considering holding a special in-service training course for employees in communications skills.
Holding this training course would be

   A. *advisable,* chiefly because government employees should receive formal training in public relations skills
   B. *inadvisable,* chiefly because the public regards such training as a *waste of the tax-payers' money*
   C. *advisable,* chiefly because such training will enable the employee to aid in drafting departmental press releases
   D. *inadvisable,* chiefly because of the great difficulty involved in developing such skills through formal instruction

9.____

10. Assume that you have extensive contact with the public. In dealing with the public, sensitivity to an individual's attitudes is important because these attitudes can be used to predict behavior.
However, the MAIN reason that attitudes CANNOT successfully predict all behavior is that

   A. attitudes are highly resistant to change
   B. an individual acquires attitudes as a function of growing up in a particular cultural environment
   C. attitudes are only one of many factors which determine a person's behavior
   D. an individual's behavior is not always observable

10.____

11. Rotation of employees from assignment to assignment is sometimes advocated by management experts.
Of the following, the MOST probable advantage to the organization of this practice is that it leads to

   A. higher specialization of duties so that excessive identification with the overall organization is reduced
   B. increased loyalty of employees to their immediate supervisors
   C. greater training and development of employees
   D. intensified desire of employees to obtain additional, outside formal education

11.____

12. Usually, a supervisor should attempt to standardize the work for which he is responsible.
The one of the following which is a BASIC reason for doing this is to

   A. eliminate the need to establish priorities
   B. permit the granting of exceptions to rules and special circumstances
   C. facilitate the taking of action based on applicable standards
   D. learn the identity of outstanding employees

12.____

13. The differences between line and staff authority are often quite ambiguous.
Of the following, the ESSENTIAL difference is that

   A. *line authority* is exercised by first-level supervisors; staff authority is exercised by higher-level supervisors and managerial staff
   B. *staff authority* is the right to issue directives; line authority is entirely consultative
   C. *line authority* is the power to make decisions regarding intra-agency matters; staff authority involves decisions regarding inter-agency matters
   D. *staff authority* is largely advisory; line authority is the right to command

13.____

14. Modern management theory stresses work-centered motivation as one way of increasing the productivity of employees.
    The one of the following which is PARTICULARLY characteristic of such motivation is that it

    A. emphasizes the crucial role of routinization of procedures
    B. stresses the satisfaction to be found in performing work
    C. features the value of wages and fringe benefits
    D. uses a firm but fair method of discipline

14.____

15. The agency's informal communications network is called the *grapevine*.
    If employees are learning about important organizational developments primarily through the grapevine, this is MOST likely an indication that

    A. official channels of communication are not functioning so efficiently as they should
    B. supervisory personnel are making effective use of the grapevine to communicate with subordinates
    C. employees already have a clear understanding of the agency's policies and procedures
    D. upward formal channels of communication within the agency are informing management of employee grievances

15.____

16. Of the following, a flow chart is BEST described as a chart which shows

    A. the places through which work moves in the course of the job process
    B. which employees perform specific functions leading to the completion of a job
    C. the schedules for production and how they eliminate waiting time between jobs
    D. how work units are affected by the actions of related work units

16.____

17. Evaluation of the results of training is necessary in order to assess its value.
    Of the following, the BEST technique for the supervisor to use in determining whether the training under consideration actually resulted in the desired modification of the behavior of the employee concerned is through

    A. inference   B. job analysis
    C. observation   D. simulation

17.____

18. The usual distinction between line and staff authority is that staff authority is mainly advisory, whereas line authority is the right to command. However, a third category has been suggested–prescriptive–to distinguish those personnel whose functions may be formally defined as staff but in practice exercise considerable authority regarding decisions relating to their specialties.
    The one of the following which indicates the MAJOR purpose of creating this third category is to

    A. develop the ability of each employee to perform a greater number of tasks
    B. reduce line-staff conflict
    C. prevent over-specialization of functions
    D. encourage decision-making by line personnel

18.____

19. It is sometimes considered desirable to train employees to a standard of proficiency higher than that deemed necessary for actual job performance.
The MOST likely reason for such overtraining would be to

    A. eliminate the need for standards
    B. increase the value of refresher training
    C. compensate for previous lack of training
    D. reduce forgetting or loss of skill

19._____

20. Assume that you have been directed to immediately institute various new procedures in the handling of records.
Of the following, the BEST method for you to use to insure that your subordinates know exactly what to do is to

    A. circulate a memorandum explaining the new procedures and have your subordinates initial it
    B. explain the new procedures to one or two subordinates and ask them to tell the others
    C. have a meeting with your subordinates to give them copies of the procedures and discuss it with them
    D. post the new procedures where they can be referred to by all those concerned

20._____

21. A supervisor decided to hold a problem-solving conference with his entire staff and distributed an announcement and agenda one week before the meeting.
Of the following, the BEST reason for providing each participant with an agenda is that

    A. participants will feel that something will be accomplished
    B. participants may prepare for the conference
    C. controversy will be reduced
    D. the top man should state the expected conclusions

21._____

22. In attempting to motivate employees, rewards are considered preferable to punishment PRIMARILY because

    A. punishment seldom has any effect on human behavior
    B. punishment usually results in decreased production
    C. supervisors find it difficult to punish
    D. rewards are more likely to result in willing cooperation

22._____

23. In an attempt to combat the low morale in his organization, a high-level supervisor publicized an *open-door* policy to allow employees who wished to do so to come to him with their complaints.
Which of the following is LEAST likely to account for the fact that no employee came in with a complaint?

    A. Employees are generally reluctant to go over the heads of their immediate supervisors.
    B. The employees did not feel that management would help them.
    C. The low morale was not due to complaints associated with the job.
    D. The employees felt that, they had more to lose than to gain.

23._____

24. It is MOST desirable to use written instructions rather than oral instructions for a particu-   24.____
    lar job when

    A. a mistake on the job will not be serious
    B. the job can be completed in a short time
    C. there is no need to explain the job minutely
    D. the job involves many details

25. You have been asked to prepare for public distribution a statement dealing with a contro-   25.____
    versial matter.
    Of the following approaches, the one which would usually be MOST effective is to
    present your department's point of view

    A. as tersely as possible with no reference to any other matters
    B. developed from ideas and facts well known to most readers
    C. and show all the statistical data and techniques which were used in arriving at it
    D. in such a way that the controversial parts are omitted

_____

KEY (CORRECT ANSWERS)

1.	D		11.	C
2.	D		12.	C
3.	C		13.	D
4.	C		14.	B
5.	A		15.	A
6.	D		16.	A
7.	A		17.	C
8.	B		18.	B
9.	A		19.	D
10.	C		20.	C

21.	B
22.	D
23.	C
24.	D
25.	B

_____

TEST 3

DIRECTIONS: Each question or incomplete statement is followed by several suggested answers or completions. Select the one that BEST answers the question or completes the statement. *PRINT THE LETTER OF THE CORRECT ANSWER IN THE SPACE AT THE RIGHT.*

1. An administrator who supervises other supervisors makes it a practice to set deadline dates for completion of assignments.
   A NATURAL consequence of setting deadline dates is that

   A. supervisors will usually wait until the deadline date before they give projects their wholehearted attention
   B. projects are completed sooner than if no deadline dates are set
   C. such dates are ignored even though they are conspicuously posted
   D. the frequency of errors sharply increases resulting in an inability to meet deadlines

   1.____

2. Assume that you are chairing a meeting of the members of your staff. You throw out a question to the group. No one answers your question immediately, so that you find yourself faced with silence.
   In the circumstances, it would probably be BEST for you to

   A. ask the member of the group who appears to be least attentive to repeat the question
   B. change the topic quickly
   C. repeat the question carefully, pronouncing each word, and if there is still no response, repeat the question an additional time
   D. wait for an answer since someone will usually say something to break the tension

   2.____

3. Assume that you are holding a meeting with the members of your staff. John, a member of the unit, keeps sidetracking the subject of the discussion by bringing up extraneous matters. You deal with the situation by saying to him after he has raised an immaterial point, *"That's an interesting point John, but can you show me how it ties in with what we're talking about?"*
   Your approach in this situation would GENERALLY be considered

   A. *bad;* you have prevented the group from discussing not only extraneous matters but pertinent material as well
   B. *bad;* you have seriously humiliated John in front of the entire group
   C. *good;* you have pointed out how the discussion is straying from the main topic
   D. *good;* you have prevented John from presenting extraneous matters at future meetings

   3.____

4. Assume that a senior supervisor is asked to supervise a group of staff personnel. The work of one of these staff men meets minimum standards of acceptability. However, this staff man constantly looks for something at which to take offense. In any conversation with either a fellow staff man or with a superior, he views the slightest criticism as a grave insult.
   In this case, the senior supervisor should

   A. advise the staff man that the next time he refuses to accept criticism, he will be severely reprimanded
   B. ask members of the group for advice on how to deal with this staff man
   C. make it a practice to speak calmly, slowly, and deliberately to this staff man and question him frequently to make sure that there is no breakdown in communications
   D. recognize that professional help may be required and that this problem may not be conducive to a solution by a supervisor

   4.____

5. Assume that you discover that one of the staff in preparing certain papers has made a serious mistake which has become obvious.
   In dealing with this situation, it would be BEST for you to begin by

   A. asking the employee how the mistake happened
   B. asking the employee to read through the papers to see whether he can correct the mistake
   C. pointing out to the employee that, while an occasional error is permissible, frequent errors can prove a source of embarrassment to all concerned
   D. pointing to the mistake and asking the employee whether he realizes the consequences of the mistake

5.____

6. You desire to develop teamwork among the members of your staff. You are assigned a case which will require that two of the staff work together if the papers are to be prepared in time. You decided to assign two employees, whom you know to be close friends, to work on these papers. Your action in this regard would GENERALLY be considered

   A. *bad;* friends working together tend to do as little as they can get away with
   B. *bad;* people who are friends socially often find that the bonds of friendship disintegrate in work situations
   C. *good;* friends who are permitted to work together show their appreciation by utilizing every opportunity to reinforce the group leader's position of authority
   D. *good;* the evidence suggests that more work can be done in this way

6.____

7. You notice that all of the employees, without exception, take lunch hours which in your view are excessively long. You call each of them to your desk and point out that unless this practice is brought to a stop, appropriate action will be taken.
   The way in which you handled this problem would GENERALLY be considered

   A. *proper,* primarily because a civil servant, no matter what his professional status, owes the public a full day's work for a full day's pay
   B. *proper,* primarily because employees need to have a clear picture of the rewards and penalties that go with public employment
   C. *improper,* primarily because group problems require group discussion which need not be formal in character
   D. *improper,* primarily because professional personnel resent having such matters as lunch hours brought to their attention.

7.____

8. In communicating with superiors or subordinates, it is well to bear in mind a phenomenon known as the *halo effect.* An example of this *halo effect* occurs when we

   A. employ informal language in a formal setting as a means of attracting attention
   B. ignore the advice of someone we distrust without evaluating the advice
   C. ask people to speak up who have a tendency to speak softly or occasionally indistinctly
   D. react to a piece of good work by inquiring into the motivations of those who did the work

8.____

9. Which of the following dangers is MOST likely to arise when a work group becomes too tightly knit? The

    A. group may appoint an informal leader who gradually sets policies and standards for the group to the detriment of the agency
    B. group may be reluctant to accept new employees as members
    C. quantity and quality of work produced may tend to diminish sharply despite the group's best efforts
    D. group may focus too strongly on employee benefits at inappropriate times

9.____

10. The overall managerial problem has become more complex because each group of management specialists will tend to view the interests of the enterprise in terms which are compatible with the survival or the increase of its special function. That is, each group will have a trained capacity for its own function and a *trained incapacity* to see its relation to the whole.
The *trained incapacity* to which the foregoing passage refers PROBABLY results from

    A. an imbalance in the number of specialists as compared with the number of generalists
    B. development by each specialized group of a certain dominant value or goal that shapes its entire way of doing things
    C. low morale accompanied by lackadaisical behavior by large segments of the managerial staff
    D. supervisory failure to inculcate pride in workmanship

10.____

11. Of the following, the MOST important responsibility of a supervisor in charge of a section is to

    A. establish close personal relationships with each of his subordinates in the section
    B. insure that each subordinate in the section knows the full range of his duties and responsibilities
    C. maintain friendly relations with his immediate supervisor
    D. protect his subordinates from criticism from any source

11.____

12. The BEST way to get a good work output from employees is to

    A. hold over them the threat of disciplinary action or removal
    B. maintain a steady, unrelenting pressure on them
    C. show them that you can do anything they can do faster and better
    D. win their respect and liking so they want to work for you

12.____

13. Supervisors should GENERALLY

    A. lean more toward management than toward their subordinates
    B. lean neither toward subordinates nor management
    C. lean more toward their subordinates than toward their management
    D. maintain a proper balance between management and subordinates

13.____

14. For a supervisor in charge of a section to ask occasionally the opinion of a subordinate concerning a problem is

    A. *desirable;* but it would be even better if the subordinate were consulted routinely on every problem
    B. *desirable;* subordinates may make good suggestions and will be pleased by being consulted
    C. *undesirable;* subordinats may be resentful if their advice is not followed
    D. *undesirable;* the supervisor should not attempt to shift his responsibilities to subordinates

14.____

15. The PRIMARY responsibility of a supervisor is to

    A. gain the confidence and make friends of all his subordinates
    B. get the work done properly
    C. satisfy his superior and gain his respect
    D. train the men in new methods for doing the work

15.____

16. In starting a work simplification study, the one of the following steps that should be taken FIRST is to

    A. break the work down into its elements
    B. draw up a chart of operations
    C. enlist the interest and cooperation of the personnel
    D. suggest alternative procedures

16.____

17. Of the following, the MOST important value of a manual of procedures is that it usually

    A. eliminates the need for on-the-job training
    B. decreases the span of control which can be exercised by individual supervisory personnel
    C. outlines methods of operation for ready reference
    D. provides concrete examples of work previously performed by employees

17.____

18. Reprimanding a subordinate when he has done something wrong should be done PRIMARILY in order to

    A. deter others from similar acts
    B. improve the subordinate in future performance
    C. maintain discipline
    D. uphold departmental rules

18.____

19. Most of the training of new employees in a public agency is USUALLY accomplished by

    A. formal classes
    B. general orientation
    C. internship
    D. on-the-job activities

19.____

20. You find that delivery of a certain item cannot possibly be made to a using agency by the date the using agency requested.
Of the following, the MOST advisable course of action for you to take FIRST is to

    A. cancel the order and inform the using agency
    B. discuss the problem with the using agency
    C. notify the using agency to obtain the item through direct purchase
    D. schedule the delivery for the earliest possible date

20.____

21. Assume that one of your subordinates has gotten into the habit of regularly and routinely referring every small problem which arises in his work to you.
In order to help him overcome this habit, it is generally MOST advisable for you to

    A. advise him that you do not have time to discuss each problem with him and that he should do whatever he wants
    B. ask your subordinate for his solution and approve any satisfactory approach that he suggests
    C. refuse to discuss such routine problems with him
    D. tell him that he should consider looking for another position if he does not feel competent to solve such routine problems

21.____

22. The BEST of the following reasons for developing understudies to supervisory staff is that this practice

    A. assures that capable staff will not leave their jobs since they are certain to be promoted
    B. helps to assure continued efficiency when persons in important positions leave their jobs
    C. improves morale by demonstrating to employees the opportunities for advancement
    D. provides an opportunity for giving on-the-job training

22.____

23. When a supervisor delegates some of his work to a subordinate, the

    A. supervisor retains final responsibility for the work
    B. supervisor should not check on the work until it has been completed
    C. subordinate assumes full responsibility for the successful completion of the work
    D. subordinate is likely to lose interest and get less satisfaction from the work

23.____

24. Sometimes it is necessary to give out written orders or to post written or typed information on a bulletin board rather than to merely give spoken orders. The supervisor must decide how he will do it.
In which of the following situations would it be BETTER for him to give written rather than spoken orders?

    A. He is going to reassign a man from one unit to another under his supervision.
    B. His staff must be informed of a permanent change in a complicated operating procedure.
    C. A man must be transferred from a clerical unit to an operating unit.
    D. He must order a group of staff men to do a difficult and tedious inventory job to which most of them are likely to object.

24.____

25. Of the following symbolic patterns, which one is NOT representative of a normal direction   25.____
    in which formal organizational communications flow.

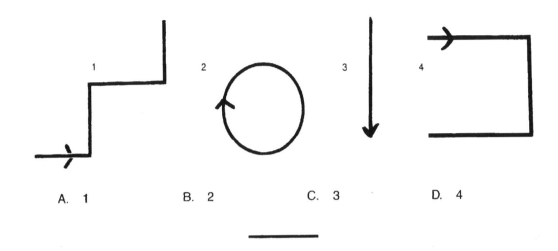

A. 1   B. 2   C. 3   D. 4

KEY (CORRECT ANSWERS)

1.	B		11.	B
2.	D		12.	D
3.	C		13.	D
4.	D		14.	B
5.	A		15.	B
6.	D		16.	C
7.	C		17.	C
8.	B		18.	B
9.	B		19.	D
10.	B		20.	B

21.	B
22.	B
23.	A
24.	B
25.	B

EXAMINATION SECTION
TEST 1

DIRECTIONS: Each question or incomplete statement is followed by several suggested answers or completions. Select the one that BEST answers the question or completes the statement. *PRINT THE LETTER OF THE CORRECT ANSWER IN THE SPACE AT THE RIGHT.*

1. *Which one* of the following generalizations is *most likely* to be INACCURATE and lead to judgmental errors in communication?

    A. A supervisor must be able to read with understanding
    B. Misunderstanding may lead to dislike
    C. Anyone can listen to another person and understand what he means
    D. It is usually desirable to let a speaker talk until he is finished

1.____

2. Assume that, as a supervisor, you have been directed to inform your subordinates about the implementation of a new procedure which will affect their work. While communicating this information, you should do all of the following EXCEPT

    A. obtain the approval of your subordinates regarding the new procedure
    B. explain the reason for implementing the new procedure
    C. hold a staff meeting at a time convenient to most of your subordinates
    D. encourage a productive discussion of the new procedure

2.____

3. Assume that you are in charge of a section that handles requests for information on matters received from the public. One day, you observe that a clerk under your supervision is using a method to log-in requests for information that is different from the one specified by you in the past. Upon questioning the clerk, you discover that instructions changing the old procedure were delivered orally by your supervisor on a day on which you were absent from the office.
Of the following, the *most appropriate* action for you to take is to

    A. tell the clerk to revert to the old procedure at once
    B. ask your supervisor for information about the change
    C. call your staff together and tell them that no existing procedure is to be changed unless you direct that it be done
    D. write a memo to your supervisor suggesting that all future changes in procedure are to be in writing and that they be directed to you

3.____

4. At the first meeting with your staff after appointment as a supervisor, you find considerable indifference and some hostility among the participants.
Of the following, the *most appropriate* way to handle this situation is to

    A. disregard the attitudes displayed and continue to make your presentation until you have completed it
    B. discontinue your presentation but continue the meeting and attempt to find out the reasons for their attitudes
    C. warm up your audience with some good natured statements and anecdotes and then proceed with your presentation
    D. discontinue the meeting and set up personal interviews with the staff members to try to find out the reason for their attitude

4.____

5. In order to start the training of a new employee, it has been a standard practice to have him read a manual of instructions or procedures.
This method is currently being replaced by the _____ method.

    A. audio-visual   B. conference
    C. lecture   D. programmed instruction

5._____

6. Of the following subjects, the *one* that can usually be *successfully* taught by a first-line supervisor who is training his subordinates is:

    A. Theory and philosophy of manage-   B. Human relations
        ment
    C. Responsibilities of a supervisor   D. Job skills

6._____

7. Assume that as a supervisor you are training a clerk who is experiencing difficulty learning a new task.
Which one of the following would be the LEAST effective approach to take when trying to solve this problem? To

    A. ask questions which will reveal the clerk's understanding of the task
    B. take a different approach in explaining the task
    C. give the clerk an opportunity to ask questions about the task
    D. make sure the clerk knows you are watching his work closely

7._____

8. One school of management and supervision involves participation by employees in the setting of group goals and in the sharing of responsibility for the operation of the unit.
If this philosophy were applied to a unit consisting of professional and clerical personnel, one should expect

    A. the professional and clerical personnel to participate with equal effectiveness in operating areas and policy areas
    B. the professional personnel to participate with greater effectiveness than the clerical personnel in policy areas
    C. the clerical personnel to participate with greater effectiveness than the professional personnel in operating areas
    D. greater participation by clerical personnel but with less responsibility for their actions

8._____

9. With regard to productivity, high morale among employees *generally* indicates a

    A. history of high productivity
    B. nearly absolute positive correlation with high productivity
    C. predisposition to be productive under facilitating leadership and circumstances
    D. complacency which has little effect on productivity

9._____

10. Assume that you are going to organize the professionals and clerks under your supervision into work groups or teams of two or three employees.
Of the following, the step which is LEAST likely to foster the successful development of each group is to

    A. allow friends to work together in the group
    B. provide special help and attention to employees with no friends in their group
    C. frequently switch employees from group to group
    D. rotate jobs within the group in order to strengthen group identification

10._____

11. Following are four statements which might be made by an employee to his supervisor during a performance evaluation interview.
    Which of the statements BEST provides a basis for developing a plan to improve the employee's performance?

    11._____

    A. *I understand that you are dissatisfied with my work and I will try harder in the future.*
    B. *I feel that I've been making too many careless clerical errors recently.*
    C. *I am aware that I will be subject to disciplinary action if my work does not improve within one month.*
    D. *I understand that this interview is simply a requirement of your job, and not a personal attack on me.*

12. Three months ago, Mr. Smith and his supervisor, Mrs. Jones, developed a plan which was intended to correct Mr. Smith's inadequate job performance. Now, during a follow-up interview, Mr. Smith, who thought his performance had satisfactorily improved, has been informed that Mrs. Jones is still dissatisfied with his work.
    Of the following, it is *most likely* that the disagreement occurred because, when formulating the plan, they did NOT

    12._____

    A. set realistic goals for Mr. Smith Is performance
    B. set a reasonable time limit for Mr. Smith to effect his improvement in performance
    C. provide for adequate training to improve Mr. Smith's skills
    D. establish performance standards for measuring Mr. Smith's progress

13. When a supervisor delegates authority to subordinates, there are usually many problems to overcome, such as inadequately trained subordinates and poor planning.
    All of the following are means of increasing the effectiveness of delegation EXCEPT:

    13._____

    A. Defining assignments in the light of results expected
    B. Maintaining open lines of communication
    C. Establishing tight controls so that subordinates will stay within the bounds of the area of delegation
    D. Providing rewards for successful assumption of authority by a subordinate

14. Assume that one of your subordinates has arrived late for work several times during the current month. The last time he was late you had warned him that another unexcused lateness would result in formal disciplinary action.
    If the employee arrives late for work again during this month, the FIRST action you should take is to

    14._____

    A. give the employee a chance to explain this lateness
    B. give the employee a written copy of your warning
    C. tell the employee that you are recommending formal disciplinary action
    D. tell the employee that you will give him only one more chance before recommending formal disciplinary action

15. In trying to decide how many subordinates a manager can control directly, one of the determinants is how much the manager can reduce the frequency and time consumed in contacts with his subordinates.
Of the following, the factor which LEAST influences the number and direction of these contacts is:

    A. How well the manager delegates authority
    B. The rate at which the organization is changing
    C. The control techniques used by the manager
    D. Whether the activity is line or staff

15._____

16. Systematic rotation of employees through lateral transfer within a government organization to provide for managerial development is

    A. *good,* because systematic rotation develops specialists who learn to do many jobs well
    B. *bad,* because the outsider upsets the status quo of the existing organization
    C. *good,* because rotation provides challenge and organizational flexibility
    D. *bad,* because it is upsetting to employees to be transferred within a service

16._____

17. Assume that you are required to provide an evaluation of the performance of your subordinates.
Of the following factors, it is MOST important that the performance evaluation include a rating of each employees

    A. initiative   B. productivity   C. intelligence   D. personality

17._____

18. When preparing performance evaluations of your subordinates, *one* way to help assure that you are rating each employee fairly is to

    A. prepare a list of all employees and all the rating factors and rate all employees on one rating factor before going on to the next factor
    B. prepare a list of all your employees and all the rating factors and rate each employee on all factors before going on to the next employee
    C. discuss all the ratings you anticipate giving with another supervisor in order to obtain an unbiased opinion
    D. discuss each employee with his co-workers in order to obtain peer judgment of worth before doing any rating

18._____

19. A managerial plan which would include the GREATEST control is a plan which is

    A. spontaneous and geared to each new job that is received
    B. detailed and covering an extended time period
    C. long-range and generalized, allowing for various interpretations
    D. specific and prepared daily

19._____

20. Assume that you are preparing a report which includes statistical data covering   20.____
    increases in budget allocations of four agencies for the past ten years.
    For you to represent the statistical data pictorially or graphically within the report is a

   A. *poor idea,* because you should be able to make statistical data understandable
      through the use of words
   B. *good idea,* because it is easier for the reader to understand pictorial representation
      rather than quantities of words conveying statistical data
   C. *poor idea,* because using pictorial representation in a report may make the report
      too expensive to print
   D. *good idea,* because a pictorial representation makes the report appear more
      attractive than the use of many words to convey the statistical data

   ――――――

KEY (CORRECT ANSWERS)

1.	C	11.	A
2.	A	12.	B
3.	B	13.	C
4.	D	14.	A
5.	D	15.	D
6.	D	16.	C
7.	D	17.	B
8.	B	18.	A
9.	C	19.	B
10.	C	20.	B

   ――――――

TEST 2

DIRECTIONS: Each question or incomplete statement is followed by several suggested answers or completions. Select the one that BEST answers the question or completes the statement. *PRINT THE LETTER OF THE CORRECT ANSWER IN THE SPACE AT THE RIGHT.*

1. Research studies have shown that supervisors of groups with high production records USUALLY   1.____

    A. give detailed instructions, constantly check on progress, and insist on approval of all decisions before implementation
    B. do considerable paperwork and other work similar to that performed by subordinates
    C. think of themselves as team members on the same level as others in the work group
    D. perform tasks traditionally associated with managerial functions

2. Mr. Smith, a bureau chief, is summoned by his agency's head in a conference to discuss Mr. Jones, an accountant who works in one of the divisions of his bureau. Mr. Jones has committed an error of such magnitude as to arouse the agency head's concern.
After agreeing with the other conferees that a severe reprimand would be the appropriate punishment, Mr. Smith should   2.____

    A. arrange for Mr. Jones to explain the reasons for his error to the agency head
    B. send a memorandum to Mr. Jones, being careful that the language emphasizes the nature of the error rather than Mr. Jones' personal faults
    C. inform Mr. Jones' immediate supervisor of the conclusion reached at the conference, and let the supervisor take the necessary action
    D. suggest to the agency head that no additional action be taken against Mr. Jones because no further damage will be caused by the error

3. Assume that Ms. Thomson, a unit chief, has determined that the findings of an internal audit have been seriously distorted as a result of careless errors. The audit had been performed by a group of auditors in her unit and the errors were overlooked by the associate accountant in charge of the audit. Ms. Thomson has decided to delay discussing the matter with the associate accountant and the staff who performed the audit until she verifies certain details, which may require prolonged investigation.
Ms. Thomson's method of handling this situation is   3.____

    A. *appropriate;* employees should not be accused of wrongdoing until all the facts have been determined
    B. *inappropriate;* the employees involved may assume that the errors were considered unimportant
    C. *appropriate;* employees are more likely to change their behavior as a result of disciplinary action taken after a *cooling off* period
    D. *inappropriate;* the employees involved may have forgotten the details and become emotionally upset when confronted with the facts

4. After studying the financial situation in his agency, an administrative accountant decides   4.____
   to recommend centralization of certain accounting functions which are being performed
   in three different bureaus of the organization.
   The one of the following which is *most likely* to be a DISADVANTAGE if this recom-
   mendation is implemented is that

   A. there may be less coordination of the accounting procedure because central direc-
      tion is not so close to the day-to-day problems as the personnel handling them in
      each specialized accounting unit
   B. the higher management levels would not be able to make emergency decisions in
      as timely a manner as the more involved, lower-level administrators who are closer
      to the problem
   C. it is more difficult to focus the attention of the top management in order to resolve
      accounting problems because of the many other activities top management is
      involved in at the same time
   D. the accuracy of upward and inter-unit communication may be reduced because
      centralization may require insertion of more levels of administration in the chain of
      command

5. Of the following assumptions about the role of conflict in an organization, the *one* which   5.____
   is the MOST accurate statement of the approach of modern management theorists is
   that conflict

   A. can usually be avoided or controlled
   B. serves as a vital element in organizational change
   C. works against attainment of organizational goals
   D. provides a constructive outlet for problem employees

6. Which of the following is generally regarded as the BEST approach for a supervisor to fol-   6.____
   low in handling grievances brought by subordinates?

   A. Avoid becoming involved personally
   B. Involve the union representative in the first stage of discussion
   C. Settle the grievance as soon as possible
   D. Arrange for arbitration by a third party

7. Assume that supervisors of similar-sized accounting units in city, state, and federal   7.____
   offices were interviewed and observed at their work. It was found that the ways they
   acted in and viewed their roles tended to be very similar, regardless of who employed
   them.
   Which of the following is the BEST explanation of this similarity?

   A. A supervisor will ordinarily behave in conformance to his own self-image
   B. Each role in an organization, including the supervisory role, calls for a distinct type
      of personality
   C. The supervisory role reflects an exceptionally complex pattern of human response
   D. The general nature of the duties and responsibilities of the supervisory position
      determines the role

8. Which of the following is NOT consistent with the findings of recent research about the characteristics of successful top managers?   8._____

    A. They are *inner-directed* and not overly concerned with pleasing others
    B. They are challenged by situations filled with high risk and ambiguity
    C. They tend to stay on the same job for long periods of time
    D. They consider it more important to handle critical assignments successfully than to do routine work well

9. As a supervisor you have to give subordinate operational guidelines.
Of the following, the BEST reason for providing them with information about the overall objectives within which their operations fit is that the subordinates will   9._____

    A. be more likely to carry out the operation according to your expectations
    B. know that there is a legitimate reason for carrying out the operation in the way you have prescribed
    C. be more likely to handle unanticipated problems that may arise without having to take up your time
    D. more likely to transmit the operating instructions correctly to their subordinates

10. A supervisor holds frequent meetings with his staff.
Of the following, the BEST approach he can take in order to elicit productive discussions at these meetings is for him to   10._____

    A. ask questions of those who attend
    B. include several levels of supervisors at the meetings
    C. hold the meetings at a specified time each week
    D. begin each meeting with a statement that discussion is welcomed

11. Of the following, the MOST important action that a supervisor can take to increase the productivity of a subordinate is to   11._____

    A. increase his uninterrupted work time
    B. increase the number of reproducing machines available in the office
    C. provide clerical assistance whenever he requests it
    D. reduce the number of his assigned tasks

12. Assume that, as a supervisor, you find that you often must countermand or modify your original staff memos. If this practice continues, *which one* of the following situations is MOST likely to occur? The   12._____

    A. staff will not bother to read your memos   B. office files will become cluttered
    C. staff will delay acting on your memos   D. memos will be treated routinely

13. In making management decisions the committee approach is often used by managers.
Of the following, the BEST reason for using this approach is to   13._____

    A. prevent any one individual from assuming too much authority
    B. allow the manager to bring a wider range of experience and judgment to bear on the problem
    C. allow the participation of all staff members, which will make them feel more committed to the decisions reached
    D. permit the rapid transmission of information about decisions reached to the staff members concerned

14. In establishing standards for the measurement of the performance of a management   14._____
project team, it is MOST important for the project manager to

    A. identify and define the objectives of the project
    B. determine the number of people who will be assigned to the project team
    C. evaluate the skills of the staff who will be assigned to the project team
    D. estimate fairly accurately the length of time required to complete each phase of the project

15. It is virtually impossible to tell an employee either that he is not so good as another   15._____
employee or that he does not measure up to a desirable level of performance, without
having him feel threatened, rejected, and discouraged.
In accordance with the foregoing observation, a supervisor who is concerned about
the performance of the less efficient members of his staff should realize that

    A. he might obtain better results by not discussing the quality and quantity of their
work with them, but by relying instead on the written evaluation of their performance to motivate their improvement
    B. since he is required to discuss their performance with them, he should do so in
words of encouragement and in so friendly a manner as to not destroy their morale
    C. he might discuss their work in a general way, without mentioning any of the specif-
ics about the quality of their performance, with the expectation that they would
understand the full implications of his talk
    D. he should make it a point, while telling them of their poor performance, to mention
that their work is as good as that of some of the other employees in the unit

16. Some advocates of management-by-objectives procedures in public agencies have   16._____
been urging that this method of operations be expanded to encompass all agencies of
the government, for one or more of the following reasons, not all of which may be correct:
    I. The MBO method is likely to succeed because it embraces the practice of
setting near-term goals for the subordinate manager, reviewing accomplish-
ments at an appropriate time, and repeating this process indefinitely
    II. Provision for authority to perform the tasks assigned as goals in the MBO
method is normally not needed because targets are set in quantitative or
qualitative terms and specific times for accomplishment are arranged in
short-term, repetitive intervals
    III. Many other appraisal-of-performance programs failed because both super-
visors and subordinates resisted them, while the MBO approach is not instituted until there is an organizational commitment to it
    IV. Personal accountability is clearly established through the MBO approach
because verifiable results are set up in the process of formulating the targets
Which of the choices below includes ALL of the foregoing statements that are COR-
RECT?

    A. I and III   B. II and IV
    C. I,II,III,IV   D. I,III,IV

17. In preparing an organizational structure, the PRINCIPAL guideline for locating staff units   17.____
is to place them

    A. all under a common supervisor
    B. as close as possible to the activities they serve
    C. as close to the chief executive as possible without over-extending his span of control
    D. at the lowest operational level

18. The relative importance of any unit in a department can be LEAST reliably judged by the   18.____

    A. amount of office space allocated to the unit
    B. number of employees in the unit
    C. rank of the individual who heads the unit
    D. rank of the individual to whom the unit head reports directly

19. Those who favor Planning-Programming-Budgeting Systems (PPBS) as a new method   19.____
of governmental financial administration emphasize that PPBS

    A. applies statistical measurements which correlate highly with criteria
    B. makes possible economic systems analysis, including an explicit examination of alternatives
    C. makes available scarce government resources which can be coordinated on a government-wide basis and shared between local units of government
    D. shifts the emphasis in budgeting methods to an automated system of data processing

20. The term applied to computer processing which processes data concurrently with a   20.____
given activity and provides results soon enough to influence the selection of a course of
action is

    A. realtime processing   B. batch processing
    C. random access processing   D. integrated data processing

KEY (CORRECT ANSWERS)

1.	D	11.	A
2.	C	12.	C
3.	B	13.	B
4.	D	14.	A
5.	B	15.	B
6.	C	16.	D
7.	D	17.	B
8.	C	18.	B
9.	C	19.	B
10.	A	20.	A

INTERPRETING STATISTICAL DATA
GRAPHS, CHARTS AND TABLES
EXAMINATION SECTION
TEST 1

DIRECTIONS: Each question or incomplete statement is followed by several suggested answers or completions. Select the one that BEST answers the question or completes the statement. *PRINT THE LETTER OF THE CORRECT ANSWER IN THE SPACE AT THE RIGHT.*

Questions 1-3.

DIRECTIONS: Questions 1 through 3 are to be answered SOLELY on the basis of the following table.

QUARTERLY SALES REPORTED BY MAJOR INDUSTRY GROUPS					
DECEMBER 2011 - FEBRUARY 2013					
Reported Sales, Taxable & Non-Taxable (In Millions)					
Industry Groups	12/11-2/12	3/12-5/12	6/12-8/12	9/12-11/12	12/12-2/13
Retailers	2,802	2,711	2,475	2,793	2,974
Wholesalers	2,404	2,237	2,269	2,485	2,512
Manufacturers	3,016	2,888	3,001	3,518	3,293
Services	1,034	1,065	984	1,132	1,092

1. The trend in total reported sales may be described as

    A. downward   B. downward and upward
    C. horizontal   D. upward

1._____

2. The two industry groups that reveal a similar seasonal pattern for the period December 2011 through November 2012 are

    A. retailers and manufacturers
    B. retailers and wholesalers
    C. wholesalers and manufacturers
    D. wholesalers and service

2._____

3. Reported sales were at a MINIMUM between

    A. December 2011 and February 2012
    B. March 2012 and May 2012
    C. June 2012 and August 2012
    D. September 2012 and November 2012

3._____

TEST 2

DIRECTIONS: Each question or incomplete statement is followed by several suggested answers or completions. Select the one that BEST answers the question or completes the statement. *PRINT THE LETTER OF THE CORRECT ANSWER IN THE SPACE AT THE RIGHT.*

Questions 1-4.

DIRECTIONS: Questions 1 through 4 are to be answered SOLELY on the basis of the following information.

The income elasticity of demand for selected items of consumer demand in the United States are:

Item	Elasticity
Airline Travel	5.66
Alcohol	.62
Dentist Fees	1.00
Electric Utilities	3.00
Gasoline	1.29
Intercity Bus	1.89
Local Bus	1.41
Restaurant Meals	.75

1. The demand for the item listed below that would be MOST adversely affected by a decrease in income is   1.____

   A. alcohol
   C. gasoline
   B. electric utilities
   D. restaurant meals

2. The item whose relative change in demand would be the same as the relative change in income would be   2.____

   A. dentist fees
   C. restaurant meals
   B. gasoline
   D. none of the above

3. If income increases by 12 percent, the demand for restaurant meals may be expected to increase by   3.____

   A. 9 percent
   C. 16 percent
   B. 12 percent
   D. none of the above

4. On the basis of the above information, the item whose demand would be MOST adversely affected by an increase in the sales tax from 7 percent to 8 percent to be passed on to the consumer in the form of higher prices   4.____

   A. would be airline travel
   C. would be gasoline
   B. would be alcohol
   D. cannot be determined

TEST 3

Questions 1-3.

DIRECTIONS: Questions 1 through 3 are to be answered SOLELY on the basis of the following graphs depicting various relationships in a single retail store.

GRAPH I
RELATIONSHIP BETWEEN NUMBER OF CUSTOMERS
STORE AND TIME OF DAY

NO. OF CUSTOMERS

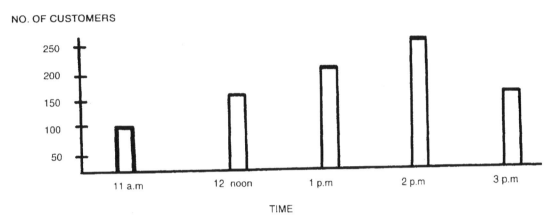

TIME

GRAPH II
RELATIONSHIP BETWEEN NUMBER OF CHECK-OUT LANES AVAILABLE
IN STORE AND WAIT TIME FOR CHECK-OUT

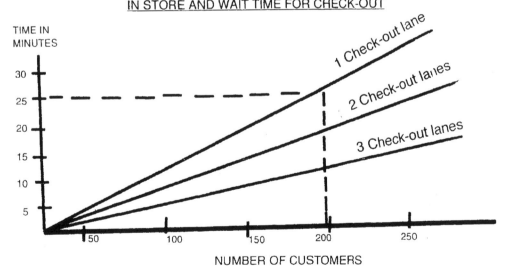

NUMBER OF CUSTOMERS

Note the dotted lines in Graph II. They demonstrate that, if there are 200 people in the store and only 1 check-out lane is open, the wait time will be 25 minutes.

1. At what time would a person be most likely NOT to have to wait more than 15 minutes if   1.___
    only one check-out lane is open?

    A.   11 A.M.   B.   12 Noon   C.   1 P.M.   D.   3 P.M.

2. At what time of day would a person have to wait the LONGEST to check out if 3 check-   2.___
    out lanes are available?

    A.   11 A.M.   B.   12 Noon   C.   1 P.M.   D.   2 P.M.

3. The difference in wait times between 1 and 3 check-out lanes at 3 P.M. is MOST   3.___
    NEARLY

    A.   5   B.   10   C.   15   D.   20

—————

TEST 4

DIRECTIONS: Each question or incomplete statement is followed by several suggested answers or completions. Select the one that BEST answers the question or completes the statement. *PRINT THE LETTER OF THE CORRECT ANSWER IN THE SPACE AT THE RIGHT.*

Questions 1-4.

DIRECTIONS: Questions 1 through 4 are to be answered SOLELY on the basis of the graph below.

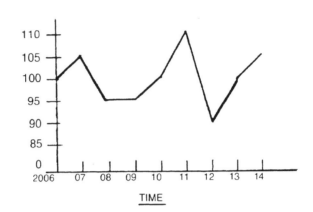

1. Of the following, during what four-year period did the average output of computer operators fall BELOW 100 sheets per hour?

    A. 2007-10   B. 2008-11   C. 2010-13   D. 2011-14

    1.____

2. The average percentage change in output over the previous year's output for the years 2009 to 2012 is MOST NEARLY

    A. 2   B. 0   C. -5   D. -7

    2.____

3. The difference between the actual output for 2002 and the projected figure based upon the average increase from 2006-2011 is MOST NEARLY

    A. 18   B. 20   C. 22   D. 24

    3.____

4. Assume that after constructing the above graph you, an analyst, discovered that the average number of entries per sheet in 2012 was 25 (instead of 20) because of the complex nature of the work performed during that period.
The average output in cards per hour for the period 2010-13, expressed in terms of 20 items per sheet, would then be MOST NEARLY

    A. 95   B. 100   C. 105   D. 110

    4.____

TEST 5

Questions 1-3.

DIRECTIONS: Questions 1 through 3 are to be answered on the basis of the following data assembled for a cost-benefit analysis.

	Cost	Benefit
No program	0	0
Alternative W	$ 3,000	$ 6,000
Alternative X	$10,000	$17,000
Alternative Y	$17,000	$25,000
Alternative Z	$30,000	$32,000

1. From the point of view of selecting the alternative with the best cost benefit ratio, the BEST alternative is Alternative   1._____

    A. W   B. X   C. Y   D. Z

2. From the point of view of selecting the alternative with the best measure of net benefit, the BEST alternative is Alternative   2._____

    A. W   B. X   C. Y   D. Z

3. From the point of view of pushing public expenditure to the point where marginal benefit equals or exceeds marginal cost, the BEST alternative is Alternative   3._____

    A. W   B. X   C. Y   D. Z

TEST 6

DIRECTIONS: Each question or incomplete statement is followed by several suggested answers or completions. Select the one that BEST answers the question or completes the statement. *PRINT THE LETTER OF THE CORRECT ANSWER IN THE SPACE AT THE RIGHT.*

Questions 1-3.

DIRECTIONS: Questions 1 through 3 are to be answered SOLELY on the basis of the following data.

A series of cost-benefit studies of various alternative health programs yields the following results:

Program	Benefit	Cost
K	30	15
L	60	60
M	300	150
N	600	500

In answering Questions 1 and 2, assume that all programs can be increased or decreased in scale without affecting their individual benefit-to-cost ratios.

1. The benefit-to-cost ratio of Program M is   1.____

   A. 10:1   B. 5:1   C. 2:1   D. 1:2

2. The budget ceiling for one or more of the programs included in the study is set at 75   2.____
   units.
   It may MOST logically be concluded that

   A. Programs K and L should be chosen to fit within the budget ceiling
   B. Program K would be the most desirable one that could be afforded
   C. Program M should be chosen rather than Program K
   D. the choice should be between Programs M and K

3. If no assumptions can be made regarding the effects of change of scale, the MOST logi-   3.____
   cal conclusion, on the basis of the data available, is that

   A. more data are needed for a budget choice of program
   B. Program K is the most preferable because of its low cost and good benefit-to-cost
       ratio
   C. Program M is the most preferable because of its high benefits and good benefit-to-
       cost ratio
   D. there is no difference between Programs K and M, and either can be chosen for
       any purpose

TEST 7

DIRECTIONS: Each question or incomplete statement is followed by several suggested answers or completions. Select the one that BEST answers the question or completes the statement. *PRINT THE LETTER OF THE CORRECT ANSWER IN THE SPACE AT THE RIGHT.*

Questions 1-6.

DIRECTIONS: Questions 1 through 6 are to be answered SOLELY on the basis of the information contained in the charts below which relate to the budget allocations of City X, a small suburban community. The charts depict the annual budget allocations by Department and by expenditures over a five-year period.

CITY X BUDGET IN MILLIONS OF DOLLARS
TABLE I. Budget Allocations By Department

Department	2007	2008	2009	2010	2011
Public Safety	30	45	50	40	50
Health and Welfare	50	75	90	60	70
Engineering	5	8	10	5	8
Human Resources	10	12	20	10	22
Conservation & Environment	10	15	20	20	15
Education & Development	15	25	35	15	15
TOTAL BUDGET	120	180	225	150	180

TABLE II. Budget Allocations by Expenditures

Category	2007	2008	2009	2010	2011
Raw Materials & Machinery	36	63	68	30	98
Capital Outlay	12	27	56	15	18
Personal Services	72	90	101	105	64
TOTAL BUDGET	120	180	225	150	180

1. The year in which the SMALLEST percentage of the total annual budget was allocated to the Department of Education and Development is

   A. 2007   B. 2008   C. 2010   D. 2011

1.___

2. Assume that in 2010 the Department of Conservation and Environment divided its annual budget into the three categories of expenditures and in exactly the same proportion as the budget shown in Table II for the year 2010. The amount allocated for capital outlay in the Department of Conservation and Environment's 2010 budget was MOST NEARLY _____ million.

   A. $2   B. $4   C. $6   D. $10

2.___

3. From the year 2008 to the year 2010, the sum of the annual budgets for the Departments   3.____
   of Public Safety and Engineering showed an overall _____ million.

   A.   decline; $8   B.   increase; $7
   C.   decline; $15   D.   increase; $22

4. The LARGEST dollar increase in departmental budget allocations from one year to the   4.____
   next was in _____ from _____.

   A.   Public Safety; 2007 to 2008
   B.   Health and Welfare; 2007 to 2008
   C.   Education and Development; 2009 to 2010
   D.   Human Resources; 2009 to 2010

5. During the five-year period, the annual budget of the Department of Human Resources   5.____
   was GREATER than the annual budget for the Department of Conservation and Environment in _____ of the years.

   A.   none   B.   one   C.   two   D.   three

6. If the total City X budget increases at the same rate from 2011 to 2012 as it did from   6.____
   2010 to 2011, the total City X budget for 2012 will be MOST NEARLY _____ million.

   A. $180   B. $200   C. $210   D. $215

TEST 8

Questions 1-3.

DIRECTIONS: Questions 1 through 3 are to be answered SOLELY on the basis of the following information.

Assume that in order to encourage Program A, the State and Federal governments have agreed to make the following reimbursements for money spent on Program A, provided the unreimbursed balance is paid from City funds.

During Fiscal Year 2011-2012 - For the first $2 million expended, 50% Federal reimbursement and 30% State reimbursement; for the next $3 million, 40% Federal reimbursement and 20% State reimbursement; for the next $5 million, 20% Federal reimbursement and 10% State reimbursement. Above $10 million expended, no Federal or State reimbursement.

During Fiscal Year 2012-2013 - For the first $1 million expended, 30% Federal reimbursement and 20% State reimbursement; for the next $4 million, 15% Federal reimbursement and 10% State reimbursement. Above $5 million expended, no Federal or State reimbursement.

1. Assume that the Program A expenditures are such that the State reimbursement for Fiscal Year 2011-2012 will be $1 million.
   Then, the Federal reimbursement for Fiscal Year 2011-2012 will be

   A. $1,600,000
   B. $1,800,000
   C. $2,000,000
   D. $2,600,000

   1.____

2. Assume that $8 million were to be spent on Program A in Fiscal Year 2012-2013.
   The TOTAL amount of unreimbursed City funds required would be

   A. $3,500,000
   B. $4,500,000
   C. $5,500,000
   D. $6,500,000

   2.____

3. Assume that the City desires to have a combined total of $6 million spent in Program A during both the Fiscal Year 2011-2012 and the Fiscal Year 2012-2013.
   Of the following expenditure combinations, the one which results in the GREATEST reimbursement of City funds is _____ in Fiscal Year 2011-2012 and _____ in Fiscal Year 2012-2013.

   A. $5 million; $1 million
   B. $4 million; $2 million
   C. $3 million; $3 million
   D. $2 million; $4 million

   3.____

KEY (CORRECT ANSWERS)

TEST 1

1. D
2. C
3. C

TEST 2

1. B
2. A
3. A
4. D

TEST 3

1. A
2. D
3. B

TEST 4

1. A
2. B
3. C
4. C

TEST 5

1. A
2. C
3. C

TEST 6

1. C
2. D
3. A

TEST 7

1. D
2. A
3. A
4. B
5. B
6. D

TEST 8

1. B
2. D
3. A

INTERPRETING STATISTICAL DATA
GRAPHS, CHARTS AND TABLES
TEST 1

DIRECTIONS: Each question or incomplete statement is followed by several suggested answers or completions. Select the one that BEST answers the question or completes the statement. *PRINT THE LETTER OF THE CORRECT ANSWER IN THE SPACE AT THE RIGHT.*

1.   The following chart shows the number of persons employed in a certain industry for each   1._____
year from 2007 through 2012.

	Thousands of Employees
2007	5.7
2008	6.8
2009	7.0
2010	7.1
2011	7.4
2012	6.4

In making a forecast of future trends, the one of the following steps which should be taken FIRST is to
   A.   take the six-year average
   B.   fit a curvilinear trend to the data
   C.   fit a straight line, omitting 2012 as an *outlier,* i.e., as an unusually low reading
   D.   check on what happened to the industry in 2012

2.   Of the following concepts, the one which CANNOT be represented suitably by a pie chart   2._____
is

   A.   percent shares
   B.   shares in absolute units
   C.   time trends
   D.   successive totals over time, with their shares

3.   A pictogram is ESSENTIALLY another version of a(n)_____ chart.   3._____

   A.   plain bar   B.   component bar
   C.   pie   D.   area

4.   A time series for a certain cost is presented in a graph. It is drawn so that the vertical   4._____
(cost) axis starts at a point well above zero.
This is a legitimate method of presentation for some purposes, but it may have the effect of

   A.   hiding fixed components of the cost
   B.   exaggerating changes which, in actual amounts, may be insignificant
   C.   magnifying fixed components of the cost
   D.   impairing correlation analysis

5. Certain budgetary data may be represented by bar, area or volume charts. 5.____
   Which one of the following BEST expresses the most appropriate order of usefulness?

   A. Descends from bar to volume and area charts, the last two being about the same
   B. Descends from volume to area to bar charts
   C. Depends on the nature of the data presented
   D. Descends from bar to area to volume charts

Questions 6-7.

DIRECTIONS: Questions 6 and 7 are to be answered on the basis of the layout below.

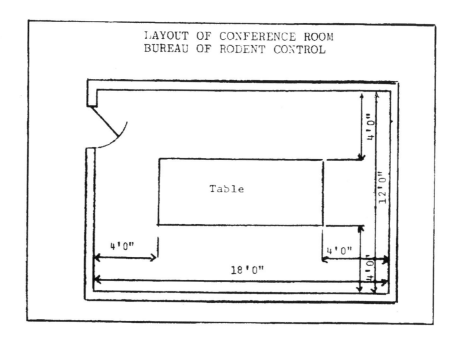

6. The LARGEST number of persons that can be accommodated in the area shown in the 6.____
   layout is

   A. 16   B. 10   C. 8   D. 6

7. Assume that the Bureau's programs undergo expansion and the Director indicates that 7.____
   the feasibility of increasing the size of the conference room should be explored.
   For every two additional persons that are to be accommodated, the analyst should recommend that _____ be added to table length and _____ be added to room length.

   A. 2'-6"; 2'-6"   B. 5'-0"; 5'-0"
   C. 2'-6"; 5'-0"   D. 5'-0"; 2'-6"

Questions 8-9.

DIRECTIONS: Questions 8 and 9 are to be answered on the basis of the following groups, both of which depict the same information in different ways. The x and y axes in graphs A and B are not necessarily drawn in the same scale. The points along the curves on both graphs represent corresponding points and are the upper limits of class intervals.

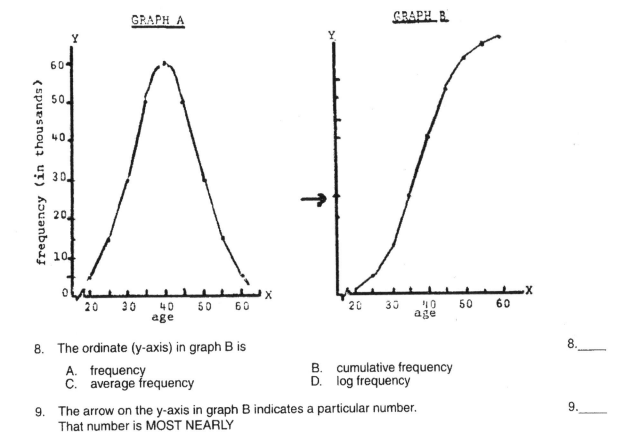

8.   The ordinate (y-axis) in graph B is   8.____

       A.   frequency   B.   cumulative frequency
       C.   average frequency   D.   log frequency

9.   The arrow on the y-axis in graph B indicates a particular number.   9.____
       That number is MOST NEARLY

       A.   100   B.   50,000   C.   100,000   D.   150,000

Questions 10-11.

DIRECTIONS: Questions 10 and 11 are to be answered on the basis of the graphs below.

ROAD REPAIR COSTS IF PERFORMED BY
CITY STAFF OR AN OUTSIDE CONTRACTOR

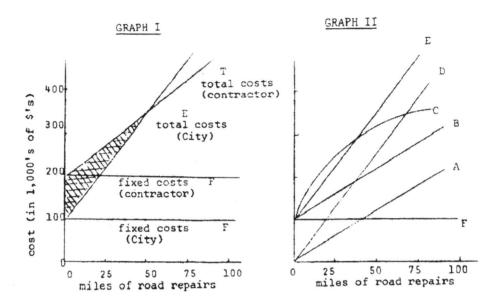

10. In Graph I, the vertical distance between lines E and T within the crosshatched area rep-   10._____
    resents the _____ than 50 miles is performed by the city.

    A. savings to the city if work of less
    B. loss to the city if work of less
    C. savings to the city if work of more
    D. loss to the city if work of more

11. Graph II is identical to Graph I except that contractor costs have been eliminated. Total   11._____
    costs (line E) are the sum of fixed costs (line F) a.nd variable costs. Variable costs are
    represented by line

    A. A   B. B   C. C   D. D

Questions 12-13.

DIRECTIONS: Questions 12 and 13 are to be answered on the basis of the following chart. In
              a hypothetical problem involving four criteria and four alternatives, the follow-
              ing data have been assembled.

Cost Criterion	Effectiveness Criterion	Timing Criterion	Feasibility Criterion
Alternative A $500,000	50 units	3 months	probably feasible
Alternative B $300,000	100 units	6 months	probably feasible
Alternative C $400,000	50 units	12 months	probably infeasible
Alternative D $200,000	75 units	3 months	probably infeasible

12. On the basis of the above data, it appears that the one alternative which is dominated by another alternative is Alternative   12._____

    A. A   B. B   C. C   D. D

13. If the feasibility constraint is absolute and fixed, then the critical trade-off is between lower cost _____ on the other.   13._____

    A. on the one hand and faster timing and higher effectiveness
    B. and higher effectiveness on one hand and faster timing
    C. and faster timing on the one hand and higher effectiveness
    D. on the one hand and higher effectiveness

14. The following illustration depicts the structure of a municipal agency.   14._____

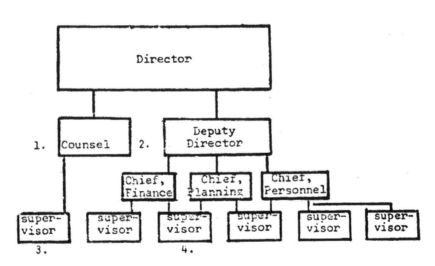

In the above illustration, which individual would generally be expected to encounter the MOST difficulty in carrying out his organizational functions?
    A. 1   B. 2   C. 3   D. 4

Questions 15-16.

DIRECTIONS: Questions 15 and 16 are to be answered on the basis of the information given
on the report forms pictured below and on the following page.

Chart I and Chart II are parts of the Field Patrol Sheets of two Parking Enforcement
Agents. They show the number of violations issued on a particular day. Chart III is the Tally
Sheet for that day prepared by the Senior Parking Enforcement Agent from the Field Patrol
Sheets of the entire squad.

CHART I

Area or Post	TYPE OF VIOLATION											
	MTrs	B/S	D/P	Hyd	N/S	N/Sp	Taxi	Curb	N/P	Alt	Other	Total
19	2	3	2	2	3	3	0	1	1	5	1	23
21	4	0	2	0	1	2	2	0	5	9	1	26
Totals	6	3	4	2	4	5	2	1	6	14	2	49

2/4	100	PEA Browne
Date	Badge	Signature

TC8-61   Checked by _____ Date _____

CHART II

Area or Post	TYPE OF VIOLATION											
	MTrs	B/S	D/P	Hyd	N/S	N/Sp	Taxi	Curb	N/P	Alt	Other	Total
31	8	2	0	0	3	2	2	0	4	5	0	26
33	7	0	1	2	3	1	2	0	6	3	0	25
Totals	15	2	1	2	6	3	4	0	10	8	0	51

2/4	101	PEA Grey
Date	Badge	Signature

TC8-61   Checked by _____ Date _____

TRAFFIC CONTROL BUREAU
SENIORS TALLY SHEET   Enf. 23A

Name	Mtrs Ptld	Mtrs	Bus Stop	Dble Park	Hyd	No Stand	No Stop	Taxi Stand	Curb	No Park	Alt Park	Other	Total
Green		18	2	3	1	6	0	0	0	4	10	1	45
Browne		6	3	4	2	4	5	2	1	6	14	2	49
White		12	0	0	0	2	1	1	0	8	8	1	33
Black		20	5	2	3	8	7	5	1	5	4	0	60
Grey		15	2	1	2	9	3	4	0	10	8	0	51
Redding		17	0	1	3	7	5	3	0	8	6	0	50
TOTAL		88	12	11	11	36	21	15	2	41	50	4	288

15. The Senior Parking Enforcement Agent who prepared Chart III made an error in transfer-   15.____
ring the violation totals from the Field Patrol Sheets to the Seniors Tally Sheet. Which
one of the following PROPERLY describes the Tally Sheet entry if this error were corrected? Parking Enforcement Agent

    A.   Browne's overall total of summonses issued would be 50
    B.   Browne's total of summonses issued for Double-Parking violations would be 3
    C.   Grey's total number of summonses issued for meter violations would be 6
    D.   Grey's total number of summonses issued for No Standing violations would be 6

16. The parking enforcement agent who issued the MOST summonses for bus stop and taxi   16.____
stand violations is

    A.   Black   B.   Redding   C.   White   D.   Browne

17. During a period of probation in which records were kept for 360 children fourteen to eigh-   17.____
teen years of age, probation officers found that the group committed certain offenses, as
shown in the following table:

I.Q.	No. of Offenders	No. of Offenses	Offenses Per Offender
61-80	125	338	2.7
81-100	160	448	2.8
101 & over	75	217	2.9

According to the foregoing data,

    A.   the more intelligent offenders are no more law-abiding than, and perhaps not so
law-abiding as, the dull offenders
    B.   brighter offenders present no more difficult problems than less intelligent offenders
    C.   the majority of this probation group is found to be above the average in intelligence
of a normal group of young persons within this age range
    D.   the relationship between the effectiveness of probation work and the number of
offenders is in inverse ratio

18.   18.____

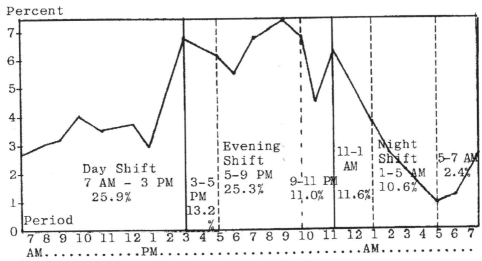

The percent for each hour is charted at the beginning of the hour. For example, 2.6% at the extreme left is for 7:00 A.M. to 7:59 A.M.

A certain police department has analyzed its need for police service and has computed the percentage distributions as shown on the chart on the preceding page. Despite good supervisory effort, there is a significant decrease in the amount of police service provided during the half-hour surrounding shift changes. The police commander wishes to minimize this effect.

To accomplish its objective, taking into account the distribution of need for police services, which one of the following is the BEST time for this department to schedule its three principal shift changes? (Assume 8-hour shifts.)

- A. A. 4:00 A.M., Noon, 8:00 P.M.
- B. 4:00 A.M., 1:00 P.M., 9:00 P.M.
- C. 6:00 A.M., 2:00 P.M., 10:00 P.M.
- D. 7:00 A.M., 3:00 P.M., 11:00 P.M.

19. An inspector on a painting contract has to keep records on the progress of the work completed by a painting contractor .   19._____
The following is the progress of the work completed by a contractor at the end of 8 months.

Apartment Size	Estimated Number of Apartments	Number of Apartments Painted
3 rooms	120	100
4 rooms	160	140
5 rooms	120	40

The percentage of work completed on a room basis is MOST NEARLY
A. 62%   B. 66%   C. 70%   D. 74%

20. Assume that an officer reported the following amounts of toll monies collected during each day of a five-day period: 20._____

Tuesday	$3,247.50
Wednesday	$2,992.50
Thursday	$3,917.50
Friday	$4,862.50
Saturday	$1,675.00

The TOTAL amount of toll money collected during this period was
A. $15,702.50   B. $16,485.00
C. $16,695.00   D. $16,997.50

21. Suppose that during a two-hour period in a toll booth an officer collected the following: 21._____

Type of Money	Number of Bills
$20 bills	2
$10 bills	5
$5 bills	23
$1 bills	269

The TOTAL amount of money the officer collected was
A. $299   B. $464   C. $474   D. $501

Questions 22-23.

DIRECTIONS: Questions 22 and 23 are to be answered SOLELY on the basis of the information shown below which indicates the charges for hospital services and physician services given in a hospital and a patient's annual income for each of four consecutive years.

Year	Patient's Annual Income	Charges for Hospital Services and Physician Services Given in a Hospital
2009	$45,000	$11,100
2010	$46,500	$11,970
2011	$64,500	$16,230
2012	$70,500	$17,325

22. A hospitalized patient may qualify for Medicaid benefits when the charges for hospital services and for physician services given in the hospital exceed 25 percent of the patient's annual income.
According to the information shown above, the one of the following that indicates ONLY those years in which the patient qualifies for Medicaid benefits is

    A. 2010, 2011
    C. 2010, 2012
    B. 2009, 2010, 2012
    D. 2010, 2011, 2012

22.____

23. The one of the following that is the patient's average annual income for the entire four-year period shown above is MOST NEARLY

    A. $48,375   B. $49,125   C. $56,025   D. $56,625

23.____

Questions 24-25.

DIRECTIONS: Questions 24 and 25 are to be answered SOLELY on the basis of the information shown below, which gives the hospital bill and the amount paid by an Insurance Plan for each of four patients.

Patient's Name	Hospital Bill	Amount Paid by the Insurance Plan Toward Hospital Bill
Mr. Harris	$ 8,753	$5,952
Mr. W. Smith	$ 4,504	$3,285
Mr. T. Jones	$ 7,211	$5,048
Mr. M. White	$12,255	$8,712

24. According to the information given above, which patient, when compared with the other three patients, had the HIGHEST percentage of his bill paid by the Insurance Plan?

    A. Mr. W. Smith
    C. Mr. T. Jones
    B. Mr. D. Harris
    D. Mr. M. White

24.____

25. The average amount paid by the Insurance Plan toward the hospital bills of the four patients shown above is MOST NEARLY

    A. $5,269   B. $5,499   C. $5,749   D. $5,766

25.____

KEY (CORRECT ANSWERS)

1.	D	11.	D
2.	C	12.	C
3.	A	13.	B
4.	B	14.	D
5.	D	15.	D
6.	B	16.	A
7.	A	17.	A
8.	B	18.	C
9.	C	19.	B
10.	A	20.	C

21.	C
22.	A
23.	D
24.	A
25.	C

TEST 2

DIRECTIONS: Each question or incomplete statement is followed by several suggested
answers or completions. Select the one that BEST answers the question or
completes the statement. *PRINT THE LETTER OF THE CORRECT ANSWER
IN THE SPACE AT THE RIGHT.*

Questions 1-2.

DIRECTIONS: Questions 1 and 2 are to be answered on the basis of the information contained in the chart below.

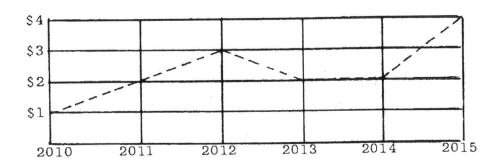

1. According to the above chart, the increase in the average price of the commodity from   1._____
    2012 to 2015 was APPROXIMATELY

    A. 25%   B. 33 1/3%   C. 50%   D. 75%

2. According to the above chart, the increase in the average price of the commodity from   2._____
    2010 to 2012 was APPROXIMATELY

    A. 20%   B. 30%   C. 200%   D. 300%

Questions 3-4.

DIRECTIONS: Questions 3 and 4 are to be answered SOLELY on the basis of the information
contained in the chart below, which shows supply and demand of a commodity
from January 1, 2011 to January 1, 2015.

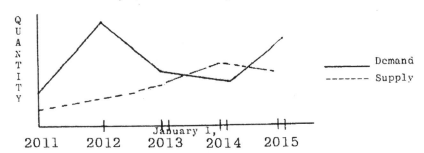

3. The above chart indicates that there was a seller's market during most of each of the following years EXCEPT   3.____

     A. 2011   B. 2012   C. 2013   D. 2014

4. According to the above chart, in the absence of price controls or other artificial or   4.____
unusual circumstances, when would the price of the commodity have been the HIGH-
EST?
January 1,

     A. 2011   B. 2012   C. 2013   D. 2014

5. In order to pay its employees, the Convex Company obtained bills and coins in the following denominations: 5.____

Denomination	$20	$10	$5	$1	$.50	$.25	$.10	$.05	$.01
Number	317	122	38	73	69	47	39	25	36

What was the TOTAL amount of cash obtained?
A. $7,874.76   B. $7,878.00
C. $7,889.25   D. $7,924.35

6. Suppose that a business you are investigating presents the following figures: 6.____

Year	Net Income	Tax Rate On Net Income
2014	$55,000	20%
2015	$55,000	30%
2016	$65,000	20%
2017	$52,000	25%
2018	$62,000	30%
2019	$68,000	25%

According to these figures, it is MOST accurate to say that
A. less tax was due in 2018 than in 2019
B. more tax was due in 2014 than in 2017
C. the same amount of tax was due in 2014 and 2015
D. the same amount of tax was due in 2016 and 2017

7. The table below shows the total amount of money owed on the bills sent to each of four   7.____
different accounts and the total amount of money which has been received from each of
these accounts.

Name of Account	Amount Owed	Amount Received
Arnold	$55,989	$37,898
Barry	$97,276	$79,457
Carter	$62,736	$47,769
Daley	$77,463	$59,534

The balance of an account is determined by subtracting the amount received from the
amount owed.
Based on this method of determining a balance, the account with the LARGEST balance
is
     A. Arnold   B. Barry   C. Carter   D. Daley

8. A work sheet for a booth audit has the readings shown below for four turnstiles: 8._____

Turnstile No.	Opening Readings	Readings For Audit
1	26178	26291
2	65489	65752
3	72267	72312
4	45965	46199

With a fare of $1.00, what is the cash value of the TOTAL difference between the Opening Readings and the Readings for Audit for the four turnstiles?

A. $635   B. $653   C. $654   D. $675

Questions 9-10.

DIRECTIONS: Questions 9 and 10 are to be answered SOLELY on the basis of the information contained in the following table.

COMPARISON OF CUNY ATTRITION RATES FOR FALL 2010 DAY FRESHMEN THROUGH FALL 2011

Colleges	Open Admissions (a)	Regular (b)	Overall
Senior	30%	14%	21%
Community	40%	34%	39%
Total	36%	20%	29%

a.   Represents senior college students admitted with high school averages below 80 and community college students admitted with high school averages below 75
b.   Represents senior college students admitted with averages of 80 and above and community college students admitted with averages of 75 and above

9. The category of students who remained in the City University in the GREATEST proportion were   9._____

A.   regular students in community colleges
B.   open admissions students in community colleges
C.   regular students in senior colleges
D.   open admissions students in senior colleges

10. Regular admission to a senior college was on the basis of an academic average   10._____

A.   above 70   B.   of 80 or above
C.   above 75   D.   above 85

Questions 11-12.

DIRECTIONS: Questions 11 and 12 are to be answered SOLELY on the basis of the information given below.

Time Scores

Maximum qualifying time	15 minutes
Minimum qualifying time (subtract)	5 minutes
Range in qualifying time	10 minutes

<u>Weighted Point Scores (Weight = 10)</u>

Maximum weighted score	10 points
Minimum qualifying score (subtract	7 points
Range in weighted scores	3 points

From the foregoing, it is apparent that a simple conversion table can be prepared by giving the maximum qualifying time a minimum qualifying weighted score of 7 points and
crediting three-tenths additional weighted points for each minute less than 15.

11. On the basis of the above paragraph, it is apparent that if the maximum *time* taken by   11._____
    any candidate on the task was 15 minutes,

    A. the test was too easy
    B. too much weight was given to the *time* portion
    C. less time should have been given for the task
    D. no one failed the *time* portion of the test

12. The BEST of the following interpretations of the above paragraph is that any candidate   12._____
    completing the task in 8 minutes would have received a weighted score for *time* of
    _____ points.

    A. 9.1   B. 8.5   C. 8.2   D. 7.9

Questions 13-14.

DIRECTIONS: Questions 13 and 14 are to be answered on the basis of the following illustra-
              tion. Assume that the figures in the chart are cubes.

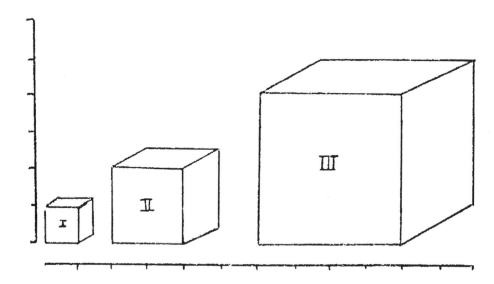

13. In the illustration above, how many times GREATER is the quantity represented by Fig-   13._____
    ure III than the quantity represented by Figure II?

    A. 2   B. 4   C. 8   D. 16

14. The illustration above illustrates a progression in quantity BEST described as   14.____

    A. arithmetic   B. geometric
    C. discrete   D. linear

Questions 15-16.

DIRECTIONS: Questions 15 and 16 are to be answered SOLELY on the basis of the following summary of salary increases applicable to a group of employees in a college office.

Hourly Rate 6/30/12	Increase 7/1/12	Increase 7/1/13
$10.20	$1.40/hr.	$1.40/hr.
$11.20	$1.20/hr.	$1.20/hr.
$12.20	$1.20/hr.	$1.20/hr.

Hourly Rate 6/30/12	Increase 7/1/12	Increase 7/1/13
$13.20	$1.00/hr.	$1.00/hr.
$14.20	$1.00/hr.	$1.00/hr.
$15.20	$1.00/hr.	$1.00/hr.

15. A college office employee with an hourly salary of $14.20 as of June 30, 2012 worked for   15.____
    32 hours during the week of April 16, 2013.
    Her GROSS salary for that week was

    A. $422.40   B. $454.40   C. $486.40   D. $518.40

16. A college office employee was earning an hourly salary of $12.20 in June of 2012.   16.____
    The percentage increase in her hourly salary as of July 2, 2013 will be MOST NEARLY
    _____ percent.

    A. 10   B. 15   C. 20   D. 25

17. An experiment was conducted to measure the error rate of typists. The results follow: 17.____

Typists	Percent of Total Output	Error Rate (in percent)
A	30	1.00
B	30	1.50
C	40	0.50

The error rate (in percent) for the three typists combined
    A. is 0.95
    B. is 1.00
    C. is 3.00
    D. cannot be calculated from the given data

Question 18.

DIRECTIONS: Question 18 is to be answered on the basis of the information given below.

At midnight on January 31, the following bodies were remaining:

Adults	Infants	Stillbirths	Amputations
37	23	40	21

On February 1st, from 12:01 A.M. to 12:00 midnight, the following bodies were received:

Adults	Infants	Stillbirths	Amputations
24	13	18	8

In addition, the following bodies were claimed:

Adults	Infants	Stillbirths	Amputations
33	9	4	2

18. What is the number of cases remaining at midnight on February 1?   18.____

	Adults	Infants	Stillbirths	Amputations
A.	31	26	41	23
B.	28	27	54	27
C.	29	28	48	25
D.	27	29	62	28

Questions 19-25.

DIRECTIONS: Questions 19 through 25 are to be answered SOLELY on the basis of the following information.

ACCIDENTS

During one month, a certain division reported the number of accidents from various causes as follows:

Falls	6
Flying objects.............................	5
Handling objects	4
Striking objects	3
Assaults	2
Stepping on objects	1

19. The GREATEST cause of accidents was   19.____

    A. striking objects   B. handling objects
    C. flying objects   D. falls

20. The accidents over which the injured person had LEAST control were those due to   20.____

    A. handling objects   B. falls
    C. assaults   D. flying objects

21. The accidents due to flying objects exceeded those due to striking objects by   21.____

    A. 8   B. 6   C. 3   D. 2

22. The TOTAL number of accidents as shown was   22.____

    A. 19   B. 20   C. 21   D. 22

23. The MOST likely cause for an accident to a station porter is   23.____

    A. stepping on objects   B. falls
    C. striking objects   D. assaults

24. The accidents which would MOST likely result in disciplinary action are those due to   24.____

    A. stepping on objects   B. assaults
    C. striking objects   D. falls

25. The TOTAL number of accidents involving objects was   25.____

    A. 8   B. 12   C. 13   D. 21

KEY (CORRECT ANSWERS)

1. B		11. D	
2. C		12. A	
3. C		13. C	
4. B		14. B	
5. A		15. C	
6. D		16. C	
7. A		17. A	
8. C		18. B	
9. C		19. D	
10. B		20. D	

21. D
22. C
23. B
24. B
25. C

PHILOSOPHY, PRINCIPLES, PRACTICES AND TECHNICS
OF
SUPERVISION, ADMINISTRATION, MANAGEMENT AND ORGANIZATION

TABLE OF CONTENTS

TABLE OF CONTENTS (CONTINUED)

PHILOSOPHY, PRINCIPLES, PRACTICES, AND TECHNICS
OF
SUPERVISION, ADMINISTRATION, MANAGEMENT AND ORGANIZATION

I. MEANING OF SUPERVISION

The extension of the democratic philosophy has been accompanied by an extension in the scope of supervision. Modern leaders and supervisors no longer think of supervision in the narrow sense of being confined chiefly to visiting employees, supplying materials, or rating the staff. They regard supervision as being intimately related to all the concerned agencies of society, they speak of the supervisor's function in terms of "growth", rather than the "improvement," of employees.

This modern concept of supervision may be defined as follows:

Supervision is leadership and the development of leadership within groups which are cooperatively engaged in inspection, research, training, guidance and evaluation.

II. THE OLD AND THE NEW SUPERVISION

TRADITIONAL
1. Inspection
2. Focused on the employee
3. Visitation
4. Random and haphazard
5. Imposed and authoritarian
6. One person usually

MODERN
1. Study and analysis
2. Focused on aims, materials, methods, supervisors, employees, environment
3. Demonstrations, intervisitation, workshops, directed reading, bulletins, etc.
4. Definitely organized and planned (scientific)
5. Cooperative and democratic
6. Many persons involved (creative)

III THE EIGHT (8) BASIC PRINCIPLES OF THE NEW SUPERVISION

1. *PRINCIPLE OF RESPONSIBILITY*
   Authority to act and responsibility for acting must be joined.
   a. If you give responsibility, give authority.
   b. Define employee duties clearly.
   c. Protect employees from criticism by others.
   d. Recognize the rights as well as obligations of employees.
   e. Achieve the aims of a democratic society insofar as it is possible within the area of your work.
   f. Establish a situation favorable to training and learning.
   g. Accept ultimate responsibility for everything done in your section, unit, office, division, department.
   h. Good administration and good supervision are inseparable.

2. PRINCIPLE OF AUTHORITY

The success of the supervisor is measured by the extent to which the power of authority is not used.

a. Exercise simplicity and informality in supervision.
b. Use the simplest machinery of supervision.
c. If it is good for the organization as a whole, it is probably justified.
d. Seldom be arbitrary or authoritative.
e. Do not base your work on the power of position or of personality.
f. Permit and encourage the free expression of opinions.

3. PRINCIPLE OF SELF-GROWTH

The success of the supervisor is measured by the extent to which, and the speed with which, he is no longer needed.

a. Base criticism on principles, not on specifics.
b. Point out higher activities to employees.
c. Train for self-thinking by employees, to meet new situations.
d. Stimulate initiative, self-reliance and individual responsibility.
e. Concentrate on stimulating the growth of employees rather than on removing defects.

4. PRINCIPLE OF INDIVIDUAL WORTH

Respect for the individual is a paramount consideration in supervision.

a. Be human and sympathetic in dealing with employees.
b. Don't nag about things to be done.
c. Recognize the individual differences among employees and seek opportunities to permit best expression of each personality.

5. PRINCIPLE OF CREATIVE LEADERSHIP

The best supervision is that which is not apparent to the employee.

a. Stimulate, don't drive employees to creative action.
b. Emphasize doing good things.
c. Encourage employees to do what they do best.
d. Do not be too greatly concerned with details of subject or method.
e. Do not be concerned exclusively with immediate problems and activities.
f. Reveal higher activities and make them both desired and maximally possible.
g. Determine procedures in the light of each situation but see that these are derived from a sound basic philosophy.
h. Aid, inspire and lead so as to liberate the creative spirit latent in all good employees.

6. PRINCIPLE OF SUCCESS AND FAILURE

There are no unsuccessful employees, only unsuccessful supervisors who have failed to give proper leadership.

a. Adapt suggestions to the capacities, attitudes, and prejudices of employees.
b. Be gradual, be progressive, be persistent.
c. Help the employee find the general principle; have the employee apply his own problem to the general principle.
d. Give adequate appreciation for good work and honest effort.
e. Anticipate employee difficulties and help to prevent them.
f. Encourage employees to do the desirable things they will do anyway.
g. Judge your supervision by the results it secures.

7. *PRINCIPLE OF SCIENCE*

Successful supervision is scientific, objective, and experimental. It is based on facts, not on prejudices.

a. Be cumulative in results.
b. Never divorce your suggestions from the goals of training.
c. Don't be impatient of results.
d. Keep all matters on a professional, not a personal level.
e. Do not be concerned exclusively with immediate problems and activities.
f. Use objective means of determining achievement and rating where possible.

8. *PRINCIPLE OF COOPERATION*

Supervision is a cooperative enterprise between supervisor and employee.

a. Begin with conditions as they are.
b. Ask opinions of all involved when formulating policies.
c. Organization is as good as its weakest link.
d. Let employees help to determine policies and department programs.
e. Be approachable and accessible - physically and mentally.
f. Develop pleasant social relationships.

IV. WHAT IS ADMINISTRATION?

Administration is concerned with providing the environment, the material facilities, and the operational procedures that will promote the maximum growth and development of supervisors and employees. (Organization is an aspect, and a concomitant, of administration.)

There is no sharp line of demarcation between supervision and administration; these functions are intimately interrelated and, often, overlapping. They are complementary activities.

1. *PRACTICES COMMONLY CLASSED AS "SUPERVISORY"*

a. Conducting employees conferences
b. Visiting sections, units, offices, divisions, departments
c. Arranging for demonstrations
d. Examining plans
e. Suggesting professional reading
f. Interpreting bulletins
g. Recommending in-service training courses
h. Encouraging experimentation
i. Appraising employee morale
j. Providing for intervisitation

2. *PRACTICES COMMONLY CLASSIFIED AS "ADMINISTRATIVE"*

a. Management of the office
b. Arrangement of schedules for extra duties
c. Assignment of rooms or areas
d. Distribution of supplies
e. Keeping records and reports
f. Care of audio-visual materials
g. Keeping inventory records
h. Checking record cards and books
i. Programming special activities
j. Checking on the attendance and punctuality of employees

3. *PRACTICES COMMONLY CLASSIFIED AS BOTH "SUPERVISORY" AND "ADMINISTRATIVE"*
   a. Program construction
   b. Testing or evaluating outcomes
   c. Personnel accounting
   d. Ordering instructional materials

V. RESPONSIBILITIES OF THE SUPERVISOR

A person employed in a supervisory capacity must constantly be able to improve his own efficiency and ability. He represents the employer to the employees and only continuous self-examination can make him a capable supervisor.

Leadership and training are the supervisor's responsibility. An efficient working unit is one in which the employees work with the supervisor. It is his job to bring out the best in his employees. He must always be relaxed, courteous and calm in his association with his employees. Their feelings are important, and a harsh attitude does not develop the most efficient employees.

VI. COMPETENCIES OF THE SUPERVISOR

1. Complete knowledge of the duties and responsibilities of his position.
2. To be able to organize a job, plan ahead and carry through.
3. To have self-confidence and initiative.
4. To be able to handle the unexpected situation and make quick decisions.
5. To be able to properly train subordinates in the positions they are best suited for.
6. To be able to keep good human relations among his subordinates.
7. To be able to keep good human relations between his subordinates and himself and to earn their respect and trust.

VII. THE PROFESSIONAL SUPERVISOR-EMPLOYEE RELATIONSHIP

There are two kinds of efficiency: one kind is only apparent and is produced in organizations through the exercise of mere discipline; this is but a simulation of the second, or true, efficiency which springs from spontaneous cooperation. If you are a manager, no matter how great or small your responsibility, it is your job, in the final analysis, to create and develop this involuntary cooperation among the people whom you supervise. For, no matter how powerful a combination of money, machines, and materials a company may have, this is a dead and sterile thing without a team of willing, thinking and articulate people to guide it.

The following 21 points are presented as indicative of the exemplary basic relationship that should exist between supervisor and employee:

1. Each person wants to be liked and respected by his fellow employee and wants to be treated with consideration and respect by his superior.
2. The most competent employee will make an error. However, in a unit where good relations exist between the supervisor and his employees, tenseness and fear do not exist. Thus, errors are not hidden or covered up and the efficiency of a unit is not impaired.
3. Subordinates resent rules, regulations, or orders that are unreasonable or unexplained.
4. Subordinates are quick to resent unfairness, harshness, injustices and favoritism.
5. An employee will accept responsibility if he knows that he will be complimented for a job well done, and not too harshly chastised for failure; that his supervisor will check the cause of the failure, and, if it was the supervisor's fault, he will assume the blame therefore. If it was the employee's fault, his supervisor will explain the correct method or means of handling the responsibility.

6. An employee wants to receive credit for a suggestion he has made, that is used. If a suggestion cannot be used, the employee is entitled to an explanation. The supervisor should not say "no" and close the subject.
7. Fear and worry slow up a worker's ability. Poor working environment can impair his physical and mental health. A good supervisor avoids forceful methods, threats and arguments to get a job done.
8. A forceful supervisor is able to train his employees individually and as a team, and is able to motivate them in the proper channels.
9. A mature supervisor is able to properly evaluate his subordinates and to keep them happy and satisfied.
10. A sensitive supervisor will never patronize his subordinates.
11. A worthy supervisor will respect his employees' confidences.
12. Definite and clear-cut responsibilities should be assigned to each executive.
13. Responsibility should always be coupled with corresponding authority.
14. No change should be made in the scope or responsibilities of a position without a definite understanding to that effect on the part of all persons concerned.
15. No executive or employee, occupying a single position in the organization, should be subject to definite orders from more than one source.
16. Orders should never be given to subordinates over the head of a responsible executive. Rather than do this, the officer in question should be supplanted.
17. Criticisms of subordinates should, whoever possible, be made privately, and in no case should a subordinate be criticized in the presence of executives or employees of equal or lower rank.
18. No dispute or difference between executives or employees as to authority or responsibilities should be considered too trivial for prompt and careful adjudication.
19. Promotions, wage changes, and disciplinary action should always be approved by the executive immediately superior to the one directly responsible.
20. No executive or employee should ever be required, or expected, to be at the same time an assistant to, and critic of, another.
21. Any executive whose work is subject to regular inspection should, whever practicable, be given the assistance and facilities necessary to enable him to maintain an independent check of the quality of his work.

VIII. MINI-TEXT IN SUPERVISION, ADMINISTRATION, MANAGEMENT, AND ORGANIZATION

A. BRIEF HIGHLIGHTS

Listed concisely and sequentially are major headings and important data in the field for quick recall and review.

1. *LEVELS OF MANAGEMENT*

Any organization of some size has several levels of management. In terms of a ladder the levels are:

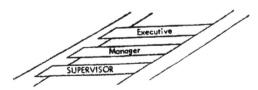

The first level is very important because it is the beginning point of management leadership.

2. WHAT THE SUPERVISOR MUST LEARN

A supervisor must learn to:
(1) Deal with people and their differences
(2) Get the job done through people
(3) Recognize the problems when they exist
(4) Overcome obstacles to good performance
(5) Evaluate the performance of people
(6) Check his own performance in terms of accomplishment

3. A DEFINITION OF SUPERVISOR

The term supervisor means any individual having authority, in the interests of the employer, to hire, transfer, suspend, lay-off, recall, promote, discharge, assign, reward, or discipline other employees or responsibility to direct them, or to adjust their grievances, or effectively to recommend such action, if, in connection with the foregoing, exercise of such authority is not of a merely routine or clerical nature but requires the use of independent judgment.

4. ELEMENTS OF THE TEAM CONCEPT

What is involved in teamwork? The component parts are:

(1) Members	(3) Goals	(5) Cooperation
(2) A leader	(4) Plans	(6) Spirit

5. PRINCIPLES OF ORGANIZATION

(1) A team member must know what his job is.
(2) Be sure that the nature and scope of a job are understood.
(3) Authority and responsibility should be carefully spelled out.
(4) A supervisor should be permitted to make the maximum number of decisions affecting his employees.
(5) Employees should report to only one supervisor.
(6) A supervisor should direct only as many employees as he can handle effectively.
(7) An organization plan should be flexible.
(8) Inspection and performance of work should be separate.
(9) Organizational problems should receive immediate attention.
(10) Assign work in line with ability and experience.

6. THE FOUR IMPORTANT PARTS OF EVERY JOB

(1) Inherent in every job is the *accountability* for results.
(2) A second set of factors in every job is *responsibilities.*
(3) Along with duties and responsibilities one must have the *authority* to act within certain limits without obtaining permission to proceed.
(4) No job exists in a vacuum. The supervisor is surrounded by key *relationships.*

7. PRINCIPLES OF DELEGATION

Where work is delegated for the first time, the supervisor should think in terms of these questions:
(1) Who is best qualified to do this?
(2) Can an employee improve his abilities by doing this?
(3) How long should an employee spend on this?
(4) Are there any special problems for which he will need guidance?
(5) How broad a delegation can I make?

8. PRINCIPLES OF EFFECTIVE COMMUNICATIONS

(1) Determine the media
(2) To whom directed?
(3) Identification and source authority
(4) Is communication understood?

9. PRINCIPLES OF WORK IMPROVEMENT

(1) Most people usually do only the work which is assigned to them
(2) Workers are likely to fit assigned work into the time available to perform it
(3) A good workload usually stimulates output
(4) People usually do their best work when they know that results will be reviewed or inspected
(5) Employees usually feel that someone else is responsible for conditions of work, workplace layout, job methods, type of tools/equipment, and other such factors
(6) Employees are usually defensive about their job security
(7) Employees have natural resistance to change
(8) Employees can support or destroy a supervisor
(9) A supervisor usually earns the respect of his people through his personal example of diligence and efficiency

10. AREAS OF JOB IMPROVEMENT

The areas of job improvement are quite numerous, but the most common ones which a supervisor can identify and utilize are:

(1) Departmental layout
(2) Flow of work
(3) Workplace layout
(4) Utilization of manpower
(5) Work methods
(6) Materials handling
(7) Utilization
(8) Motion economy

11. SEVEN KEY POINTS IN MAKING IMPROVEMENTS

(1) Select the job to be improved
(2) Study how it is being done now
(3) Question the present method
(4) Determine actions to be taken
(5) Chart proposed method
(6) Get approval and apply
(7) Solicit worker participation

12. CORRECTIVE TECHNIQUES OF JOB IMPROVEMENT

Specific Problems	General Improvement	Corrective Techniques
(1) Size of workload	(1) Departmental layout	(1) Study with scale model
(2) Inability to meet schedules	(2) Flow of work	(2) Flow chart study
(3) Strain and fatigue	(3) Work plan layout	(3) Motion analysis
(4) Improper use of men and skills	(4) Utilization of manpower	(4) Comparison of units produced to standard allowance
(5) Waste, poor quality, unsafe conditions	(5) Work methods	(5) Methods analysis
(6) Bottleneck conditions that hinder output	(6) Materials handling	(6) Flow chart & equipment study
(7) Poor utilization of equipment and machine	(7) Utilization of equipment	(7) Down time vs. running time
(8) Efficiency and productivity of labor	(8) Motion economy	(8) Motion analysis

13. A PLANNING CHECKLIST

(1) Objectives	(6) Resources	(11) Safety
(2) Controls	(7) Manpower	(12) Money
(3) Delegations	(8) Equipment	(13) Work
(4) Communications	(9) Supplies and materials	(14) Timing of improvements
(5) Resources	(10) Utilization of time	

14. FIVE CHARACTERISTICS OF GOOD DIRECTIONS

In order to get results, directions must be:

(1) Possible of accomplishment	(3) Related to mission	(5) Unmistakably clear
(2) Agreeable with worker interests	(4) Planned and complete	

15. TYPES OF DIRECTIONS

(1) Demands or direct orders	(3) Suggestion or implication
(2) Requests	(4) Volunteering

16. CONTROLS

A typical listing of the overall areas in which the supervisor should establish controls might be:

(1) Manpower	(3) Quality of work	(5) Time	(7) Money
(2) Materials	(4) Quantity of work	(6) Space	(8) Methods

17. ORIENTING THE NEW EMPLOYEE

(1) Prepare for him	(3) Orientation for the job
(2) Welcome the new employee	(4) Follow-up

18. CHECKLIST FOR ORIENTING NEW EMPLOYEES

	Yes	No
(1) Do your appreciate the feelings of new employees when they first report for work?	___	___
(2) Are you aware of the fact that the new employee must make a big adjustment to his job?	___	___
(3) Have you given him good reasons for liking the job and the organization?	___	___
(4) Have you prepared for his first day on the job?		
(5) Did you welcome him cordially and make him feel needed?		
(6) Did you establish rapport with him so that he feels free to talk and discuss matters with you?		
(7) Did you explain his job to him and his relationship to you?	___	___
(8) Does he know that his work will be evaluated periodically on a basis that is fair and objective?	___	___
(9) Did you introduce him to his fellow workers in such a way that they are likely to accept him?	___	___
(10) Does he know what employee benefits he will receive?	___	___
(11) Does he understand the importance of being on the job and what to do if he must leave his duty station?		
(12) Has he been impressed with the importance of accident prevention and safe practice?	___	___
(13) Does he generally know his way around the department?	___	___
(14) Is he under the guidance of a sponsor who will teach the right ways of doing things?	___	___
(15) Do you plan to follow-up so that he will continue to adjust successfully to his job?	___	___

19. *PRINCIPLES OF LEARNING*
      (1) Motivation   (2) Demonstration or explanation   (3) Practice

20. *CAUSES OF POOR PERFORMANCE*
      (1) Improper training for job
      (2) Wrong tools
      (3) Inadequate directions
      (4) Lack of supervisory follow-up
      (5) Poor communications
      (6) Lack of standards of performance
      (7) Wrong work habits
      (8) Low morale
      (9) Other

21. *FOUR MAJOR STEPS IN ON-THE-JOB INSTRUCTION*
      (1) Prepare the worker
      (2) Present the operation
      (3) Tryout performance
      (4) Follow-up

22. *EMPLOYEES WANT FIVE THINGS*
      (1) Security   (2) Opportunity   (3) Recognition   (4) Inclusion   (5) Expression

23. *SOME DON'TS IN REGARD TO PRAISE*
      (1) Don't praise a person for something he hasn't done
      (2) Don't praise a person unless you can be sincere
      (3) Don't be sparing in praise just because your superior withholds it from you
      (4) Don't let too much time elapse between good performance and recognition of it

24. *HOW TO GAIN YOUR WORKERS' CONFIDENCE*
    Methods of developing confidence include such things as:
      (1) Knowing the interests, habits, hobbies of employees
      (2) Admitting your own inadequacies
      (3) Sharing and telling of confidence in others
      (4) Supporting people when they are in trouble
      (5) Delegating matters that can be well handled
      (6) Being frank and straightforward about problems and working conditions
      (7) Encouraging others to bring their problems to you
      (8) Taking action on problems which impede worker progress

25. *SOURCES OF EMPLOYEE PROBLEMS*
    On-the-job causes might be such things as:
      (1) A feeling that favoritism is exercised in assignments
      (2) Assignment of overtime
      (3) An undue amount of supervision
      (4) Changing methods or systems
      (5) Stealing of ideas or trade secrets
      (6) Lack of interest in job
      (7) Threat of reduction in force
      (8) Ignorance or lack of communications
      (9) Poor equipment
     (10) Lack of knowing how supervisor feels toward employee
     (11) Shift assignments

    Off-the-job problems might have to do with:
      (1) Health   (2) Finances   (3) Housing   (4) Family

26. *THE SUPERVISOR'S KEY TO DISCIPLINE*

There are several key points about discipline which the supervisor should keep in mind:

(1) Job discipline is one of the disciplines of life and is directed by the supervisor.
(2) It is more important to correct an employee fault than to fix blame for it.
(3) Employee performance is affected by problems both on the job and off.
(4) Sudden or abrupt changes in behavior can be indications of important employee problems.
(5) Problems should be dealt with as soon as possible after they are identified.
(6) The attitude of the supervisor may have more to do with solving problems than the techniques of problem solving.
(7) Correction of employee behavior should be resorted to only after the supervisor is sure that training or counseling will not be helpful.
(8) Be sure to document your disciplinary actions.
(9) Make sure that you are disciplining on the basis of facts rather than personal feelings.
(10) Take each disciplinary step in order, being careful not to make snap judgments, or decisions based on impatience.

27. *FIVE IMPORTANT PROCESSES OF MANAGEMENT*

(1) Planning   (2) Organizing   (3) Scheduling
(4) Controlling   (5) Motivating

28. *WHEN THE SUPERVISOR FAILS TO PLAN*

(1) Supervisor creates impression of not knowing his job
(2) May lead to excessive overtime
(3) Job runs itself -- supervisor lacks control
(4) Deadlines and appointments missed
(5) Parts of the work go undone
(6) Work interrupted by emergencies
(7) Sets a bad example
(8) Uneven workload creates peaks and valleys
(9) Too much time on minor details at expense of more important tasks

29. *FOURTEEN GENERAL PRINCIPLES OF MANAGEMENT*

(1) Division of work
(2) Authority and responsibility
(3) Discipline
(4) Unity of command
(5) Unity of direction
(6) Subordination of individual interest to general interest
(7) Remuneration of personnel
(8) Centralization
(9) Scalar chain
(10) Order
(11) Equity
(12) Stability of tenure of personnel
(13) Initiative
(14) Esprit de corps

30. *CHANGE*

Bringing about change is perhaps attempted more often, and yet less well understood, than anything else the supervisor does. How do people generally react to change? (People tend to resist change that is imposed upon them by other individuals or circumstances.

Change is characteristic of every situation. It is a part of every real endeavor where the efforts of people are concerned.

A. Why do people resist change?
> People may resist change because of:
>> (1) Fear of the unknown
>> (2) Implied criticism
>> (3) Unpleasant experiences in the past
>> (4) Fear of loss of status
>> (5) Threat to the ego
>> (6) Fear of loss of economic stability

B. How can we best overcome the resistance to change?
> In initiating change, take these steps:
>> (1) Get ready to sell
>> (2) Identify sources of help
>> (3) Anticipate objections
>> (4) Sell benefits
>> (5) Listen in depth
>> (6) Follow up

B. BRIEF TOPICAL SUMMARIES

I. WHO/WHAT IS THE SUPERVISOR?

1. The supervisor is often called the "highest level employee and the lowest level manager."
2. A supervisor is a member of both management and the work group. He acts as a bridge between the two.
3. Most problems in supervision are in the area of human relations, or people problems.
4. Employees expect: Respect, opportunity to learn and to advance, and a sense of belonging, and so forth.
5. Supervisors are responsible for directing people and organizing work. Planning is of paramount importance.
6. A position description is a set of duties and responsibilities inherent to a given position.
7. It is important to keep the position description up-to-date and to provide each employee with his own copy.

II. THE SOCIOLOGY OF WORK

1. People are alike in many ways; however, each individual is unique.
2. The supervisor is challenged in getting to know employee differences. Acquiring skills in evaluating individuals is an asset.
3. Maintaining meaningful working relationships in the organization is of great importance.
4. The supervisor has an obligation to help individuals to develop to their fullest potential.
5. Job rotation on a planned basis helps to build versatility and to maintain interest and enthusiasm in work groups.
6. Cross training (job rotation) provides backup skills.
7. The supervisor can help reduce tension by maintaining a sense of humor, providing guidance to employees, and by making reasonable and timely decisions. Employees respond favorably to working under reasonably predictable circumstances.
8. Change is characteristic of all managerial behavior. The supervisor must adjust to changes in procedures, new methods, technological changes, and to a number of new and sometimes challenging situations.
9. To overcome the natural tendency for people to resist change, the supervisor should become more skillful in initiating change.

III. PRINCIPLES AND PRACTICES OF SUPERVISION

1. Employees should be required to answer to only one superior.
2. A supervisor can effectively direct only a limited number of employees, depending upon the complexity, variety, and proximity of the jobs involved.
3. The organizational chart presents the organization in graphic form. It reflects lines of authority and responsibility as well as interrelationships of units within the organization.
4. Distribution of work can be improved through an analysis using the "Work Distribution Chart."
5. The "Work Distribution Chart" reflects the division of work within a unit in understandable form.
6. When related tasks are given to an employee, he has a better chance of increasing his skills through training.
7. The individual who is given the responsibility for tasks must also be given the appropriate authority to insure adequate results.
8. The supervisor should delegate repetitive, routine work. Preparation of recurring reports, maintaining leave and attendance records are some examples.
9. Good discipline is essential to good task performance. Discipline is reflected in the actions of employees on the job in the absence of supervision.
10. Disciplinary action may have to be taken when the positive aspects of discipline have failed. Reprimand, warning, and suspension are examples of disciplinary action.
11. If a situation calls for a reprimand, be sure it is deserved and remember it is to be done in private.

IV. DYNAMIC LEADERSHIP

1. A style is a personal method or manner of exerting influence.
2. Authoritarian leaders often see themselves as the source of power and authority.
3. The democratic leader often perceives the group as the source of authority and power.
4. Supervisors tend to do better when using the pattern of leadership that is most natural for them.
5. Social scientists suggest that the effective supervisor use the leadership style that best fits the problem or circumstances involved.
6. All four styles -- telling, selling, consulting, joining -- have their place. Using one does not preclude using the other at another time.
7. The theory X point of view assumes that the average person dislikes work, will avoid it whenever possible, and must be coerced to achieve organizational objectives.
8. The theory Y point of view assumes that the average person considers work to be as natural as play, and, when the individual is committed, he requires little supervision or direction to accomplish desired objectives.
9. The leader's basic assumptions concerning human behavior and human nature affect his actions, decisions, and other managerial practices.
10. Dissatisfaction among employees is often present, but difficult to isolate. The supervisor should seek to weaken dissatisfaction by keeping promises, being sincere and considerate, keeping employees informed, and so forth.
11. Constructive suggestions should be encouraged during the natural progress of the work.

V. PROCESSES FOR SOLVING PROBLEMS

1. People find their daily tasks more meaningful and satisfying when they can improve them.
2. The causes of problems, or the key factors, are often hidden in the background. Ability to solve problems often involves the ability to isolate them from their backgrounds. There is some substance to the cliché that some persons "can't see the forest for the trees."
3. New procedures are often developed from old ones. Problems should be broken down into manageable parts. New ideas can be adapted from old ones.

4. People think differently in problem-solving situations. Using a logical, patterned approach is often useful. One approach found to be useful includes these steps:

    (a) Define the problem   (d) Weigh and decide
    (b) Establish objectives   (e) Take action
    (c) Get the facts   (f) Evaluate action

VI. TRAINING FOR RESULTS

1. Participants respond best when they feel training is important to them.
2. The supervisor has responsibility for the training and development of those who report to him.
3. When training is delegated to others, great care must be exercised to insure the trainer has knowledge, aptitude, and interest for his work as a trainer.
4. Training (learning) of some type goes on continually. The most successful supervisor makes certain the learning contributes in a productive manner to operational goals.
5. New employees are particularly susceptible to training. Older employees facing new job situations require specific training, as well as having need for development and growth opportunities.
6. Training needs require continuous monitoring.
7. The training officer of an agency is a professional with a responsibility to assist supervisors in solving training problems.
8. Many of the self-development steps important to the supervisor's own growth are equally important to the development of peers and subordinates. Knowledge of these is important when the supervisor consults with others on development and growth opportunities.

VII. HEALTH, SAFETY, AND ACCIDENT PREVENTION

1. Management-minded supervisors take appropriate measures to assist employees in maintaining health and in assuring safe practices in the work environment.
2. Effective safety training and practices help to avoid injury and accidents.
3. Safety should be a management goal. All infractions of safety which are observed should be corrected without exception.
4. Employees' safety attitude, training and instruction, provision of safe tools and equipment, supervision, and leadership are considered highly important factors which contribute to safety and which can be influenced directly by supervisors.
5. When accidents do occur they should be investigated promptly for very important reasons, including the fact that information which is gained can be used to prevent accidents in the future.

VIII. EQUAL EMPLOYMENT OPPORTUNITY

1. The supervisor should endeavor to treat all employees fairly, without regard to religion, race, sex, or national origin.
2. Groups tend to reflect the attitude of the leader. Prejudice can be detected even in very subtle form. Supervisors must strive to create a feeling of mutual respect and confidence in every employee.
3. Complete utilization of all human resources is a national goal. Equitable consideration should be accorded women in the work force, minority-group members, the physically and mentally handicapped, and the older employee. The important question is: "Who can do the job?"
4. Training opportunities, recognition for performance, overtime assignments, promotional opportunities, and all other personnel actions are to be handled on an equitable basis.

IX. IMPROVING COMMUNICATIONS

1. Communications is achieving understanding between the sender and the receiver of a message. It also means sharing information -- the creation of understanding.
2. Communication is basic to all human activity. Words are means of conveying meanings; however, real meanings are in people.
3. There are very practical differences in the effectiveness of one-way, impersonal, and two-way communications. Words spoken face-to-face are better understood. Telephone conversations are effective, but lack the rapport of person-to-person exchanges. The whole person communicates.
4. Cooperation and communication in an organization go hand in hand. When there is a mutual respect between people, spelling out rules and procedures for communicating is unnecessary.
5. There are several barriers to effective communications. These include failure to listen with respect and understanding, lack of skill in feedback, and misinterpreting the meanings of words used by the speaker. It is also common practice to listen to what we want to hear, and tune out things we do not want to hear.
6. Communication is management's chief problem. The supervisor should accept the challenge to communicate more effectively and to improve interagency and intra-agency communications.
7. The supervisor may often plan for and conduct meetings. The planning phase is critical and may determine the success or the failure of a meeting.
8. Speaking before groups usually requires extra effort. Stage fright may never disappear completely, but it can be controlled.

X. SELF-DEVELOPMENT

1. Every employee is responsible for his own self-development.
2. Toastmaster and toastmistress clubs offer opportunities to improve skills in oral communications.
3. Planning for one's own self-development is of vital importance. Supervisors know their own strengths and limitations better than anyone else.
4. Many opportunities are open to aid the supervisor in his developmental efforts, including job assignments; training opportunities, both governmental and non-governmental -- to include universities and professional conferences and seminars.
5. Programmed instruction offers a means of studying at one's own rate.
6. Where difficulties may arise from a supervisor's being away from his work for training, he may participate in televised home study or correspondence courses to meet his self-develop- ment needs.

XI. TEACHING AND TRAINING

A. The Teaching Process

Teaching is encouraging and guiding the learning activities of students toward established goals. In most cases this process consists in five steps: preparation, presentation, summarization, evaluation, and application.

1. Preparation

Preparation is twofold in nature; that of the supervisor and the employee.
Preparation by the supervisor is absolutely essential to success. He must know what, when, where, how, and whom he will teach. Some of the factors that should be considered are:

(1) The objectives	(5) Employee interest
(2) The materials needed	(6) Training aids
(3) The methods to be used	(7) Evaluation
(4) Employee participation	(8) Summarization

Employee preparation consists in preparing the employee to receive the material. Probably the most important single factor in the preparation of the employee is arousing and maintaining his interest. He must know the objectives of the training, why he is there, how the material can be used, and its importance to him.

2. Presentation

In presentation, have a carefully designed plan and follow it.
The plan should be accurate and complete, yet flexible enough to meet situations as they arise. The method of presentation will be determined by the particular situation and objectives.

3. Summary

A summary should be made at the end of every training unit and program. In addition, there may be internal summaries depending on the nature of the material being taught. The important thing is that the trainee must always be able to understand how each part of the new material relates to the whole.

4. Application

The supervisor must arrange work so the employee will be given a chance to apply new knowledge or skills while the material is still clear in his mind and interest is high. The trainee does not really know whether he has learned the material until he has been given a chance to apply it. If the material is not applied, it loses most of its value.

5. Evaluation

The purpose of all training is to promote learning. To determine whether the training has been a success or failure, the supervisor must evaluate this learning.

In the broadest sense evaluation includes all the devices, methods, skills, and techniques used by the supervisor to keep him self and the employees informed as to their progress toward the objectives they are pursuing. The extent to which the employee has mastered the knowledge, skills, and abilities, or changed his attitudes, as determined by the program objectives, is the extent to which instruction has succeeded or failed.

Evaluation should not be confined to the end of the lesson, day, or program but should be used continuously. We shall note later the way this relates to the rest of the teaching process.

B. Teaching Methods

A teaching method is a pattern of identifiable student and instructor activity used in presenting training material.

All supervisors are faced with the problem of deciding which method should be used at a given time.

As with all methods, there are certain advantages and disadvantages to each method.

1. Lecture

The lecture is direct oral presentation of material by the supervisor. The present trend is to place less emphasis on the trainer's activity and more on that of the trainee.

2. Discussion

Teaching by discussion or conference involves using questions and other techniques to arouse interest and focus attention upon certain areas, and by doing so creating a learning situation. This can be one of the most valuable methods because it gives the employees 'an opportunity to express their ideas and pool their knowledge.

3. Demonstration

The demonstration is used to teach how something works or how to do something. It can be used to show a principle or what the results of a series of actions will be. A well-staged demonstration is particularly effective because it shows proper methods of performance in a realistic manner.

4. Performance

Performance is one of the most fundamental of all learning techniques or teaching methods. The trainee may be able to tell how a specific operation should be performed but he cannot be sure he knows how to perform the operation until he has done so.

5. Which Method to Use

Moreover, there are other methods and techniques of teaching. It is difficult to use any method without other methods entering into it. In any learning situation a combination of methods is usually more effective than anyone method alone.

Finally, evaluation must be integrated into the other aspects of the teaching-learning process. It must be used in the motivation of the trainees; it must be used to assist in developing understanding during the training; and it must be related to employee application of the results of training.

This is distinctly the role of the supervisor.

BASIC FUNDAMENTALS OF A FINANCIAL STATEMENT

TABLE OF CONTENTS

BASIC FUNDAMENTALS
OF A FINANCIAL STATEMENT

COMMENTARY

The ability to read and understand a financial statement is a basic requirement for the accountant, auditor, account clerk, bookkeeper, bank examiner. budget examiner, and, of course, for the executive who must manage and administer departmental affairs.

FINANCIAL REPORTS

Are financial reports really as difficult as all that? Well, if you know they are not so difficult because you have worked with them before, this section will be of auxiliary help for you. However, if you find financial statements a bit murky, but realize their great importance to you, we ought to get along fine together. For "mathematics," all we'll use is fourth-grade arithmetic.

Accountants, like all other professionals, have developed a specialized vocabulary. Sometimes this is helpful and sometimes plain confusing (like their practice of calling the income account, "Statement of Profit and Loss," when it is bound to be one or the other). But there are really only a score or so technical terms that you will have to get straight in mind. After that is done, the whole foggy business will begin to clear and in no time at all you'll be able to talk as wisely as the next fellow.

BALANCE SHEET

Look at the sample balance sheet printed on page 2, and we'll have an insight into how it is put together. This particular report is neither the simplest that could be issued, nor the most complicated. It is a good average sample of the kind of report issued by an up-to-date manufacturing company.

Note particularly that the *balance sheet* represents the situation as it stood on one particular day, December 31, not the record of a year's operation. This balance sheet is broken into two parts: on the left are shown *ASSETS* and on the right *LIABILITIES.* Under the asset column, you will find listed the value of things the company owns or are owed to the company. Under liabilities, are listed the things the company owes to others, plus reserves, surplus, and the stated value of the stockholders' interest in the company.

One frequently hears the comment, "Well, I don't see what a good balance sheet is anyway, because the assets and liabilities are always the same whether the company is successful or not."

It is true that they always balance and, by itself, a balance sheet doesn't tell much until it is analyzed. Fortunately, we can make a balance sheet tell its story without too much effort -- often an extremely revealing story, particularly, if we compare the records of several years. ASSETS The first notation on the asset side of the balance sheet is *CURRENT* ASSETS (item 1). In general, current assets include cash and things that can be turned into cash in a hurry, or that, in the normal course of business, will be turned into cash in the reasonably near future, usually within a year.

Item 2 on our sample sheet is *CASH.* Cash is just what you would expect -bills and silver in the till and money on deposit in the bank.

UNITED STATES GOVERNMENT SECURITIES is item 3. The general practice is to show securities listed as current assets at cost or market value, whichever is lower. The figure, for all reasonable purposes, represents the amount by which total cash could be easily increased if the company wanted to sell these securities.

The next entry is *ACCOUNTS RECEIVABLE* (item 4). Here we find the total amount of money owed to the company by its regular business creditors and collectable within the next year. Most of the money is owed to the company by its customers for goods that the company delivered on credit. If this were a department store instead of a manufacturer, what you owed the store on your charge account would be included here. Because some people fail to pay their bills, the company sets up a reserve for doubtful accounts, which it subtracts from all the money owed.

THE ABC MANUFACTURING COMPANY, INC.
CONSOLIDATED BALANCE SHEET – DECEMBER 31

Item			Item			
1. CURRENT ASSETS			16. CURRENT LIABILITIES			
2. Cash			17. Accts. Payable		$ 300,000	
3. U.S. Government Securities			18. Accrued Taxes		800,000	
4. Accounts Receivable (less reserves)	2,000,000		19. Accrued Wages, Interest and Other Expenses		370,000	
5. Inventories (at lower of cost or market)	2,000,000		20. Total Current Liabilities		$1,470,000	
6. Total Current Assets	$7,000,000		21. FIRST MORTGAGE SINK-ING FUND BONDS, 3 1/2% DUE 2002		2,000,000	
7. INVESTMENT IN AFFIL-IATED COMPANY Not consolidated (at cost, not in ex-cess of net assets)	200,000		22. RESERVE FOR CON-TINGENCIES		200,000	
8. OTHER INVESTMENTS At cost, less than market	100,000		23. CAPITAL STOCK:			
9. PLANT IMPROVEMENT FUND	550,000		24. 5% Preferred Stock (author-ized and issued 10,000 shares of $100 par value)	$1,000,000		
10. PROPERTY, PLANT AND EQUIPMENT: Cost $8,000,000			25. Common stock (author-ized and issued 400,000 shares of no par value)	1,000,000		
11. Less Reserve for Deprecia-tion 5,000,000					2,000,000	
12. NET PROPERTY	3,000,000		26. SURPLUS:			
13. PREPAYMENTS	50,000		27. Earned	3,530,000		
14. DEFERRED CHARGES	100,000		28. Capital (arising from sale of common capital stock at price in excess of stated value	1,900,000		
15. PATENTS AND GOODWILL	100,000				5,430,000	
TOTAL	$11,100,000		TOTAL		$11,100,000	

Item 5, *INVENTORIES,* is the value the company places on the supplies it owns. The inventory of a manufacturer may contain raw materials that it uses in making the things it sells, partially finished goods in process of manufacture and, finally, completed merchandise that it is ready to sell. Several methods are used to arrive at the value placed on these various items. The most common is to value them at their cost or present market value, whichever is lower. You can be reasonably confident, however, that the figure given is an honest and significant one for the particular industry if the report is certified by a reputable firm of public accountants.

Next on the asset side is *TOTAL CURRENT ASSETS* (item 6). This is an extremely important figure when used in connection with other items in the report, which we will come to presently. Then we will discover how to make total current assets tell their story.

INVESTMENT IN AFFILIATED COMPANY (item 7) represents the cost to our parent company of the capital stock of its *subsidiary* or affiliated company. A subsidiary is simply one company that is controlled by another. Most corporations that own other companies outright, lump the figures in a *CONSOLIDATED BALANCE SHEET.* This means that, under cash, for example, one would find a total figure that represented *all* of the cash of the parent company and of its wholly owned subsidiary. This is a perfectly reasonable procedure because, in the last analysis, all of the money is controlled by the same persons.

Our typical company shows that it has *OTHER INVESTMENTS* (item 8), in addition to its affiliated company. Sometimes good marketable securities other than Government bonds are carried as current assets, but the more conservative practice is to list these other security holdings separately. If they have been bought as a permanent investment, they would always be shown by themselves. "At cost, less than market" means that our company paid $100,000 for these other investments, but they are now worth more.

Among our assets is a *PLANT IMPROVEMENT FUND* (item 9). Of course, this item does not appear in all company balance sheets, but is typical of *special funds* that companies set up for one purpose or another. For example, money set aside to pay off part of the bonded debt of a company might be segregated into a special fund. The money our directors have put aside to improve the plant would often be invested in Government bonds.

FIXED ASSETS

The next item (10), is *PROPERTY, PLANT AND EQUIPMENT,* but it might just as well be labeled *Fixed Assets* as these terms are used more or less interchangeably. Under item 10, the report gives the value of land, buildings, and machinery and such movable things as trucks, furniture, and hand tools. Historically, probably more sins were committed against this balance sheet item than any other.

In olden days, cattlemen used to drive their stock to market in the city. It was a common trick to stop outside of town, spread out some salt for the cattle to make them thirsty and then let them drink all the water they could hold. When they were weighed for sale, the cattlemen would collect cash for the water the stock had drunk. Business buccaneers, taking the cue from their farmer friends, would often "write up" the value of their fixed assets. In other words, they would increase the value shown on the balance sheet, making the capital stock appear to be worth a lot more than it was. *Watered stock* proved a bad investment for most stockholders. The practice has, fortunately, been stopped, though it took major financial reorganizations to squeeze the water out of some securities.

The most common practice today is to list fixed assets at cost. Often, there is no ready market for most of the things that fall under this heading, so it is not possible to give market value. A good report will tell what is included under fixed assets and how it has been valued. If the value has been increased by *write-up* or decreased by *write-down,* a footnote explanation is usually given. A *write-up* might occur, for instance, if the value of real estate increased substantially. A *write-down* might follow the invention of a new machine that put an important part of the company's equipment out of date.

DEPRECIATION

Naturally, all of the fixed property of a company will wear out in time (except, of course, non-agricultural land). In recognition of this fact, companies set up a *RESERVE FOR DEPRECIATION* (item 11). If a truck costs $4,000 and is expected to last four years, it will be depreciated at the rate of $1,000 a year.

Two other terms also frequently occur in connection with depreciation -*depletion* and *obsolescence.* Companies may lump depreciation, depletion, and obsolescence under a single title, or list them separately.

Depletion is a term used primarily by mining and oil companies (or any of the so-called extractive industries). Depletion means exhaust or use up. As the oil or other natural resource is used up, a reserve is set up, to compensate for the natural wealth the company no longer owns. This reserve is set up in recognition of the fact that, as the company sells its natural product, it must get back not only the cost of extracting but also the original cost of the natural resource.

Obsolescence represents the loss in value because a piece of property has gone out of date before it wore out. Airplanes are modern examples of assets that tend to get behind the times long before the parts wear out. (Women and husbands will be familiar with the speed at which ladies' hats "obsolesce.")

In our sample balance sheet we have placed the reserve for depreciation under fixed assets and then subtracted, giving us *NET PROPERTY* (item 12), which we add into the asset column. Sometimes, companies put the reserve for depreciation in the liability column. As you can see, the effect is just the same whether it is *subtracted* from assets or *added* to liabilities.

The manufacturer, whose balance sheet we use, rents a New York showroom and pays his rent yearly, in advance. Consequently, he has listed under assets *PREPAYMENTS* (item 13). This is listed as an asset because he has paid for the use of the showroom, but has not yet received the benefit from its use. The use is something coming to the firm in the following year and, hence, is an asset. The dollar value of this asset will decrease by one-twelfth each month during the coming year.

DEFERRED CHARGES (item 14) represents a type of expenditure similar to prepayment. For example, our manufacturer brought out a new product last year, spending $100,000 introducing it to the market. As the benefit from this expenditure will be returned over months or even years to come, the manufacturer did not think it reasonable to charge the full expenditure against costs during the year. He has *deferred* the charges and will write them off gradually.

INTANGIBLES

The last entry in our asset column is *PATENTS AND GOODWILL* (item 15). If our company were a young one, set up to manufacture some new patented prod uct, it would probably carry its patents at a substantial figure. In fact, *intangibles* of both old and new companies are often of great but generally unmeasurable worth.

Company practice varies considerably in assigning value to intangibles. Procter & Gamble, despite the tremendous goodwill that has been built up for IVORY SOAP, has reduced all of its intangibles to the nominal $1. Some of the big cigarette companies, on the contrary, place a high dollar value on the goodwill their brand names enjoy. Companies that spend a good deal for research and the development of new products are more inclined than others to reflect this fact in the value assigned to patents, license agreements, etc.

LIABILITIES

The liability side of the balance sheet appears a little deceptive at first glance. Several of the entries simply don't sound like liabilities by any ordinary definition of the term.

The first term on the liability side of any balance sheet is usually CURRENT LIABILITIES (item 16). This is a companion to the Current Assets item across the page and includes all debts that fall due within the next year. The relation between current assets and current liabilities is one of the most revealing things to be gotten from the balance sheet, but we will go into that quite thoroughly later on.

ACCOUNTS PAYABLE (item 17) represents the money that the company owes to its ordinary business creditors -- unpaid bills for materials, supplies, insurance, and the like. Many companies itemize the money they owe in a much more detailed fashion than we have done, but, as you will see, the totals are the most interesting thing to us.

Item 18, ACCRUED TAXES, is the tax bill that the company estimates it still owes for the past year. We have lumped all taxes in our balance sheet, as many companies do. However, sometimes you will find each type of tax given separately. If the detailed procedure is followed, the description of the tax is usually quite sufficient to identify the separate items.

Accounts Payable was defined as the money the company owed to its regular business creditors. The company also owes, on any given day, wages to its own employees; interest to its bondholders and to banks from which it may have borrowed money; fees to its attorneys; pensions, etc. These are all totaled under ACCRUED WAGES, INTEREST AND OTHER EXPENSES (item 19).

TOTAL CURRENT LIABILITIES (item 20) is just the sum of everything that the company owed on December 31 and which must be paid sometime in the next twelve months.

It is quite clear that all of the things discussed above are liabilities. The rest of the entries on the liability side of the balance sheet, however, do not seem at first glance to be liabilities.

Our balance sheet shows that the company, on December 31, had $2,000,000 of 3 1/2 percent First Mortgage BONDS outstanding (item 21). Legally, the money received by a company when it sells bonds is considered a loan to the company. Therefore, it is obvious that the company owes to the bondholders an amount equal to the face value or the call price of the bonds it has outstanding. The call price is a figure usually larger than the face value of the bonds at which price the company can call the bonds in from the bondholders and pay them off before they ordinarily fall due. The date that often occurs as part of the name of a bond is the date at which the company has promised to pay off the loan from the bondholders.

RESERVES

The next heading, RESERVE FOR CONTINGENCIES (item 22), sounds more like an asset than a liability. "My reserves," you might say, "are dollars in the bank, and dollars in the bank are assets."

No one would deny that you have something there. In fact, the corporation treasurer also has his reserve for contingencies balanced by either cash or some kind of unspecified investment on the asset side of the ledger. His reason for setting up a reserve on the liability side of the balance sheet is a precaution against making his financial position seem better than it is. He decided that the company might have to pay out this money during the coming year if certain things happened. If he did not set up the "reserve," his surplus would appear larger by an amount equal to his reserve.

A very large reserve for contingencies or a sharp increase in this figure from the previous year should be examined closely by the investor. Often, in the past, companies tried to hide their true earnings by transferring funds into a contingency reserve. As a reserve looks somewhat like a true liability, stockholders were confused about the real value of their securities. When a reserve is not set up for protection against some very probable loss or expenditure, it should be considered by the investor as part of surplus.

CAPITAL STOCK

Below reserves there is a major heading, *CAPITAL STOCK* (item 23). Companies may have one type of security outstanding, or they may have a dozen. All of the issues that represent shares of ownership are capital, regardless of what they are called on the balance sheet -- preferred stock, preference stock, common stock, founders' shares, capital stock, or something else.

Our typical company has one issue of 5 per cent *PREFERRED STOCK* (item 24). It is called *preferred* because those who own it have a right to dividends and assets before the *common* stockholders -- that is, the holders are in a preferred position as owners. Usually, preferred stockholders do not have a voice in company affairs unless the company fails to pay them dividends at the promised rate. Their rights to dividends are almost always *cumulative*. This simply means that all past dividends must be paid before the other stockholders can receive anything. Preferred stockholders are not creditors of the company so it cannot properly be said that the company *owes* them the value of their holdings. However, in case the company decided to go out of business, preferred stockholders would have a prior claim on anything that was left in the company treasury after all of the creditors, including the bondholders, were paid off. In practice, this right does not always mean much, but it does explain why the book value of their holdings is carried as a liability.

COMMON STOCK (item 25) is simple enough as far as definition is concerned it represents the rights of the ordinary owner of the company. Each company has as many owners as it has stockholders. The proportion of the company that each stockholder owns is determined by the number of shares he has. However, neither the book value of a no-par common stock, nor the par value of an issue that has a given par, can be considered as representing either the original sale price, the market value, or what would be left for the stockholders if the company were liquidated.

A profitable company will seldom be dissolved. Once things have taken such a turn that dissolution appears desirable, the stated value of the stock is generally nothing but a fiction. Even if the company is profitable as a going institution, once it ceases to function even its tangible assets drop in value because there is not usually a ready market for its inventory of raw materials and semi-finished goods, or its plant and machinery.

SURPLUS

The last major heading on the liability side of the balance sheet is *SURPLUS* (item 26). The surplus, of course, is not a liability in the popular sense at all. It represents, on our balance sheet, the difference between the stated value of our common stock and the net assets behind the stock.

Two different kinds of surplus frequently appear on company balance sheets, and our company has both kinds. The first type listed is *EARNED* surplus (item 27). Earned surplus is roughly similar to your own savings. To the corporation, earned surplus is that part of net income which has not been paid to stockholders as dividends. It still *belongs* to you, but the directors have decided that it is best for the company and the stockholders to keep it in the business. The surplus may be invested in the plant just as you might invest part of your savings in your home. It may also be in cash or securities.

In addition to the earned surplus, our company also has a *CAPITAL* surplus (item 28) of $1,900.00, which the balance sheet explains arose from selling the stock at a higher cost per share than is given as its stated value. A little arithmetic shows that the stock is carried on the books at $2.50 a share while the capital surplus amounts to $4.75 a share. From this we know that the company actually received an average of $7.25 net a share for the stock when it was sold.

WHAT DOES THE BALANCE SHEET SHOW?

Before we undertake to analyze the balance sheet figures, a word on just what an investor can expect to learn is in order. A generation or more ago, before present accounting standards had gained wide acceptance, considerable imagination went into the preparation of balance sheets. This, naturally, made the public skeptical of financial reports. Today, there is no substantial ground for skepticism. The certified public accountant, the listing requirements of the national stock exchanges, and the regulations of the Securities and Exchange Commission have, for all practical purposes, removed the grounds for doubting the good faith of financial reports.

The investor, however, is still faced with the task of determining the significance of the figures. As we have already seen, a number of items are based, to a large degree, upon estimates, while others are, of necessity, somewhat arbitrary.

NET WORKING CAPITAL

There is one very important thing that we can find from the balance sheet and accept with the full confidence that we know what we are dealing with. That is net working capital, sometimes simply called working capital.

On the asset side of our balance sheet we have added up all of the current assets and show the total as item 6. On the liability side, item 20 gives the total of current liabilities. *Net working capital* or *net current assets* is the difference left after subtracting current liabilities from current assets. If you consider yourself an investor rather than a speculator, you should always insist that any company in which you invest have a comfortable amount of working capital. The ability of a company to meet its obligations with ease, expand its volume as business expands and take advantage of opportunities as they present themselves, is, to an important degree, determined by its working capital.

Probably the question in your mind is: *"Just what does 'comfortable amount' of working capital mean?"* Well, there are several methods used by analysts to judge whether a particular company has a sound working capital position. The first rough test for an industrial company is to compare the working capital figure with the current liability total. Most analysts say that minimum safety requires that net working capital at least equal current liabilities. Or, put another way, that current assets should be at least twice as large as current liabilities.

There are so many different kinds of companies, however, that this test requires a great deal of modification if it is to be really helpful in analyzing companies in different industries. To help you interpret the *current position* of a company in which you are considering investing, the *current ratio* is more helpful than the dollar total of working capital. The current ratio is current assets divided by current liabilities.

In addition to working capital and current ratio, there are two other ways of testing the adequacy of the current position. *Net quick assets* provide a rigorous and important test of a company's ability to meet its current obligations. Net quick assets are found by taking total current assets (item 6) and subtracting the value of inventories (item 5). A well-fixed industrial company should show a reasonable excess of quick assets over current liabilities..

Finally, many analysts say that a good industrial company should have at least as much working capital (current assets less current liabilities) as the total book value of its bonds and preferred stock. In other words, current liabilities, bonded debt, and preferred stock *altogether* should not exceed the current assets.

INVENTORY AND INVENTORY TURNOVER

In the recent past, there has been much talk of inventories. Many commentators have said that these carry a serious danger to company earnings if management allows them to increase too much. Of course, this has always been true, but present high prices have made everyone more inventory-conscious than usual.

There are several dangers in a large inventory position. In the first place, a sharp drop in price may cause serious losses; also, a large inventory may indicate that the company has accumulated a big supply of unsalable merchandise. The question still remains, however: *"What do we mean by large inventory?"*

As you certainly realize, an inventory is large or small only in terms of the yearly turnover and the type of business. We can discover the annual turnover of our sample company by dividing inventories (item 5) into total annual sales (item "a" on the income account).

It is also interesting to compare the value of the inventory of a company being studied with total current assets. Again, however, there is considerable variation between different types of companies, so that the relationship becomes significant only when compared with similar companies.

NET BOOK VALUE OF SECURITIES

There is one other very important thing that can be gotten from the balance sheet, and that is the net book or equity value of the company's securities. We can calculate the net book value of each of the three types of securities our company has outstanding by a little very simple arithmetic. *Book value means the value at which something is carried on the books of the company.*

The full rights of the bondholders come before any of the rights of the stockholders, so, to find the net book value or net tangible assets backing up the bonds we add together the balance sheet value of the bonds, preferred stock, common stock, reserve, and surplus. This gives us a total of $9,630,000. (We would not include contingency reserve if we were reasonably sure the contingency was going to arise, but, as general reserves are often equivalent to surplus, it is, usually, best to treat the reserve just as though it were surplus.) However, part of this value represents the goodwill and patents carried at $100,000, which is not a tangible item, so, to be conservative, we subtract this amount, leaving $9,530,000 as the total net book value of the bonds. This is equivalent to $4,765 for each $1,000 bond, a generous figure. To calculate the net book value of the preferred stock, we must eliminate the face value of the bonds, and then, following the same procedure, add the value of the preferred stock, common stock, reserve, and surplus, and subtract goodwill. This gives us a total net book value for the preferred stock of $7,530,000 or $753 for each share of $100 par value preferred. This is also very good coverage for the preferred stock, but we must examine current earnings before becoming too enthusiastic about the *value* of any security.

The net book value of the common stock, while an interesting figure, is not so important as the coverage on the senior securities. In case of liquidation, there is seldom much left for the common stockholders because of the normal loss in value of company assets when they are put up for sale, as mentioned before. The book value figure, however, does give us a basis for comparison with other companies. Comparisons of net book value over a period of years also show us if the company is a soundly growing one or, on the other hand, is losing ground. Earnings, however, are our important measure of common stock values, as we will see shortly.

The net book value of the common stock is found by adding the stated value of the common stock, reserves, and surplus and then subtracting patents and goodwill. This gives us a total net book value of $6,530,000. As there are 400,000 shares of common outstanding, each share has a net book value of $16.32. You must be careful not to be misled by book value figures, particularly of common stock. Profitable companies (Coca-Cola, for example) often show a very low net book value and very substantial earnings. Railroads, on the other hand, may show a high book value for their common stock but have such low or irregular earnings that the market price of the stock is much less than its apparent book value. Banks, insurance companies, and investment -trusts are exceptions to what we have said about common stock net book value. As their assets are largely liquid (i.e., cash, accounts receivable, and marketable securities), the book value of their common stock sometimes indicates its value very accurately.

PROPORTION OF BONDS, PREFERRED AND COMMON STOCK

Before investing, you will want to know the proportion of each kind of security issued by the company you are considering. A high proportion of bonds reduces the attractiveness of both the preferred and common stock, while too large an amount of preferred detracts from the value of the common.

The *bond ratio* is found by dividing the face value of the bonds (item 21), or $2,000,000, by the total value of the bonds, preferred stock, common stock, reserve, and surplus, or $9,630,000. This shows that bonds amount to about 20 per cent of the total of bonds, capital, and surplus.

The *preferred stock ratio* is found in the same way, only we divide the stated value of the preferred stock by the total of the other five items. Since we have half as much preferred stock as we have bonds, the preferred ratio is roughly 10.

Naturally, the *common stock ratio* will be the difference between 100 per cent and the totals of the bonds and preferred, or 70 per cent in our sample company. You will want to remember that the most valuable method of determining the common stock ratio is in combination with reserve and surplus. The surplus, as we have noted, is additional backing for the common stock and usually represents either original funds paid in to the company in excess of the stated value of the common stock (capital surplus), or undistributed earnings (earned surplus).

Most investment analysts carefully examine industrial companies that have more than about a quarter of their capitalization represented by bonds, while common stock should total at least as much as all senior securities (bonds and preferred issues). When this is not the case, companies often find it difficult to raise new capital. Banks don't like to lend them money because of the already large debt, and it is sometimes difficult to sell common stock because of all the bond interest or preferred dividends that must be paid before anything is available for the common stockholder.

Railroads and public utility companies are exceptions to most of the rules of thumb that we use in discussing The ABC Manufacturing Company, Inc. Their situation is different because of the tremendous amounts of money they have invested in their fixed assets., their small inventories and the ease with which they can collect their receivables. Senior securities of railroads and utility companies frequently amount to more than half of their capitalization. Speculators often interest themselves in companies that have a high proportion of debt or preferred stock because of the *leverage factor*. A simple illustration will show why. Let us take, for example, a company with $10,000,000 of 4 per cent bonds outstanding. If the company is earning $440,000 before bond interest, there will be only $40,000 left for the common stock ($10,000,000 at 4% equals $400,000). However, an increase of only 10 per cent in earnings (to $484,000) will leave $84,000 for common stock dividends, or an increase of more than 100 per cent. If there is only a small common issue, the increase in earnings per share would appear very impressive.

You have probably already noticed that a decline of 10 per cent in earnings would not only wipe out everything available for the common stock, but result in the company being unable to cover its full interest on its bonds without dipping into surplus. This is the great danger of so-called high leverage stocks and also illustrates the fundamental weakness of companies that have a disproportionate amount of debt or preferred stock. Investors would do well to steer clear of them. Speculators, however, will continue to be fascinated by the market opportunities they offer.

THE INCOME ACCOUNT

The fundamental soundness of a company, as shown by its balance sheet, is important to investors, but of even greater interest is the record of its operation. Its financial structure shows much of its ability to weather storms and pick up speed when times are good. It is the income record, however, that shows us how a company is actually doing and gives us our best guide to the future.

The *Consolidated Income and Earned Surplus* account of our company is stated on the next page. Follow the items given there and we will find out just how our company earned its money, what it did with its earnings, and what it all means in terms of our three classes of securities. We have used a combined income and surplus account because that is the form most frequently followed by industrial companies. However, sometimes the two statements are given separately. Also, a variety of names are used to describe this same part of the financial report. Sometimes it is called profit and loss account, sometimes *record of earnings,* and, often, simply *income account.* They are all the same thing.

The details that you will find on different income statements also vary a great deal. Some companies show only eight or ten separate items, while others will give a page or more of closely spaced entries that break down each individual type of revenue or cost. We have tried to strike a balance between extremes; give the major items that are in most income statements, omitting details that are only interesting to the expert analyst.

The most important source of revenue always makes up the first item on the income statement. In our company, it is *Net Sales* (item "a"). If it were a railroad or a utility instead of a manufacturer, this item would be called *gross revenues.* In any case, it represents the money paid into the company by its customers. Net sales are given to show that the figure represents the amount of money actually received after allowing for discounts and returned goods.

Net sales or gross revenues, you will note, is given before any kind of miscellaneous revenue that might have been received from investments, the sale of company property, tax refunds, or the like. A well-prepared income statement is always set up this way so that the stockholder can estimate the success of the company in fulfilling its major job of selling goods or service. If this were not so, you could not tell whether the company was really losing or making money on its operations, particularly over the last few years when tax rebates and other unusual things have often had great influence on final net income figures.

COST OF SALES

A general heading, *Cost of Sales, Expenses and Other Operating Charges* (item "b") is characteristic of a manufacturing company, but a utility company or railroad would call all of these things *operating expenses.*

The most important subdivision is *Cost of Goods Sold* (item "c"). Included under cost of goods sold are all of the expenses that go directly into the manufacture of the products the company sells -- raw materials, wages, freight, power, and rent. We have lumped these expenses together, as many companies do. Sometimes, however, you will find each item listed separately. Analyzing a detailed income account is a pretty technical operation and had best be left to the expert.

The ABC Manufacturing Company, Inc.
CONSOLIDATED INCOME AND EARNED SURPLUS
For the Year Ended December 31

Item			
a.	Sales		$10,000,000
b.	COST OF SALES, EXPENSES AND OTHER OPERATING CHARGES:		
c.	Cost of Goods Sold	$7,000,000	
d.	Selling, Administrative & Gen. Expenses	500,000	
e.	Depreciation	200,000	
f.	Maintenance and Repairs	400,000	
g.	Taxes (Other than Federal Inc. Taxes)	300,000	8,400,000
h.	NET PROFIT FROM OPERATIONS		$ 1,600,000
i.	OTHER INCOME:		
j.	Royalties and Dividends	$ 250,000	
k.	Interest	25,000	275,000
l.	TOTAL		$ 1,875,000
m.	INTEREST CHARGES:		
n.	Interest on Funded Debt	$ 70,000	
o.	Other Interest	20,000	90,000
p.	NET INCOME BEFORE PROVISION FOR FED. INCOME TAXES		$ 1,785,000
q.	PROVISION FOR FEDERAL INCOME TAXES		678,300
r.	NET INCOME		$ 1,106,700
s.	DIVIDENDS:		
t.	Preferred Stock - $5.00 Per Share	$ 50,000	
u.	Common Stock - $1.00 Per Share	400,000	
v.	PROVISION FOR CONTINGENCIES	200,000	650,000
w.	BALANCE CARRIED TO EARNED SURPLUS		$ 456,700
x.	EARNED SURPLUS – JANUARY 1		3,073,000
y.	EARNED SURPLUS – DECEMBER 31		$ 3,530,000

We have shown separately, opposite "d," the *Selling, Administrative and General Expenses* of the past year. Unfortunately, there is little uniformity among companies in their treatment of these important non-manufacturing costs. Our figure includes the expenses of management; that is, executive salaries and clerical costs; commissions and salaries paid to salesmen; advertising expenses, and the like.

Depreciation ("e") shows us the amount that the company transferred from income during the year to the depreciation reserve that we ran across before as item "11" on the balance sheet (page 2). Depreciation must be charged against income unless the company is going to live on its own fat, something that no company can do for long and stay out of bankruptcy.

MAINTENANCE

Maintenance and Repairs (item "f") represents the money spent to keep the plant in good operating order. For example, the truck that we mentioned under depreciation must be kept running day by day. The cost of new tires, recharging the battery, painting and mechanical repairs are all maintenance costs. Despite this day-to-day work on the truck, the company must still provide for the time when it wears out -- hence, the reserve for depreciation.

You can readily understand from your own experience the close connection between maintenance and depreciation. If you do not take good care of your own car, you will have to buy a new one sooner than you would had you maintained it well. Corporations face the same problem with all of their equipment. If they do not do a good job of maintenance, much more will have to be set aside for depreciation to replace the abused tools and property.

Taxes are always with us. A profitable company always pays at least two types of taxes. One group of taxes are paid without regard to profits, and include real estate taxes, excise taxes, social security, and the like (item "g"). As these payments are a direct part of the cost of doing business, they must be included before we can determine the *Net Profit From Operations* (item "h").

Net Profit from Operations (sometimes called *gross profit)* tells us what the company made from manufacturing and selling its products. It is an interesting figure to investors because it indicates .how efficiently and successfully the company operates in its primary purpose as a creator of wealth. As a glance at the income account will tell you, there are still several other items to be deducted before the stockholder can hope to get anything. You can also easily imagine that for many companies these other items may spell the difference between profit and loss. For these reasons, we use net profit from operations as an indicator of progress in manufacturing and merchandising efficiency, not as a judge of the investment quality of securities.

Miscellaneous Income not connected with the major purpose of the company is generally listed after net profit from operations. There are quite a number of ways that corporations increase their income, including interest and dividends on securities they own, fees for special services performed, royalties on patents they allow others to use, and tax refunds. Our income statement shows *Other Income* as item "i," under which is shown income from *Royalties and Dividends* (item "j"), and, as a separate entry, *Interest* (item "k") which the company received from its bond investments. The *Total* of other income (item t1t?) shows us how much The ABC Manufacturing Company received from so-called *outside activities.* Corporations with diversified interests often receive tremendous amounts of *other income.*

INTEREST CHARGES

There is one other class of expenses that must be deducted from our income before we can determine the base on which taxes are paid, and that is *Interest Charges* (item "m"). As our company has $2,000,000 worth of 3 1/2 per cent bonds outstanding, it will pay *Interest on Funded Debt* of $70,000 (item "n"). During the year, the company also borrowed money from the bank, on which it, of course, paid interest, shown as *Other Interest* (item "o").

Net Income Before Provision for Federal Income Taxes (item "p") is an interesting figure for historical comparison. It shows us how profitable the company was in all of its various operations. A comparison of this entry over a period of years will enable you to see how well the company had been doing as a business institution before the Government stepped in for its share of net earnings. Federal taxes have varied so much in recent years that earnings before taxes are often a real help in judging business progress.

A few paragraphs back we mentioned that a profitable corporation pays two general types of taxes. We have already discussed those that are paid without reference to profits. *Provision for Federal Income Taxes* (item "q") is ordinarily figured on the total income of the company after normal business expenses, and so appears on our income account below these charges. Bond interest, for example, as it is payment on a loan, is deducted beforehand. Preferred and common stock dividends, which are *profits* that go to owners of the company, come after all charges and taxes.

NET INCOME

After we have deducted all of our expenses and income taxes from total income, we get *Net Income* (item "r"). Net income is the most interesting figure of all to the investor. Net income is the amount available to pay dividends on the preferred and common stock. From the balance sheet, we have learned a good deal about the company's stability and soundness of structure; from net profit from operations, we judge whether the company is improving in industrial efficiency. Net income tells us whether the securities of the company are likely to be a profitable investment.

The figure given for a single year is not nearly all of the story, however. As we have noted before, the historical record is usually more important than the figure for any given year. This is just as true of net income as any other item. So many things change from year to year that care must be taken not to draw hasty conclusions. During the war, Excess Profits Taxes had a tremendous effect on the earnings of many companies. In the next few years, *carryback tax credits* allowed some companies to show a net profit despite the fact that they had operated at a loss. Even net income can be a misleading figure unless one examines it carefully. A rough and easy way of judging how *sound* a figure it is would be to compare it with previous years.

The investor in stocks has a vital interest in *Dividends* (item "s"). The first dividend that our company must pay is that on its *Preferred Stock* (item "t"). Some companies will even pay preferred dividends out of earned surplus accumulated in the past if the net income is not large enough, but such a company is skating on thin ice unless the situation is most unusual.

The directors of our company decided to pay dividends totaling $400,000 on the *Common Stock,* or $1 a share (item "u"). As we have noted before, the amount of dividends paid is not determined by net income, but by a decision of the stockholders' representatives - the company's directors. Common dividends, just like preferred dividends, can be paid out of surplus if there is little or no net income. Sometimes companies do this if they have a long history of regular payments and don't want to spoil the record because of some special temporary situation that caused them to lose money. This occurs even less frequently and is more *dangerous* than paying preferred dividends out of surplus.

It is much more common, on the contrary, to *plough earnings back into the business* -- a phrase you frequently see on the financial pages and in company reports. The directors of our typical company have decided to pay only $1 on the common stock, though net income would have permitted them to pay much more. They decided that the company should *save* the difference.

The next entry on our income account, *Provision for Contingencies* (item "v"), shows us where our reserve for contingencies arose. The treasurer of our typical company has put the provision for contingencies after dividends. However, you will discover, if you look at very many financial reports, that it is sometimes placed above net income.

All of the net income that was not paid out as dividends, or set aside for contingencies, is shown as *Balance Carried to Earned Surplus* (item "w"). In other words, it is kept in the business. In previous years, the company had also earned more than it paid out so it had already accumulated by the beginning of the year an earned surplus of $3,073,000 (item "x"). When we total the earned surplus accumulated during the year to that which the company had at the first of the year, we get the total earned surplus at the end' of the year (item "y"). You will notice that the total here is the same as that which we ran across on the balance sheet as item 27.

Not all companies combine their income and surplus account. When they do not, you will find that *balance carried to surplus will* be the last item on the income account. The statement of consolidated surplus would appear as a third section of the corporation's financial report. A separate surplus account might be used if the company shifted funds for reserves to surplus during the year or made any other major changes in its method of treating the surplus account.

ANALYZING THE INCOME ACCOUNT

The income account, like the balance sheet, will tell us a lot more if we make a few detailed comparisons. The size of the totals on an income account doesn't mean much by itself. A company can have hundreds of millions of dollars in net sales and be a very bad investment. On the other hand, even a very modest profit in round figures may make a security attractive if there are only a small number of shares outstanding.

Before you select a company for investment, you will want to know something of its *margin of profit,* and how this figure has changed over the years. Finding the margin of profit is very simple. We just divide the net profit from operations (item "h") by net sales (item "a"). The figure we get (0.16) shows us that the company make a profit of 16 per cent from operations. By itself, though, this is not very helpful. We can make it significant in two ways.

In the first place, we can compare it with the margin of profit in previous years, and, from this comparison, learn if the company excels other companies that do a similar type of business. If the margin of profit of our company is very low in comparison with other companies in the same field, it is an unhealthy sign. Naturally, if it is high, we have grounds to be optimistic.

Analysts also frequently use *operating ratio* for the same purpose. The operating ratio is the complement of the margin of profit. The margin of profit of our typical company is 16. The operating ratio is 84. You can find the operating ratio either by subtracting the margin of profit from 100 or dividing the total of operating costs ($8,400,000) by net sales ($10,000,000).

The margin of profit figure and the operating ratio, like all of those ratios we examined in connection with the balance sheet, give us general information about the company, help us judge its prospects for the future. All of these comparisons have significance for the long term as they tell us about the fundamental economic condition of the company. But you still have the right to ask: *"Are the securities good investments for me now?"*

Investors, as opposed to speculators, are primarily interested in two things. The first is safety for their capital and the second, regularity of income. They are also interested in the rate of return on their investment but, as you will see, the rate of return will be affected by the importance placed on safety and regularity. High income implies risk. Safety must be bought by accepting a lower return.

The safety of any security is determined primarily by the earnings of the company that are available to pay interest or dividends on the particular issue. Again, though, round dollar figures aren't of much help to us. What we want to know is the relationship between the total money available and the requirements for each of the securities issued by the company.

INTEREST COVERAGE

As the bonds of our company represent part of its debt, the first thing we want to know is how easily the company can pay the interest. From the income account we see that the company had total income of $1,875,000 (item "1"). The interest charge on our bonds each year is $70,000 (3 1/2 per cent of $2,000,000 - item 21 on the balance sheet). Dividing total income by bond interest charges ($1,875,000 by $70,000) shows us that the company earned its bond interest 26 times over. Even after income taxes, bond interest was earned 17 times, a method of testing employed by conservative analysts. Before an industrial bond should be considered a safe investment, most analysts say that the company should earn interest charges several times over, so our company has a wide margin of safety.

To calculate the *preferred dividend coverage* (i.e., the number of times preferred dividends were earned), we must use net income as our base, as Federal Income Taxes and all interest charges must be paid before anything is available for stockholders. As we have 10,000 shares of $100 par value of preferred stock which pays a dividend of 5 per cent, the total dividend requirement for the preferred stock is $50,000 (items 24 on the balance sheet and "t" on the income account).

EARNINGS PER COMMON SHARE

The buyer of common stocks is often more concerned with the earnings per share of his stock than he is with the dividend. It is usually earnings per share or, rather, prospective earnings per share, that influence stock market prices. Our income account does not show the earnings available for the common stock, so we must calculate it ourselves. It is net income less preferred dividends (items "r" - "t"), or $1,056,700. From the balance sheet, we know that there are 400,000 shares outstanding, so the company earned about $2.64 per share.

All of these ratios have been calculated for a single year. It cannot be emphasized too strongly, however, that the *record* is more important to the investor than the report of any single year. By all the tests we have employed, both the bonds and the preferred stock of our typical company appear to be very good investments,, if their market prices were not too high. The investor would want to look back, however, to determine whether the operations were reasonably typical of the company.

Bonds and preferred stocks that are very safe usually sell at pretty high prices, so the yield to the investor is small. For example, if our company has been showing about the same coverage on its preferred dividends for many years and there is good reason to believe that the future will be equally kind, the company would probably replace the old 5 per cent preferred with a new issue paying a lower rate, perhaps 4 per cent.

STOCK PRICES

As the common stock does not receive a guaranteed dividend, its market value is determined by a great variety of influences in addition to the present yield of the stock measured by its dividends. The stock market, by bringing together buyers and sellers from all over the world, reflects their composite judgment of the present and future value of the stock. We cannot attempt here to write a treatise on the stock market. There is one important ratio, however, that every common stock buyer considers. That is the ratio of earnings to market price.

The so-called *price-earnings ratio is* simply the earnings per share on the common stock divided into the market price. Our typical company earned $2.64 a common share in the year, If the stock were selling at $30 a share, its price-earnings ratio would be about 11.4. This is the basic figure that you would want to use in comparing the common stock of this particular company with other similar stocks.

IMPORTANT TERMS AND CONCEPTS

LIABILITIES
> WHAT THE COMPANY OWES -- + RESERVES + SURPLUS + STOCKHOLDERS INTEREST IN THE COMPANY

ASSETS
> WHAT THE COMPANY OWNS -- + WHAT IS OWED TO THE COMPANY

FIXED ASSETS
> MACHINERY, EQUIPMENT, BUILDINGS, ETC.

EXAMPLES OF FIXED ASSETS
> DESKS, TABLES, FILING CABINETS, BUILDINGS, LAND, TIMBERLAND, CARS AND TRUCKS, LOCOMOTIVES AND FREIGHT CARS, SHIPYARDS, OIL LANDS, ORE DEPOSITS, FOUNDRIES

EXAMPLES OF:
> PREPAID EXPENSES
>> PREPAID INSURANCE, PREPAID RENT, PREPAID ROYALTIES AND PREPAID INTEREST

> DEFERRED CHARGES
>> AMORTIZATION OF BOND DISCOUNT, ORGANIZATION EXPENSE, MOVING EXPENSES, DEVELOPMENT EXPENSES

ACCOUNTS PAYABLE
> BILLS THE COMPANY OWES TO OTHERS

BONDHOLDERS ARE CREDITORS
> BOND CERTIFICATES ARE IOU'S ISSUED BY A COMPANY BACKED BY A PLEDGE

BONDHOLDERS ARE OWNERS
> A STOCK CERTIFICATE IS EVIDENCE OF THE SHAREHOLDER'S OWNERSHIP

EARNED SURPLUS
> INCOME PLOWED BACK INTO THE BUSINESS

NET SALES
> GROSS SALES MINUS DISCOUNTS AND RETURNED GOODS

NET INCOME
> = TOTAL INCOME MINUS ALL EXPENSES AND INCOME TAXES